Singers of the Century

Singers of the Century

VOLUME 3

J.B. Steane

Amadeus Press

Portland, Oregon

First published in North America in 2000 by
Amadeus Press (an imprint of Timber Press, Inc)
The Haseltine Building
133 S.W. Second Avenue, Suite 450
Portland, Oregon 97204, U.S.A.

A catalog record for this book is available
from the Library of Congress.

ISBN 1-57467-057-3

Chapters 2, 3, 4, 5, 7, 11, 23, 24, 38, 39, 42, 50 appeared first in *Opera Now*.
Chapters 10 and 13 have been slightly adapted from original versions
published in *Opera News*, and Chapters 1 and 14 from record notes compiled
for Pearl.

Sources of illustrations
(numbers refer to the pages of this book)

George Burr: 35, 75, 86, 109, 116, 119, 146, 175, 177. Colin Deane: 65, 67.
Decca: 13 (Meyer, Barcelona), 23, 31, 41 (Mike Evans), 93, 165 (Simon
Fowler), 245 (Christian Steiner). EMI: 18, 126 (Reg Wilson), 145, 149, 181
(Clive Barda), 225 (Reg Wilson). Gramophone: 20, 31, 74 (right), 81, 121, 155
(Andrew Bailey), 159 (Hanya Chlala), 166 169, 196, 197, 219 (Schaffler,
Salzburg), 221 (Clive Barda), 225, 226, 229 (Mahoudeau, Paris), 231 (J-P
Masclet), 232, 241, 245 (Christian Steiner), 246 (John Marshall). Edward
Morgan: 129, 131. Nimbus: 55, 71, 99, 104, 115, 134, 136, 145, 189, 204, 209.
Others from the author's collection.

Jacket illustrations: Nimbus: Muzio and Martinelli. Gramophone: Bartoli
(Decca; J-P Masclet); Hampson (Martin Becker).

Printed in Great Britain

Contents

Foreword   vii

Foreword

This is the third and last volume of the series, which like the century in question has run its course. The choice of singers has been personal but not, I hope, irresponsible. The self-imposed limit of 150 chapters, even with some doubling-up and in one instance a threesome, was bound to incur disappointment among admirers of the singers omitted. I do extend sympathies to them, knowing very well the feelings aroused by the neglect of a favourite. To those whose regret turns to indignation I can only suggest they find consolation in the thought that many others are absent too, and the more numerous these exclusions, the less invidious.

The arbitrary sequence of chapters will be familiar to readers of the previous volumes; and if these readers have remained faithful it can perhaps be assumed they have not been too much put out. For those who begin with Vol. 3 some explanation is due. Briefly: the series originated in an invitation from the then Editor of the magazine *Opera Now* to write for each number an article which would discuss the art and life of a singer alive or dead who had made a significant contribution to opera in the twentieth century and in whom writer and readers might find an interest.[1] A limit of roughly 1500 words was given; otherwise no conditions were attached. I began with Tauber, went on to Calvé, then Schwarzkopf, and so forth. When the first 50 articles were due to be reprinted in book-form, the question arose as to whether they should be re-ordered, or (some might say) ordered. Rather in the spirit of those conservative members of the French Assembly of whom it was said that had they been present on the day of Creation they would have cried 'Mon Dieu! je préfère le Chaos', the original dis-order was preserved. There are advantages, and it is too late to change now.

As to content, perhaps some principles have prevailed after all. It was never part of the intention to compile a rudimentary encyclopaedia. Dates and events become relevant in as far as they enter the discussion, and while the discussion has been guided towards centrality it has no pretensions to comprehensiveness. Readers who may complain that this or that aspect of a singer's work is missing are simply furthering the never-ending critical process. The word-limit brings into play the discipline of précis; on the other hand, personal, discursive and incidental elements may add something worthwhile to even the most severely-conducted critical exercise. When T.S. Eliot suggests that criticism should involve 'the common pursuit of true judgment' one may agree without necessarily wishing for the complete elimination of 'personal prejudices and cranks (tares to which we are all subject)' which is held to be a condition of its success. It may well be that something in the writer's own experience or judgment has assumed a disproportionate place in the total view; but it is better that a specific and true personal response is expressed if only because it and the response which it elicits in its own turn may become an enriching part of that 'common pursuit'.

Perhaps I should repeat the further declaration of intent stated in the Foreword to Vol. 1: that the essential purpose has been to help, 'in however limited a way', to keep 'the voices, the names and the circumstances of these remarkable people's lives in circulation'. Some reviewers of the previous volumes placed such a concern as amiably peripheral to the real interests of the musical world. In my view, the art of singing (and therefore an interest in the singers who practise it) is, or should be, one of that world's most central concerns. I read the newspapers daily and note how opera-critics 'place' singers and singing in their hierarchy of values: they are usually left to the end of the review, and if anything specific is mentioned it has normally to do with acting rather than singing. These books, 'in however limited a way', are offered as an antidote to that.

---

[1] For the bound editions I have added singers whose main distinction lay in other fields, mainly concert-work.

Coventry 2000   J.B.S.

As in Volume 2, thanks are due to John Karran and George Burr for valuable help generously given.

To Bruce Ritchie

CHAPTER 1

Giovanni Martinelli

'All'armi!'

Manrico's battle-cry, with which Martinelli himself so often rallied the troops on stage in *Il trovatore*, leaps to his defence whenever the great tenor is called into question, which he sometimes is. In my youth, to me personally his voice was the most exciting sound on earth: no *better* than Caruso's, of course, but more fascinating, the possessor of more secrets, a danger and a thrill in it, with a way of imprinting the memory, haunting the dreams, even being clearly audible in music one never heard him sing. But in youth, everybody I knew who had any interest in such things preferred Gigli, or, for that matter, Webster Booth. The fine long phrases, the fiery declamation: yes, in theory they could see all that in Martinelli's favour. The actual *sound* was something at which they looked concerned, shook their heads, and after a while plugged their ears.

Listening now, as though through the ears of a newcomer, one can recognise easily enough the deterrent qualities. In the earliest of his records, the Edisons of 1912 in which one might look for the freshness, freedom and fire of youth, there is a curious stiffness of manner, and while the top notes are certainly there, they fail to ring out quite as one is hoping they will. Then in the latest of the studio recordings, the excerpts from *Otello* made in 1939, the voice has dried out. In between those dates is singing which exhibits a fine art, yet with a tone which may be found too sharply pointed and sometimes too plangent for comfort, a sound that compels attention but makes hard listening.

For the essential Martinelli I would go first to the Improvviso from *Andrea Chénier*; or if that fiery utterance is too extreme, try 'Pourquoi me réveiller?' from an opera he never sang, Massenet's *Werther*. The song's sadness touches a nerve in the voice which was specially sensitive, and the timbre itself has a strength, purity and concentration utterly individual and, here, extremely beautiful. From that, one might move to *Guglielmo Tell*, the role of Arnoldo being one of his most admired, sung first at the Metropolitan in 1923. In all of these records the voice gleams and the passion flames, particularly in its expression of the young man's suffering. That is present too in the famous arioso from *Pagliacci*, which also, in the

1

electrically recorded version of 1927 or the Vitaphone of 1926, shows the voice as an instrument which is not just a shining point of sound but that of a dramatic tenor, a voice with breadth and body too. Canio was a role very much at the centre of Martinelli's repertoire (68 performances at the Metropolitan alone). Of a performance in Ravinia Park at Chicago in 1930 the critic Hermann Devries asked whether the lament can ever have been better sung, or indeed as well: 'surely not before or since Caruso'. He then turned to the second Act and the performance as a whole: 'Martinelli's acting,' he wrote, 'seemed the very essence of suffering ... and from now on I shall think of Martinelli as a glorious singing actor, and not as singer only.' And of that solo, the 'No, Pagliaccio non son' there is also a marvellously vivid studio recording.

Caruso's death in 1921 probably impelled Martinelli towards the heavy dramatic repertoire a little earlier and a little more exclusively than he would have chosen. In many ways it was by nature a lyric tenor's voice. The solos from *Lucia di Lammermoor* recorded in 1916 show him as a pure *lirico-spinto*, singing with poise and grace in the high Donizetti tessitura. He draws the finest possible line, firm and yet wonderfully tender (he is also master of the tenderising art of *portamento*). Edgardo was a part he kept in his repertoire till as late as 1935, when he was already preparing Otello, and in appreciation of this element in his art, another of the Chicago critics, Glenn Gunn, wrote in 1929 of Martinelli as 'the poised, serene, resourceful and commanding artist, able to subdue his magnificent voice to the lesser volume demanded by this ancient music [*sic*]; able too to sustain and adorn the lyric line'.

In two of the roles for which he won the greatest respect, Otello and Eléazar in *La Juive*, he was less concerned with vocal beauty than with the emotional force of his dramatic portrayal. As the old Jew he used a tone to match the character, sometimes lean, even desiccated, sometimes with an undertone of cantorial lament. Yet the broad, tensely charged phrases of his records from the opera have their beauty too, and of his performance on stage the terms of the *New York Herald Tribune*'s appreciation are notable. Their report from the Met in 1928 found him 'in magnificent form, his voice full, resonant, charged with emotion and yet never over-emphasised or injudiciously applied'. Of his Otello a great deal could be said,[1] and was said at the time. But on the sheer quality of voice a few of the London critics at the 1937 season at Covent Garden will suffice to show that the dry acoustic of the studio in which he recorded excerpts did him less than justice. Walter Legge wrote in the *Manchester Guardian*, 'a thread of pure gold runs through his voice'. Dyneley Hussey in the *Spectator* specified his ability to 'ravish the ear with the beauty of his final phrases in the first Act'. W.J. Turner in the *New Statesman* noted 'a voice of beautiful quality, very evenly developed throughout its range'; and Francis Toye of the *Morning Post*, having described his singing as 'splendid', added that 'even

Martinelli as Otello

the fleeting moments of harshness and cold tone were in themselves beautiful'.

He was then officially in his fifty-second year, and, though the Otello of the years immediately to follow effectively crowned his career, there is no doubt that he went on singing too long. It would have been best for his memory in the States, where his career was so firmly centred, had he

Royal Opera Covent Garden

LONDON & PROVINCIAL OPERA SOCIETY SEASON

Artistic Director: Sir Thomas Beecham, Bart.
Secretary & Manager: Charles A. Barrand

Saturday, June 26th, 1937, at 8

VERDI'S OPERA

OTELLO

In Italian

Otello	GIOVANNI MARTINELLI
Iago	LAWRENCE TIBBETT
Cassio	BEN WILLIAMS
Roderigo	OCTAVE DUA
Lodovico	GIULIO TOMEI
Montano	ARISTIDE BARACCHI
Desdemona	EIDE NORENA
Emilia	CONSTANCE WILLIS
Un Araldo	BOOTH HITCHIN

Conductor . Sir THOMAS BEECHAM, Bart.

retired shortly after the performances of *Otello* given early in 1941. Even then a sympathetic critic such as Olin Downes observed that 'his voice could not completely realise his intentions'. There were what he called 'deviations from pitch', and, though he does not say so, these had become more troublesome over several years. Even so, it was in these later performances that New Yorkers realised they had been taking him for granted for decades, and looking around could see no one to take his place. A complete recording of one of those 1941 *Otello*s shows just how fine he still could be, and the memory of him as an artist should probably have drawn its last impression from that. The voice was then still sufficiently its true self to recall Downes' words about his first Otello in the house, back in 1938. He sang the part, said Downes, 'with the art of the veteran that he is, interpreted with a conviction, a subtlety and pathos that wrung the heart'. And he added that it 'stands today as one of the finest interpretations the Metropolitan stage now knows'.

Happily, the years of decline were followed by a glowing return to public life in a different role. In 1962 he gave two lectures for the British Institute of Recorded Sound, one on Verdi, the other on his associations with composers of the verismo school. They were unforgettable occasions, and unforgettable too was the warmth of his reception. When it came to speaking of *Otello*, the opera and the role, he recited some of the lines, commanding marvellous strength and authority in the 'Esultate' and a depth of tragic utterance in the monologue, 'Dio, mi potevi scagliar', which now comes back to mind whenever the passage is acted or sung. Deep-toned and vibrant, this spoken declamation was in sound almost the antithesis of his singing, and yet in spirit the purest distillation. Five years later he was back again in London as a speaker at the National Film Theatre. Philip Hope-Wallace reported for the *Guardian* (October 10): 'Wonderful old Giovanni Martinelli, rubicund, expansive, with a magnificent white mop and swelling thorax, seems at 82 the best value in lecturers the London film and opera world is likely to see for a long time.' In between these events in London, he had celebrated his Golden Jubilee at the Met. In his speech from the stage he said that he understood there had been some fear he might want to sing. Reassuring the audience on that point, he added: 'If ever they find that Verdi did write a *King Lear* and the score is discovered I might consider making myself available.' And of course he did sing again in opera – as the Emperor in *Turandot* at Seattle in January 1967. On this occasion his speech noted that he had begun in this opera as the Prince, had been promoted to Emperor, and would now abdicate.

Wonderful old man, everybody said: ripe and mellow, replete with laughter and energy. I always think there must have been another element in his life and character, for his special gift was to embody in tone and style the sorrows that are the very soul of Italian opera. His singing had its faults, sure enough. If this were not so, there would be no need for faith (and Martinelli can inspire faith). If there were no faith there would be no need in the face of criticism to raise the banner. And with (or without) the banner, the cry still goes up: 'All'armi!'

And 'Viva Giovanni!'

[1] See *Voices, Singers and Critics*: Duckworth, 1992, pp. 174-8.

CHAPTER 2

Lucrezia Bori

In *Twilight in Italy*, D.H. Lawrence divides churches into two categories, eagle and dove. Can you do something similar with singers, I wonder. The eagles predominate, certainly among prima donnas. The dove-churches, according to Lawrence, nestle in the trees and are 'shy and hidden': nothing of the prima donna about those. Eagle-churches stand high and proud, their bells ringing imperiously and 'falling on the subservient world below': the very image of the type, from Lilli Lehmann and Nellie Melba to Maria Callas and Birgit Nilsson (to go no further). The dovecote-cloisters harbour no Wagnerians, few coloraturas, few of those chirpy soubrettes: just a few lyric sopranos, perhaps, with no aspirations towards the dramatic. I'm inclined to look among them for Lucrezia Bori.

Hear her on records, and, yes, shyness seems part of the character. A small voice, we think, and then, almost immediately, 'How did it fill the Metropolitan?' It was in that vast house (the old Met, of course) that she sang, as one of the acknowledged *prime donne* among eagles, from 1912 to 1936. On the roster of Italian tenors who sang with her were Caruso, Martinelli, Gigli and Lauri-Volpi, none of them lightweights. She undertook a busy schedule, and while Mimì was the role she sang most often, others with an important place in her career included Violetta, Mélisande and Fiora in *L'amore dei tre re*. And the voice carried.[1]

The vocal personality is affectionate, sensitive, fragile, vulnerable, charming, girlish. The first impression may indeed be of girlishness with an admixture of the infantile. That was a word which entered the reviews of her early performances at the Met. 'Pallid and infantile' was Henry Krehbiel's phrase in the *Tribune*, and even eight months later W.J. Henderson of the *Sun* wrote of her as 'not a prima donna of the ideal Metropolitan type' (21 November 1913), having 'radical defects in her emission of tone' (6 April). Both of these critics changed their opinions, Krehbiel almost instantly. Bori made her debut on the opening night of the season, 11 November 1912, opposite Caruso in *Manon Lescaut*. In the first Act, according to Krehbiel, the voice 'could not assert itself at all', but in the second 'she surprised the audience, critical and uncritical alike, by the real fineness of her vocal art – by an exquisite exhibition of legato singing, by exquisite diction, impeccable intonation and moving pathos'. He also

Bori as Manon

attributed to the voice 'perfect emission' and 'ample carrying power'. Henderson took longer to be convinced, but writing of her appearance, on 2 January 1914, in the American premiere of *L'amore dei tre re*, he confessed to some astonishment: 'This young soprano grew greatly by last night's revelation. She discovered unsuspected dramatic skill and a higher command of vocal art than ever before'. Shortly after that, in one of his periodical (and mostly disenchanted) surveys, he declared, of Bori and himself, that 'For once the chronicler of the *Sun* can almost shed tears of joy at the possibility of being able to write in the not too distant future "Another real singer has arrived".'

There followed a setback, as severe (short of fatal illness or accident) as can befall a singer at this crucial stage. She developed nodes on the vocal cords – suggesting that Henderson's misgivings may not have been groundless after all – and underwent an operation in 1915. Another became necessary the following year, and after it a long period of complete silence, not even speaking. Patience, self-denial and solitude governed her life at this time, and that too must have fortified her art when the voice returned. She tended it carefully, testing eventually in the small jewel of an opera house at Monte Carlo. In January 1921 she returned to the Metropolitan, amid rejoicing.

In Lawrence's essay he finds the churches of the dove 'gathered into a silence of their own in the very midst of the town', strangely elusive. Elusive too was the church of the eagle, but when at last he came upon it 'it was another world ... suspended above the village, like the lowest step of heaven, of Jacob's ladder'.

Bori, so fragile in her appeal, emerges, as one comes to know her, as strong. More eagle than dove after all. It is so with her singing as we become familiar with it on records. Several writers, among them Lanfranco Rasponi in *The Last Prima Donnas*, testify that her recordings do her no kind of justice. 'In those days,' says Rasponi, 'the microphones were unable to pick up the nuances of which her art was made.' All the more remarkable, then, that we who never heard her 'in the flesh' can hear her in our minds so very clearly: much more clearly, indeed, and with more subtlety of nuance, than we do many singers whom we encounter 'in the flesh' and on records as our daily familiars. This too testifies to strength.

Her early records of course were made not with the microphone but the horn. The very first, for Thomas Edison in 1913, capture a warmth of tone that comes as a surprise if one knows only the Victors. From the other end of her career we can further supplement the Victors with transcripts from broadcasts, and these, technically primitive as they are, help to bring her more clearly and credibly into the present-day listener's view. One of them, Louise's 'Depuis le jour' from 1935, played at a meeting of the Recorded Vocal Art Society in London, drew from some who had heard Bori frequently at the Met a sharp cry of recognition: 'That was it! That was her!' The recording made of her farewell at the Metropolitan in 1936 is also

Saturday Afternoon, April 23, 1932, at 2 O'clock

LES CONTES D'HOFFMANN
(THE TALES OF HOFFMANN)

FANTASTIC OPERA IN THREE ACTS, PROLOGUE AND EPILOGUE

(IN FRENCH)

MUSIC *By* JACQUES OFFENBACH

OLYMPIA	LILY PONS
GIULIETTA	GRACE MOORE
ANTONIA	LUCREZIA BORI
NICKLAUSSE	GLADYS SWARTHOUT
A VOICE	DOROTHEA FLEXER
HOFFMANN	ARMAND TOKATYAN
COPPELIUS	PAVEL LUDIKAR
DAPPERTUTTO	LAWRENCE TIBBETT
MIRACLE	LEON ROTHIER
SPALANZANI	LOUIS D'ANGELO
SCHLEMIL	GEORGE CEHANOVSKY
LINDORF	ALFREDO GANDOLFI
CRESPEL	LOUIS D'ANGELO

ANDRES	
COCHENILLE	
FRANZ	ANGELO BADA
PITICHINACCIO	

NATHANAEL	MAREK WINDHEIM
HERMANN	PAOLO ANANIAN
LUTHER	GEORGE CEHANOVSKY

CONDUCTOR . . LOUIS HASSELMANS

CHORUS MASTER . . . . . GIULIO SETTI

STAGE MANAGER . . . . . ARMANDO AGNINI

SYNOPSIS OF SCENES

PROLOGUE—The Tavern of Master Luther.

ACT I. Olympia, the Mechanical Doll.
(A Ballroom in the House of Spalanzani.)

ACT II. Giulietta, the Venetian Beauty.
(A Gallery in a Palace in Venice.)

ACT III. Antonia, the Munich Maid.
(A Room in the House of Crespel in Munich.)

EPILOGUE—Same Scene as Prologue.

SCENERY DESIGNED AND PAINTED BY JOSEPH URBAN

POSITIVELY NO ENCORES ALLOWED

Correct Librettos For Sale in the Lobby

KNABE PIANO USED EXCLUSIVELY

The Metropolitan Opera on Tour at Cleveland

wonderfully vivid. In her 49th year (accepting 24 December 1887 as the date of her birth) she sings still with youth in the voice, fluent, graceful and unforced. The Gavotte from Massenet's *Manon* is a charmer, the St Sulpice scene with Richard Crooks beautifully sung (by both) and touchingly expressive. These and a few other broadcasts from the Met do for Bori's living memory the great service of taking her out of the studios. The dry acoustic and confined space of those recordings of the 1920s make it peculiarly difficult to 'see' her as in the opera house or concert hall. Yet even so, in a different sense, 'see' her is exactly what we do.

For myself, she provides one of the reasons why records have such great value. It is not so much a matter of whether one generation of singers is better than another; it is that among them are irreplaceable individuals. Bori, of all singers, is one of the easiest to 'switch on' in the mind. It is a quality she shares with Martinelli, the tenor. With these singers, colleagues for many years, timbre and style are utterly distinctive; in their different ways they have an intensity of feeling within them that almost turns the limitations of recording to their advantage. We match their concentration with our own, and remember. Anyone who knows Bori's records from the Mascagni operas, *Iris* and *L'amico Fritz* or the unforgettable *Bohème* scene with Tito Schipa will understand what this means.

Of course there are disappointments. Like most Italian-trained sopranos of the period, she had no trill or only the rudimentary suggestions of one. Despite the light girlishness which was part of her voice-character, the top notes hardly rejoice. The *Traviata* aria is sung a semitone down, and the runs of 'Sempre libera' are subject to a little simplification. She also had a large repertoire of Spanish songs (I'm told that at recitals there would be a kind of post-encore time when she would sing on and on for friends and admirers); charming examples can be found among her records, but they provide only a glimpse. There were also seven years (1929-1936) in which she made no studio recordings at all.

I fancy that in her own lifetime harm may well have been done to the 'image' people had of her voice by the prevalence of wrong playing-speeds, for at 78rpm most play a semitone high, distorting tone and vowels to give what was sometimes described as a 'pinched' sound. I also suspect that something about her voice-character, the public personality too, may have become slightly comical to a younger generation. One of her best-known records coupled two waltz-songs, 'Il bacio' and the 'Valse d'oiseau' with its 'twee-twee-twee-twee-tweet's; enchanting in their way, but not to be sung, let's say, within range of Groucho's eyebrows.

The other side of the coin is that there has probably never been an opera-singer more respected, liked and loved within the profession. She never married, and her life was given almost entirely to opera and other good causes. Most famously, she led the 'Save the Metropolitan' movement when the economic slump threatened the Met's existence. Drumming up donations, chairing meetings, broadcasting appeals, she worked tirelessly. In 1941 she turned her experience in organisation towards war work. On the Board of Directors at the Met she encouraged young singers and maintained an interest in all that was going on, taking a positive attitude in almost everything except the producer's right to distort the composer's intentions. She also became President of a foundation concerned with pensions for musicians down on their luck. And when the floods of 1957 brought disaster to Spain, her native land, and particularly to her birthplace, Valencia, she set about raising relief money in the United States. Lucrecia Borja y Gonzalez de Riancho died in New York on May 14, 1960,

10

deeply mourned. At her funeral in Valencia thousands lined the streets, to honour the benefactor they had never met and the great singer they had never heard.

---

[1] The most surprising role in her repertoire was Octavian in *Der Rosenkavalier*. She sang it in the Italian premiere of the opera at La Scala in 1911, handpicked by Strauss, who presented her with a copy of the score, with alterations in his own hand to suit her voice. Where, I wonder, is that now?

11

CHAPTER 3

Montserrat Caballé

The name of a singer is a note in the air: with Caballé an A flat, a high A flat taken softly from the octave below and perfectly placed. She holds it, holds it long, and just as it seems she must stop for breath other voices enter below. And still she holds, as they take up a hypnotic melody, snake-charmed with fascinated repulsion, for in their midst the woman with the beautiful voice is the Borgia, and the note, which we hear inwardly as the sound evoked by the singer's name, is part of the inspired finale to the Prologue of Donizetti's opera. Soloists and chorus express their horror, and the voice of the vilified woman shines over them like a halo.

Of course, any soprano who is at all worthy of the role can make something of that passage, and particularly of the held note. But it takes only a fractional misjudgement or failure of technique to spoil it: a momentary judder, a minimal error of pitch, the unavailability of an apparently limitless breath-supply. And even then, if all these conditions are met, the small matter of quality remains, and there Caballé was ideal.

Indeed, she came to us as a kind of ideal. This was in the 1960s, when memory of Callas had soured somewhat along with her voice, and when Sutherland's brilliance, purity and fullness seemed increasingly compromised by the want of a firmly drawn melodic line. Caballé, in their *bel canto* repertoire (with significant extensions), brought the rich beauty of tone lacking in Callas and a substantiality of legato which was proving elusive in Sutherland.

Conjure now a few more notes. She was never one for the very highest flights, those Ds and E flats that were Sutherland's glory and a tormentingly irresistible challenge to the tortured voice of Callas. A top C, however, is the note summoned for present savouring. Aida's aria in the third Act, 'O patria mia', has at its climax a high C marked *dolce*. Most singers of the role have preferred to believe that Verdi didn't really mean it, or perhaps that *dolce* and *fortissimo* were, in their own particular case, compatible. Nowadays more of them attempt to obey instructions, but again Caballé was one who fulfilled the ideal. Her note, as we hear it in the 1974 recording of the opera under Muti, was soft but not thin, a climax of soul rather than body, a note of love and yearning sent up through the

night sky of Egypt to the Ethiopian homeland. Moreover (for let no one suppose this to be an occasion for that odious term 'canary-fancier'), the note has its quietly climactic place within the musical phrase, just as has the phrase itself within the aria. If Caballé's note is lovely and wonderful, the whole phrase is doubly so. From its start at 'no, mai più' it rises and descends on a single breath, mindful of Verdi's warning not to hurry the semiquavers, and constructing a perfect arch of sound as Aida's wish aspires towards the highest note and as the acknowledgement of its hopelessness falls with regretful calm.

For listening to further lovely notes (but within a phrase within an aria within an opera within a great composer's work within an important movement in European culture) turn then to Leonora's 'D'amor sull' ali rosee' in *Il trovatore*, beginning with the recitative. A vivid flash of stage-presence comes first, though this is a sound-recording, made, none too satisfactorily, in a studio in Barcelona. Her darkly dramatic tone in 'Timor di me' suits this nocturnal opera, but that might still be, so to speak, a bit of external attitude-painting. The phrase 'presso a te son io, e tu nol sai' is something more: a sigh of regret from the heart where others give it as a statement of prosaic fact. 'Gemente aure ...': the line rises to an exquisite high note and ends after a miracle of sustained phrasing. People have suspicious minds, and in those days there was much talk about fiendishly clever things done in studios to improve on nature. But shortly after the release of this recital-record in 1975 Caballé sang the role of Leonora at Covent Garden. My impression then was that the two performances were practically identical. A 'private' recording preserves one of those performances, and, though the climactic phrases with the high C are not linked as in the studio, the breadth, shading, expression and beauty of tone otherwise correspond unfailingly. Faults occur in both, most especially in the substitution of a kind of flutter for a genuine trill, but in voice and in artistry both performances are treasurable.

Those are good memories of Caballé. Others are less so, and there is one I wish I had never had. In fact it survives in duplicate. The first came so unexpectedly that it was tempting to disbelieve the evidence of one's senses, for there, in public, was this famous soprano giving what seemed inescapably to be a parody of another. With a facetious, not distinctly audible announcement, she sang, as her second or third encore, the Swiss folk-song 'Gsätzli'. As many in the London audience at that time would have known, it had been the regular encore-song of Elisabeth Schwarzkopf, who learned it from her teacher Maria Ivogün: no one else sang it in those days. The performance involved facial expressions and deliberate false intonation: it was a send-up, and it gained laughs and applause. Two possible explanations were suggested: either it was a cheap, unprofessional guying of a fellow artist or it betrayed an ignorance concerning which some adviser should have enlightened her. I believed the former. Once might have been an aberration, but she repeated the enormity at a concert in Covent Garden. For years after that I would never go to a Caballé recital again.

Then in 1999 she reappeared in Britain, at Croydon's Fairfield Halls, and, after all, the offence had been perpetrated a long time ago. She had recently celebrated her 66th birthday and it seemed an occasion not to be missed. Perhaps it should have been. Over the main body of her voice, at

14

London Opera Society

Artistic Director *MICHAEL R. SCOTT*

First Subscription Series 1968-69: First Evening

Royal Festival Hall

Friday, 4th October, 1968

Lucrezia Borgia

Opera in a Prologue and Two Acts

LUCREZIA BORGIA	. .	MONTSERRAT CABALLE
DON ALFONSO	. . .	RUGGIERO RAIMONDI
GENNARO	. . . .	EDOARDO GIMENEZ
MAFFIO ORSINI	. . .	HUGUETTE TOURANGEAU
RUSTIGHELLO	. . .	DAVID LENNOX
ASTOLFO	. . . .	ERICH VIETHEER
LIVEROTTO	. . . .	ROBIN DONALD
GAZELLA .	. . . .	JOHN GIBB
PETRUCCI	. . . .	NEIL HOWLETT
VITELLOZZO .	. . .	BRUCE LOCHTIE
GUBETTA	. . . .	ERICH VIETHEER

a *mezzo forte* or louder, the wear of those years was sadly evident. Every now and than a note, a phrase – sometimes heart-stopping in its sudden beauty – would recall the singer we knew her to have been: there was something of it in her opening number, a rare aria from Donizetti's *Gabriella di Vergy* and again in 'Il est doux' from Massenet's *Hérodiade*. As the evening drew on, a kind of silliness supervened – facetious little exchanges with the conductor or the front row of the stalls, and all on an unbecoming tide of giggles. They stirred memories of her last appearance in opera at Covent Garden in 1992 as the innkeeper in Rossini's *Il viaggio a Reims*. Again, most of the ad-libbing was unintelligible but the humour of what could be heard hardly told of lost pearls, and when she landed an apple on the conductor's head the drollery seemed to have gone far enough.

It is sad to find these among one's souvenirs – and of course they also include the moment of realisation that hers was the voice arising so unpleasingly in the pop number called *Barcelona*. In John Potter's interesting and important book, *Vocal Authority* (Cambridge 1998), Caballé's contribution is contrasted to Freddie Mercury's. Mercury, he points out,

15

'sings with the directness of speech' whereas Caballé, with 'the ideological baggage of several hundred years', 'is concerned above all with making beautiful sounds in the conventional singerly way'. It would be unfortunate for the 'singerly way' if anybody thought it authentically represented by the vocalising heard in that record, and unfortunate for Caballé if anyone believed that when she really wanted to make beautiful sounds that was the best she could do.

A worse mistake lies in the notion that the 'baggage of several hundred years' lumbers a singer with the idea that 'making beautiful sounds' is an aim to be pursued to the exclusion or detriment of expression. The 'odious term' referred to earlier itself implies it, and perhaps Caballé may be enlisted in its annihilation: a canary-fancier's fancy is what she may appear to be, but that is wrong on two accounts. First, the so-called connoisseur is unlikely to approve of a singer whose faults include the lack of a real or reliable trill, and whose technique led to a kind of vocal dichotomy in which the soft floated high notes were celestial while those same notes sung at a forte became hard and relatively unsteady. But, secondly and more importantly, she was no 'canary' if that word is meant to signify song without sensibility. For one thing, she developed a repertory which it is almost impossible to acquire, let alone perform, without a modicum of intelligence (Armida, Fiordiligi, Tatiana, Isolde, Salome and the Marschallin, for instance, are not 'canary' roles). For another, recordings show that her constant practice was to work through the notes to the intelligent heart of her music. Her Turandot is an example. It is a part which, even on records, she probably should never have sung (though she did it, without immediate damage, in San Francisco and Paris), but the 'In questa reggia' has uncanny insights, imaginative and totally individual.

The artist in Caballé has no doubt been enriched, rather than encumbered, by the traditions she inherited and of which she became one of the finest latter-day exponents. Of Caballé the woman, it is as well also to remember a childhood in civil war, a struggle with poverty and discouragement, a fight against frightening illness, a generous devotion to good public causes and to her family amid a ceaselessly demanding workschedule. It is true: a note, an exquisite tone on the high A flat, may be evoked at the name of Caballé, but the 'fancier' who admires it is immediately drawn into a wider human and musical context. In fact: no 'fancier', no 'canary'.

CHAPTER 4

Alfredo Kraus

With the death of Alfredo Kraus the twentieth century lost a distinction which in its latter half it hardly expected to have. This was a tenor of the Italian type for whom the adjectives most favoured by public and critics alike were 'elegant', 'refined' and 'stylish'. His model, in the formative years, was Tito Schipa, and that of itself explains much. Among the leading tenors of his time, Schipa stood alone. Kraus came to occupy a comparable position, which he won through steadily increasing achievement and which he maintained with respect for his calling and a long-preserved, unostentatious dignity.

His name, of course, is a strange one to set among 'Italian' tenors. One wonders whether the Austrian element did something to supply what was different and distinctive about him. This appears not to have been so: his father left Vienna at the age of 18, became a citizen of Las Palmas and brought up his children as natives of the Canary Islands, their language Spanish, their culture Latin rather than Germanic. For music, there were evenings round the piano, which the boy learnt to play, while also singing in the local church choir. An interest in music and a gift for singing showed themselves early and suggested the path his future might take; but it was the sheet music of popular songs rather than the Lieder albums, and the *zarzuelas* or musical comedies of Spain rather than the operas of Mozart and Wagner, that formed his background.

In 1947 he heard a celebrated tenor for the first time 'in the flesh'. This was Helge Roswaenge, then a refugee from Europe who celebrated his 25th stage anniversary with a performance of *Pagliacci* in Las Palmas. At that time, Roswaenge, with no regular source of income, worked as a chemist, drawing on the qualifications he had gained long ago at the Polytechnic in Copenhagen. His singing provided inspiration for the young Alfredo, but if Otto Kraus, the father, also took an interest it would probably have been with the satisfaction of confirming his view that an aspiring singer needed some other profession to fall back on, and he ensured that his son continued to train as an electrical engineer.

For a singer, to be a late starter may be no bad thing. The voice has settled; the human being and potential artist is relatively mature. Kraus made his operatic debut in 1956 at the age of 28. He did not leave his home

till 1948, even then returning for two years after taking singing-lessons in Barcelona and Valencia. During those years he married and again there must have been much earnest thinking about the future; nevertheless he left for Italy in 1955. Luck then played its part, for asking his way of a compatriot in Milan he happened to mention that he was a singer in search of a teacher and was directed to his acquaintance's sister, the Spanish soprano Mercedes Llopart, whose career had taken her to La Scala where she sang the Marschallin in *Der Rosenkavalier* under Toscanini. From her,

Kraus learnt much, and later was able to show gratitude by bringing to her the young Renata Scotto, who was to be her other star-pupil.

With Scotto, Llopart had to return to basics, proscribing the more strenuous roles she was then singing (Butterfly for instance), and working towards appreciation and mastery of *bel canto*. With Kraus it seems that the foundations had been sound and the repertoire could be built up at her discretion. He would later talk with some pride of the historic line in which he stood, partly through Llopart and partly through a previous teacher, Francisco Andrés, who himself was trained in the Garcia method with links back to Lamperti and the eighteenth-century master Mancini. The famous Spanish tenor Gayarré had also been raised in this school. In 1958 Kraus was to make a film about him: a charmingly directed, naive film with plenty of singing in it, including many of the parts which Kraus would soon be making his own.

In choice of roles he was from the start exceptionally careful. His first contract, with the Italian opera at Cairo in 1956, stipulated that if he was to sing the Duke in *Rigoletto* he must also accept Cavaradossi in *Tosca*. He did so, and three years later sang Pinkerton in *Madama Butterfly* – but never again. He was *un tenore schipiano* and restricted himself even more stringently than Schipa had done. The heaviest roles he undertook throughout his career were probably Offenbach's Hoffmann and Massenet's Werther. Basically, like Schipa, he maintained a core-repertoire of about a dozen roles, rarely singing more than six in any one year.

His reputation grew steadily. Working mostly in Italy, Spain and Portugal, he made his London debut at the now defunct Stoll theatre as early as 1957, Covent Garden following two years later. He reached La Scala in 1960 and the USA in 1961. It was at about this time that the operatic world began to realise that he was probably something special. 'Not since Valletti's American advent has a lyric tenor of such technical polish and musical persuasion been heard' wrote the critic for *Opera* magazine (January 1963) of his Chicago debut in *L'elisir d'amore*. He scored a notable success in the virtuoso music of Cherubini's *Ali Baba* at La Scala, was voted 'hero of the evening' in *La favorita* at Buenos Aires, and by 1975 had earned what to many Italians seemed the ultimate accolade, the commendation of Rodolfo Celletti, Pontiff of *bel canto*. Coupling Kraus's name with that of Carlo Bergonzi, Celletti wrote of him as 'the only tenor in the last thirty years capable of giving us performances of Bellini, Donizetti and certain Verdi operas, founded on a true professional confidence and a precise stylistic vision of the romantic musical theatre of the period 1830 to 1860' (*Opera*, January 1975).

Oddly perhaps, the role which was to become most closely associated with him was of a different nationality, period and style. He sang Werther for the first time in 1966 at Piacenza, where the opera was given in Italian. Not until his first American appearances in the work did he sing it in French: that was at Chicago in 1971. It was also the opera which intro-

Kraus as Romeo in *Roméo et Juliette*

duced him to Paris, somewhat belatedly, in 1984, and there were acclaimed performances at La Scala, the Vienna Staatsoper, Covent Garden
and the Metropolitan. He also made a highly praised recording, and in
many interviews spoke of the fascination the role had for him and the
challenge it presented to the singer in having to combine the character's
introspective nature with the audience's need for communication. 'One of
the glories of the lyric stage today' was the verdict of the critic Patrick J.
Smith (*Opera*, January 1979).

My own memory of Kraus's Werther at Covent Garden (1979) is more
mixed, as is my reaction to the recording. In both, the opening solo, the
Invocation to Nature, remains a treasured possession: sung with that fine
clean line so characteristic of Kraus at his best, and also with a personal
quality that makes one yearn to hear him again. Elsewhere, contrary to
reputation, much is (and was) exaggeratedly self-pitying and emphatic. A
classic of operatic singing and of Kraus's art should be the poem of Ossian,
'Pourquoi me réveiller?', which Werther sings in Act 3. But though Kraus
begins beautifully, the emotion soon becomes too overt, the vocal line
suffers disruption, the high note is held too long, and the *diminuendo* at
the verse's end ('o souffle du printemps') draws too much attention to itself

20

as a special effect or *tour de force*. Such excesses (and they occur at several points in the recording) may be defended as excesses of the character. But here is the real problem which the role of Werther poses for its singer. It is not necessary to study the libretto very deeply before one realises (as Kraus came to) that Werther is an egoist and that what he calls his love for Charlotte is a self-dramatising, romantic obsession. In opera, however, the character is what the *music* says it is, and characterisation has to be guided by the composer's musical-dramatic intention. The music places him in a much more sympathetic light, and the drama depends on Werther's ability to gain the audience's sympathy (if not, he simply gets what he deserves and his long-drawn-out death is no tragedy). If Werther whines and suffuses his voice with self-indulgent pathos, he loses respect and, with it, sympathy. Kraus's Werther, intensely memorable, is to my mind very far from representing the qualities – refinement, elegance, feeling for style – with which he is most unanimously credited.

These are to be found much more consistently in the area delineated by Rodolfo Celletti – the period 1830 to 1860. In Bellini, Kraus's Arturo in *I puritani* is finely caught on records, one of its great assets being the placing of the voice so wonderfully matching the high tessitura. His Donizetti is still better, and among my own most cherished memories of opera at Covent Garden is his aria in *Lucrezia Borgia*, performed with Sutherland in 1980. Then, in any assessment of him, the sheer longevity of his career must have a place – it testifies to the soundness of his method. His last appearance at Covent Garden was in recital in 1996, his 70th year. The most applauded item on the programme then was 'Tombe degli avi miei' from *Lucia di Lammermoor*, where his mastery of phrasing was a lesson in itself. His voice, with its exceptional range, survived marvellously well, and even at the time of his death his engagements for stage appearances and concerts would have involved a busy future. Moreover, the voice developed so well: in early years a recurrent word among the critics was 'reedy', but his fifteen-year absence from the London house (1959-1974) highlighted for us the way in which his tone had gained body and warmth.

Ultimately, and perhaps surprisingly, warmth became his gift and his reward. A reticent, disciplined man, a dignified rather than a demonstrative presence on stage, a singer with defined, penetrative tone, he never courted publicity or encouraged a personality-cult. At his death, the mourning was heartfelt, and as his coffin lay in the Teatro Real in Madrid (its foyer turned into a chapel of rest) the honour paid him by his countryfolk expressed an affection which had grown out of respect and was felt by lovers of singing throughout the world.

CHAPTER 5

Sena Jurinac

Drifting through open dressing-room windows, the sound of singers warming up was part of the outdoor scenery before the show and during the dinner interval at the old Glyndebourne. In general no one took much notice. But on certain golden evenings in the early or mid-1950s, couples strolling across the lawn might pause, turn their heads and listen. A soprano was trying out a phrase of Fiordiligi's or Donna Anna's, quite softly it seemed and yet with a fullness of tone that might even then have been carrying towards people down by the lake, who in turn would hear and wonder. For those who knew, anticipation was deliciously enriched. Jurinac was in good voice.

A favourite throughout Europe and in the States, she was beloved at Glyndebourne. In pre-war seasons the adorable Luise Helletsgruber may have won a comparable place in the audience's affections, but in more recent times, though many internationally famous singers (Caballé, for instance, Crespin, Janowitz, Pavarotti, Souzay) have come and gone, Jurinac remains the singer most closely associated with the Sussex house and most fondly recalled by the veterans of many seasons. She was young and beautiful and in her prime: no doubt those were some of the reasons. She sang almost exclusively in Mozart, and that also refined our feelings about her. She was versatile too, singing the pageboy Cherubino as well as the Countess, Dorabella as well as Fiordiligi, Anna and Elvira in *Don Giovanni*, and in *Ariadne auf Naxos* (her single Strauss opera at Glyndebourne) a Composer who took all hearts. She became the ideal Ilia in *Idomeneo*, and in *Così fan tutte* the seemingly irreplaceable Fiordiligi: my own most treasured memories of that opera include the rise of curtain on the second scene, set in the sunshine and freshness of 'a garden by the seashore', as the stage-directions suggest, and itself something of a rarity these days, and then the finely flavoured blend of Jurinac's tone with the equally beautiful but quite distinctive voice of Nan Merriman.

Jurinac came to Britain as one of the new Viennese school, that outstanding generation of singers (most of them sopranos) who were to be found among the State Opera Company, deprived as they were of their own bombed house and singing currently at the Theater an der Wien. They visited London in 1947, where audiences at Covent Garden heard for the

first time Hilde Gueden, Emmy Loose, Elisabeth Schwarzkopf, Irmgard Seefried and Ljuba Welitsch as well as a new Dorabella in Jurinac who alternated with Elisabeth Hoengen in the role. Elisabeth Grümmer and Lisa della Casa were still to come, and of all these Jurinac was the youngest, born in 1921. Before her engagement at Vienna she had sung, with Mimì as her debut-role in 1942, at Zagreb, where she trained under the teacher of Zinka Milanov, Milka Kostrenčič. Her Viennese mother approved, her Croatian father recommended a course in medicine, and

23

wartime conditions created difficulties in all directions. Amid such circumstances a remarkable voice tends to have a will of its own, and usually it finds a way.

Many singers talk of 'the voice' as almost a thing apart: *of* themselves and yet *not* themselves, having an agenda and a strong instinct of its own. Jurinac found this will-to-survive asserting itself after her first year in Vienna. With the opera at Zagreb she had sung in an entirely suitable lyric repertoire, her roles there including Majenka in *The Bartered Bride* and the Countess in *Le nozze di Figaro*. Because Vienna was short of mezzos many of their roles came her way, and her voice, with its strong middle register, could sustain them. But in that first year she took part in more than 150 performances, and that was too much. She adjusted, and there followed what we think of as the 'Glyndebourne period', which also brought excursions into the Italian repertoire, with *La forza del destino* at Edinburgh, and, at Salzburg, *Don Carlos*. That was in 1958, the year in which nodes on the vocal cords necessitated an interval of some six months with no singing and then a cautious return in a relatively small role, Ighino in *Palestrina*. She made her second Covent Garden 'debut' the following year in *Madama Butterfly*, and though she enjoyed a great success ('she was the most honest, most heroic, and in the end most touching interpreter of the role I had ever encountered' was Lord Harewood's report), my feeling at the time was that her voice had in some degree changed; had thickened perhaps, and lost the freshness of just a few years back.

In this – phase two of her mature career – Jurinac continued to undertake a weightier repertoire. At Covent Garden her first Leonore followed, in a series of performances under Klemperer in which *Fidelio* had what reads as something of a dream-cast, with Jurinac, Vickers, Hotter and Frick in the leading roles. She herself was disappointed. 'With his heavy, pedestrian tempos he nearly drove me up the wall,' she said of Klemperer to Lanfranco Rasponi (*The Last Prima Donnas*, London 1975). Harold Rosenthal found her 'warm, noble, sincere, moving' (*Opera*, April 1961), but my own memory of her is dim, though clear enough on the others; the Fidelio who really moved me in those years was Gré Brouwenstijn (see Chapter 6), comparable in 'size' of voice but aflame with the passion of her role. Later, Jurinac took on Jenufa at Vienna and Salzburg, Tosca at Covent Garden, and Senta in *Der fliegende Holländer* at Strasburg; but again the voice asserted its will to survive and the last two roles were soon dropped. The perennial temptations of Carmen presented themselves and were again resisted. In the 1970s she took a decisive step along the road to operatic venerability, exchanging the girlish dress of Jenufa for the graveyard black of her stepmother; and again the time came when she was asked to return for more performances but decided to call it a day.

In June 1981, Jurinac gave a recital at the Wigmore Hall in London; it was the last time I heard her sing (she reappeared for some masterclasses). Her voice had remained firm and pure; but pitch troubled fairly

Wigmore Hall
Manager: William Lyne
Lessees: The Arts Council of Great Britain

Wigmore Summer Nights

Tuesday 30 June 1981 at 7.30 pm

Sena Jurinac
soprano

Geoffrey Parsons
piano

Arts Council
OF GREAT BRITAIN

persistently and she tended to sing, with chin tucked in, at the the same level of volume. This was in her Purcell, Handel and Schubert. Mendelssohn seemed to free her a little and at the end of the Harvest song, 'Erntelied', the last line actually brought a smile, a sudden rare flash of expression in the still and serenely beautiful face. With this for a breakthrough, she started to communicate in the very last group before the interval, with three early songs of Webern. Afterwards came Brahms, and after 'Therese' (not an end-of-group song) spontaneous applause: it was clear that the audience so wanted to encourage her and was so relieved to find a genuine opportunity for doing so. In 'Von ewiger Liebe', which followed, we felt we were hearing for the first time that evening the Jurinac we knew. Reger and Strauss brought the printed programme to an end, and her single encore was the Marschallin's monologue. At the phrase about the mystery at the heart of life – 'das alles ist geheim, so viel geheim' – it was as though the soul, and in a way the voice too, came free of its cage. For perhaps the first time in a long evening of singing, she raised her head.

The experience was a strange one, and I remember following it up at the weekend with an evening of records which began with the *Idomeneo* of 1956 under Pritchard, then breaking off to go back to the earlier recording, in 1951, of excerpts under Fritz Busch. The singing is not expressive, but in the early recording overwhelmingly beautiful simply as singing, and this is so with the excerpts from *Così fan tutte* a year earlier. The sheer sound of the singing is the lovely thing, and lovelier the further we go back. It is again the beauty of sound that gives value to her recording of Strauss's *Four Last Songs* from 1951. The songs themselves were still new, and Jurinac has since remarked that she sang them, in Stockholm on that occasion, almost at sight. That would explain why the singing is so external; the sound remains glorious.

Since then, of course, numerous live transcripts of her performances on stage have become readily accessible and the Jurinac collection is significantly enriched. The vocal prime is caught, for instance, in an historic occasion at Vienna, the *Don Giovanni* of 5 November 1955, the second night of the newly reopened State Opera House, Böhm conducting. Jurinac presents a Donna Elvira in whom there is no shrewishness, a tenderly caring woman, of such sympathetic warmth that the opera virtually regroups around her. Then a totally different character and a new Jurinac emerges in *L'incoronazione di Poppea*. It is performed in the edition of Erich Kraack, more like Respighi than Monteverdi but wickedly effective as a setting for the *femme fatale*, and Jurinac is there, with a new glamour in the strong middle register, where the part mostly lies. This is from Vienna, 1963, Karajan conducting. From Salzburg, and again with Karajan, we now have a *Don Carlos* (1958), and this too extends our comprehension: we can see, for instance, why she was one of those rarities, a singer of what Italians would see as the German school, whom they actually took to their hearts. The dignity has warmth, the manner re-strained but lit by passion from within. Moreover, in no country where a taste for singing survives, could the true artist fail to be recognised in the cleanness of 'take' and the noble span of phrase in the Queen's great aria, 'Tu che le vanità'.

The sight as well as the sound of Jurinac on stage is preserved in a film of *Der Rosenkavalier* from Salzburg in 1960, where she sings her Octavian to the Marschallin of Elisabeth Schwarzkopf, the voices standing out with such well-defined individuality: Schwarzkopf vibrantly feminine, Jurinac giving a boyish tone to her firm mezzo quality. Her stage presence – and the film brings it back to mind wonderfully well – had a spark in it, a liveliness and mobility that the listener who knows only her sound record-ings might not expect. She was one of the most wholesome singers of our time: thinking of her, listening to her, and now seeing her again, one can only feel the better for it.

CHAPTER 6

Gré Brouwenstijn and
Julia Varady

'That we would do, we should do when we would'.

I thought of Gré Brouwenstijn, and thought of her with affection. To write about her it would be necessary to know more of her life. But then the further thought occurred: why not take a day or two off and go to Holland where she was living? Perhaps next month, I thought, and then, when next month came, the one after that. And then on 7 January 2000, *The Times* carried her obituary. She had died on the previous 14 December, aged 84. She had been dead even while I was saying 'Next month' for the last time.

Then came a strange experience. Trying to think of her, as one does, adjusting the lenses and tone-controls of memory to focus a face and a voice, I found that a sound and sight very promptly and obediently arose – but the face and voice were those of Julia Varady. Then on a different occasion, only a little later, thoughts of Varady centred on her Fidelio. Visually, it was all quite vivid. But why was she singing against the background of a production by Wieland Wagner? Where, for that matter, had I heard Varady's Leonore, and, come to that, was I sure she had ever sung the role? And this is the thing they call memory!

But of course the vision did begin to clear, and out of the mists emerged the realisation that the 'Varady' of remembrance was Gré Brouwenstijn. This was the Leonore of a *Fidelio* performed at London's Festival Hall in 1955 by the Stuttgart State Opera. Wolfgang Windgassen was the Florestan, Gustav Neidlinger the Pizarro, both superb in their roles, and the Marcelline was an enchanting soprano, Lore Wissmann. The conductor was Ferdinand Leitner; the producer (for this was part of a season of staged performances in the Hall), Wieland Wagner.

Brouwenstijn was fairly slight of figure and certainly not weighty of voice, but she was immense in her resolution. Deeply human, she concentrated her voice to match her will-power. The voice itself had nothing of the Flagstad breadth about it: it was as though it *had* to intensify because it couldn't expand. In the last section of the solo, 'Ich folg' dem innern Triebe', the demands upon such a voice seemed cruel, and yet she emerged

Gré Brouwenstijn

The 15th performance at The Royal Opera House of " Don Carlos "

CHARACTERS IN ORDER OF APPEARANCE

ELIZABETH DE VALOIS	GRÉ BROUWENSTIJN
TEBALDO, her Page	JEANNETTE SINCLAIR
DON CARLOS, Infante of Spain	JON VICKERS
COUNT OF LERMA, a Spanish nobleman	EDGAR EVANS
A MONK	JOSEPH ROULEAU
RODRIGO, Marquis of Posa	TITO GOBBI
PHILIP II, King of Spain	BORIS CHRISTOFF
PRINCESS OF EBOLI, ⎱ Ladies in Waiting	FEDORA BARBIERI
THE COUNTESS OF AREMBERG ⎰ to Elizabeth	MARGARET LENSKY
THE GRAND INQUISITOR	MICHAEL LANGDON
THE ROYAL HERALD	ROBERT ALLMAN
A VOICE FROM HEAVEN	AVA JUNE

Flemish Deputies — Inquisitors — Ladies and Gentlemen of the Spanish Court — Pages —
Guards of Philip II — Friars — Members of the Holy Office — Soldiers — Magistrates —
Colonial Deputies

Covent Garden, May 1958

triumphantly, eyes blazing and tone uncompromised. A certain pride was inherent; this was an aristocrat among voices.

Hence, I think, the Varady connection. Among today's sopranos, she has an aristocracy of voice and style comparable to Brouwenstijn's from an earlier generation in that she sings roles which are hers not by virtue of vocal power or weight but by a concentration of tone and spirit. She holds her head high and yet her voice has a full measure of human warmth within it.

It is interesting to note the ways in which a singer becomes personally special. Often the first hearing proves decisive, and that must have been

29

so with Brouwenstijn. Of Varady, by contrast, it could almost be said that the special relationship dates from the first of many times of *not* hearing. A jinx operated to ensure that on my night she would be indisposed, and there was a certain irony about this in that her name had come to be familiar for her own substitution as Alceste at Edinburgh in place of an indisposed Janet Baker. A friend, who duly turned up at the King's Theatre and was disgusted to find that his beloved Janet was not to appear, recalled the sympathetic reassurance of the attendant who encouraged him to take his seat (others had left) and added 'I don't think you'll be disappointed, sir'. In fact so far was he from disappointment that he made a special point of the event, and later found himself for once in full agreement with Harold Rosenthal who wrote in *Opera* magazine on the pleasure he had in making the acquaintance of 'the superb Julia Varady'. Thrilled by her stage presence and dramatic involvement, Rosenthal found her voice not intrinsically beautiful but used with much feeling and intensity, an artist comparable to the late Marie Collier.

That was at the Festival of 1974. Varady's career had already run for twelve years, but Cluj Opera House in Romania was perhaps not the best place for attracting public attention, and it was not until she moved to Frankfurt and then, in 1972, to Munich that she gained wider notice. Reports came regularly to *Opera* magazine from their correspondent Greville Rothon who heard her as Leonora in *La forza del destino* and wrote that she was 'a most exciting singing-actress'. Her voice was 'striking', its usage characterised by 'a refined legato', her style by 'a passionate intensity'. Clearly she was a singer to watch.

It was in the previous year, 1973, at Munich that she had met and sung with her future husband. Cast as the troubled, unfaithful wife in Puccini's *Il tabarro* (or *Der Mantel* in German) she found herself singing to the towering Michele (or Marcel) of Dietrich Fischer-Dieskau. It is not true, apparently, that he slipped her a note proposing marriage during the course of their duet, but they did discover a mutual attraction and he himself recalled singing the part with especial ardour. A recording exists, preserving a deeply committed performance by all concerned, with Wolfgang Sawallisch conducting in a way that is sometimes more Italianate than the Italians and yet from time to time seems to uncover an Italian *Wozzeck*. Varady's is the first voice heard, and immediately thrills with its tone, tense and deep, reminding us that in childhood her voice was said to be remarkable for its contralto depth. Radiant in the love music, she shows herself a fastidious artist, bringing the instinct for beauty and refinement even to the heart of this turbulent score. And it is true that something of the urgent vibrancy that was so strong in Marie Collier's performances asserts itself here; something too of the concentrated, tragically inflected lyricism of Meta Seinemeyer. It is a heady mixture.

Her work with Fischer-Dieskau continued after their marriage in 1977 with *Arabella*, also at Munich; and soon, in 1979, was to come Aribert

30

Julia Varady

Reimann's *Lear*, in which the reconciliation scene as played by these two is among the most moving passages from opera on records. Varady also in these years sang her first Desdemona, the role of her Covent Garden debut in 1986. This was no doubt another cause of a mental association with Brouwenstijn. Varady's Otello was Vladimir Atlantov, on the stage which, years before, Brouwenstijn had shared with Ramon Vinay. The Russian tenor had an exceptionally powerful and incisive voice, and beside him Varady stood little chance in terms of sheer volume. Happily, her portrayal from the first had been conceived with other priorities in mind. Horst Koegler wrote in *Opera* of her first Desdemona in Munich as glowing with 'almost autumnal colours, floating her lovely, slender voice as if poised in mid-air'. Brouwenstijn, as I remember, was more substantial, and yet she too conveyed the sense of nobly affectionate integrity by means of a voice that had, so to speak, kept its figure, drawing a slender line of sound, and never spreading under pressure. She sang on those unforgettable nights in 1955 when the opera burst on us in its first house production since the war. Everything worked together (the handling of the chorus alone was something of a revelation), and the isolated, dignified figure of Brouwenstijn's Desdemona stood at the centre. Her voice was lovely, though uncertainties of intonation became more troublesome over the years; they

31

were especially noticeable, I recall, in the 'Ave Maria' – and yet a live recording of the solo made as late as 1968 hints only very slightly at this weakness and preserves much of the purity and refined style that were so memorable.

Cherished still more deeply is the memory of her Elisabeth de Valois in *Don Carlos*. 1957 was the centenary year of Covent Garden's existence specifically as an opera house, and the celebrations included in 1958 performances of a new production which perhaps for the first time revealed Verdi's opera as the masterpiece it is. Again, a live recording exists, but it is one I have never wanted to hear, not from fear of disillusionment but because the memory should not be diluted. Inevitably that has happened with Gobbi and Christoff (whose performances I 'hear' now as an amalgam of live memories and records), but Vickers and Brouwenstijn I want to preserve. The duets were painfully lovely; Elisabeth's aria had a vulnerable strength so that you listened intently; and probably most characteristic of all were the 'Giustizia' and the royally controlled intensity of her prayer 'Ah! Iddio su noi veglio!'.

These are passages in which it is also easy 'in the mind's ear' to hear Varady. Her legacy of recordings is a great deal larger than Brouwenstijn's, and future generations will be able to identify for themselves this aristocracy of style in a wide repertoire from Bach and Handel onwards. Rarities to take in on the way include Spontini's *Olympie*, Spohr's *Jessonda* and a gloriously sung 'scenic cantata' by the young Meyerbeer, *Gli amori di Teolinda*. There is plenty of Mozart and Strauss, and in Wagner a fine Senta and Sieglinde. Yet it is Italian opera that throws her distinction into sharpest relief: the fire burning so fiercely for example within her outwardly controlled Santuzza in *Cavalleria rusticana*. A Puccini recital recorded in 1993 has in it 'Un bel dì', 'Vissi d'arte', all the favourites to which the common touch has been brought from time out of mind and which always find something *un*common in her mixture of strength and charm, warmth and dignity. In Verdi her kinship with Brouwenstijn is most demonstrable. Their first entrances in the *Requiem* have thrilling effect out of proportion to the size of their voices – it is the concentration of timbre and emotion that does it. In the 'Pace' aria from *La forza del destino* it is the feeling for *chiaroscuro*, so fully responsive to the tensions of angst and serenity. Brouwenstijn retired in 1971, just about the time when Varady was opening up her career in Germany. It is always pleasing to find a link from one generation to another. Varady (born in 1941) is now at about the age of Brouwenstijn (born 1915) at the end of her career. There are, let us hope, more years to go; but when the time comes and some commentator looks back, it will be interesting to know where the young soprano is at present who in retrospect will be seen as having in her turn continued the distinguished line.

CHAPTER 7

Nicolai Gedda

There must be some bad reason why Gedda's name slips the mind so often. Perhaps by that I mean *my* mind, but I think there is a general tendency too. In theory, for example, the specialist record collectors who know about voices probably admire Gedda as much as they do any tenor of the post-78rpm era; but when they slip into incantatory mode, invoking the great names, the *allegro con entusiasmo* of the first dozen or so will relax into an *andante*, with a further *rallentando*, pause for thought, then *coda con brio* ... 'and Gedda!'. Of course, it has partly to do with nationality (Björling gets in early, but after him the Scandinavians are forgotten). To a much greater extent it's to do with repertoire. Not many great operatic tenors sing Verdi and Bach, Donizetti and Janáček, Gounod and Mussorgsky, Elgar, Barber, Stravinsky and (at sight if necessary) Guillaume de Machaut. Inclusiveness can have an oddly exclusive effect. The man who can encompass so much comes to mind for no one primary thing; and you end up surprised to find that he has been missed out altogether.

But first let us put some different questions. 'Who are the *smiling* tenors?' for example. Gigli, no doubt, and ...? Or 'Who are the *sweet*-voiced tenors?' Bonci, maybe, and ...? For both of these I would probably want to say 'Gedda' first. In the matter of sweetness it would have to be with reference to Gedda's relatively early years (remembering that they began relatively late). But in general Gedda sang with the lines of his face rounding upwards in a smile, and the enduring memory of his voice 'in the flesh' is of a most delightful sweetness and purity of tone.

The 'image' of his recorded voice is slightly different. Ever so slightly, and yet insistently, an unevenness of emission (not in registers or in passage-work but on individual notes) obtrudes. Stylistically he stands so firmly in the category of the refined tenor that it comes as a surprise to find an element which it would be unkind to call gawky but which, at any rate, has not the elegance one had cause to hope for. There are plentiful exceptions to this, but my strong impression is that the sound of his singing 'live' gave a pleasure that came with additional delight if for some time one had become accustomed to his voice only on records.

The records are precious of course, and often both marvellous (in the ease of his top notes, for instance) and faithful; yet a later generation, which has only the records to go by, needs to have such a testimony as this, however limited, for the real sound was more beautiful and the small flaws noted above were easily assimilated. The mind has another delicate 'separating' operation to perform. Gedda belongs to that remarkable generation of tenors who have been able to sing on, giving considerable (and not just relative) pleasure at what, for tenors, is an advanced age. Carlo Bergonzi and Alfredo Kraus were others, and at one of Gedda's late concerts I heard it suggested that if those three, with all their years, cared to, they could still collectively outsing the current trio of Carreras, Domingo and Pavarotti. It was not a remark likely to be put to the test, but it shows the faith which these singers were able to inspire. Two of the last times I myself heard Gedda (not the very last) were orchestral concerts at Birmingham and Covent Garden. The programmes were substantially the same, and it was interesting to hear them in sequence. The first had some most beautiful singing of operatic arias in the first half, but then after the interval, in the selection of songs from Viennese operetta, he seemed vocally tired. At Covent Garden it was the other way round. The arias went rather less well, but the second half was magic: the vitality seemed unquenchable and the voice had cleared itself of the slight 'frog' that had sometimes affected tone and pitch in the arias. Both of these were happy and touching occasions; yet the memory has to put them affectionately to one side in the search back through the years for the true Gedda sound, the sweetness that characterised it so distinctively.

The voice I strive to catch – and just about can – is the pure lyric Duke of Mantua whose 'E il sol dell'anima', 'Parmi veder le lagrime' and 'Bella figlia dell'amore', but for the matter of language (which was English), seemed to belong to the era of those early records, rarer to the hearing then than they are now, which, if so lucky as to possess, one would play and replay till they were known by heart.

That was in 1954, and a long time elapsed before a concert performance of *Die Zauberflöte* under Klemperer brought this sound back to the ears 'live' and again showed it to be better than the records. Mind, the records were something. That youth and sweetness in the character of Grigory the monk or (as he becomes) Dmitri the pretender in *Boris Godunov* was a revelation: they almost tilted the balance of the opera, and in doing so gave it a hero that cannot have been intended for it. And then there were those operettas with Otto Ackermann conducting and Elisabeth Schwarzkopf at her most radiant: these had the sweetness and the smile in conjunction. Then the Callas *Butterfly*, Gedda's Act 1 Pinkerton being an utter charmer, as of course he should be or the thing makes no sense. In fact his recordings came so thick and fast that one began to take him for granted and forgot to be grateful. But then, in 1966, came another 'live' reminder, with the marvellous *Benvenuto Cellini* at Covent Garden. That surely was the time when Gedda reached the height of his powers.

In this part, his voice put on weight and showed its resilience: the

Gedda as Lenski in *Eugene Onegin*

production restored passages that had traditionally been cut, and it made a long evening. Gedda was not usually credited with any very remarkable talent as an actor, but he certainly carried conviction here. The abiding impression was of vitality which suited both Berlioz and the Renaissance. He always had a certain dominance on stage, partly because, to put it indecorously, he has quite a large head. The features are well defined, the face providing a vivid focal point. It was a clever stroke of casting, as well as an imaginative gesture of affection, that brought him back in 1997, his 72nd year, to take the short but effective role of Abdisu in Pfitzner's *Palestrina*. The production was strongly cast, but I find it difficult now to 'see' any of the other characters; no trouble at all with the aged Patriarch of Assyria.

From the 1970s onwards he gave an increasing number of recitals, and it was in these that one realised most clearly the breadth of his accomplishment. He might on one date give a straightforward Lieder recital, memorable for its Brahms ('Im Waldeseinsamkeit' especially) and Strauss ('Wie sollten wir geheim sie halten'). Then would come an ingenious *Songs of the North* programme, with Glinka, Mussorgsky and Tchaikowsky for Russia, Grieg and Sibelius principal among the Scandinavians. Often he would include a French group, beautiful in finesse and use of the language. His prowess as a linguist was of course another powerful asset. His English was excellent – when he sang in the premiere of Samuel Barber's *Vanessa* at the Metropolitan they remarked that in a cast of native English speakers he was the one whose words came across most clearly. He would also sing Dvořák's *Gypsy Songs* in Czech, and his recording of Janáček's *One Who Vanished* is one of the best.

The mood of his concerts, the expression which dominates them in memory, was of eagerness. He was a man with something to share, and there was a certain impetuosity in his delivery. There could be sadness too and a poetic luxury of meditation – the lingering phrases of Tchaikowsky's 'After the ball' and the despair of his tones in Rachmaninov's 'Christ is risen' were unforgettable. Often one wonders about the interaction between the private life and the artistic, and Gedda's recently published autobiography (*My Life and Art*, Amadeus, 1999) shows a man who from childhood has been a prey to anxieties. He concludes that the experience of suffering can be beneficial: 'Singing while having to contend with personal problems is dreadful, but after living through a crisis you notice that you have in fact developed in human terms, assuming of course that you have not snapped under the strain.' Or as Burl Ives used to put it, 'Takes a worried man to sing a worried song.' Perhaps it was this underlay of melancholy that made the smile in his voice so vivid and potent.

For myself, though there is little likelihood of impressions dimming, I have two *aides-mémoires*. One is a compact disc: the young singer in his ardent prime giving a song recital at the Salzburg Festival of 1961. The other is a printed programme. On the last time I heard him he sang at St

John's in London. Among his encores was Rachmaninov's 'In the silence of the night', its high note and diminuendo still beautifully taken; and at the end a voice from the audience dropped into the silence of the hall the Russian word 'Horozho'. It was quietly spoken, almost an involuntary murmur of appreciation. In the applause which followed, it seemed to swell into an expression of the whole audience's gratitude for the gift and achievements of a lifetime.

CHAPTER 8

Gérard Souzay

There are singers whose voices seem hardly to change though the years become decades and the decades themselves mount up to a not inconsiderable portion of a century. Gérard Souzay has not been one of those. As an observer, with no 'inside' knowledge of a personal kind and no quasi-technical theories to offer, I have found it extremely puzzling. The voice we knew first from records in the immediate post-war years ranked in quality with the most beautiful of all; it sounded as though well trained and seemed to come under no undue stress. It had most especially a quality which singers often forfeit when they cease to be gifted amateurs and start to perform professionally: a natural generosity of sound, which teaching hardens, concentrating the tone to give it penetrative edge, often developing a carapace of a harder, and sometimes objectionably metallic, substance. There was obviously nothing even faintly amateurish about Souzay's production or style even in the very early years when his first records were released on 78s; but the voice itself had the freshness, the bloom and naturalness of the good amateur. If as an amateur oneself, one tried to imitate Souzay, it would involve (vainly) 'centralising' the tone, aiming at a gentle resonance located in the easy middle of the voice and then encouraged to bloom in the upper and lower registers, which lent themselves less readily. If a singer of the past were mentally invoked it might be Herbert Janssen in his records from the 1930s; and, as with him so with Souzay, a very light, almost imperceptible flicker of quick vibrato formed part of the voice's character and its natural attractiveness. And it seemed to me that Souzay's voice remained in that condition until sometime in the late 1960s.

I remember hearing him in the Festival Hall in 1960 itself and even then being surprised by the depth of tone (the initial impression was almost of a bass-baritone) and also by the extent to which the aureole of gentle resonance (if that is a fair term for it) seemed to have thinned, to reveal the strong metal at the centre. But this was still a beautiful sound, whereas some ten years later, or roughly by the age of fifty, the production appeared to have changed, the legato to be compromised and the now harder tone to be its former self only on certain notes and in certain passages, usually quiet or loud rather than in the medium-volume range.

38

This process accelerated till neither on records nor 'live' could I identify the sound with the one I still knew as 'Souzay'. The style was assured, the manner expressive but the voice itself gave sadly limited pleasure, and that of an altered kind.

This did matter. The point needs making because the theory of perform-ance in French song is that voice and singing as such are of secondary importance, the primary need being for clear and intelligent communica-tion of meaning. French teaching and commentary constantly assert the primacy of the words. This is the *thrust* of opinion: usually the professors will cover themselves with a saving clause, much as English adjudicators do at singing-competitions, to the effect that, while a beautiful voice is highly desirable and 'of course' the singer must know how to produce it, nevertheless (and we gather this is the important bit) the singer has to communicate meaning, and that this involves giving full attention to the words. It is a point, or an emphasis, made with regard to all song, but is applied with particular insistence to the *mélodie*. In Reynaldo Hahn's influential and symptomatic lectures *On Singers and Singing* (1913-14)

39

we come upon constant reminders: 'and let us remember that our wish, above all, is for singing to be simply a more beautiful form of speech, ever inspired by the spoken word'. Hahn, 'let us remember', used habitually to sing with a cigarette in one corner of his mouth. Other major teachers and influences upon singers of Souzay's generation include the mezzo-soprano Claire Croiza, who reportedly said: 'In singing, one may prefer either the sound or the word. No sound however beautiful will ever give me personally the joy that I get from a perfectly enunciated vowel'. If such a claim were merely autobiographical (as that one is in form) it would merely state a point of view, but from a major representative of a national school it has to be taken seriously. It illustrates also the process whereby for so long the French art-song has acquired a mystique: if a perfectly enunciated vowel is the primary source of pleasure, how can a foreigner aspire either to the perfection itself or even a just critical appreciation of it? Those who implied that they possessed this refinement of appreciation were *ipso facto* connoisseurs who would wince as though stung whenever they detected a vowel that was less than perfect. As with most mystiques there is a great deal of silliness, and so there is in the sentence attributed (by an admirer) to Croiza – after all, a vowel, when pronounced, *is* a sound and on its own has no more meaning than a high B flat.

Souzay was brought up as a singer with this at the very least constituting an important element in the climate of opinion. Its practical force, one would think, must surely be to make an established singer set even more value upon the word (and 'the spoken word' at that, according to Hahn) as the principal means of expressiveness in music. Whether evenness of voice-production came to seem of less importance, or whether some other cause was at work in his later vocal development I cannot say; but whereas his mastery of expression through the word seemed not to have diminished, I had no doubt as to the diminution of my own pleasure in his singing – which is not too oblique a commentary, perhaps, on these precepts concerning the primacy of 'the word'.

A mystique is nothing if not a mystery, and a further mystery (or puzzle, at least) arises from the entry under Souzay in *Grove* (*Dictionary of Music and Musicians*, 1980). This was written by Martin Cooper, an authority on French music and source of the remark attributed above to Claire Croiza. He refers to Souzay's period of study with Pierre Bernac and adds that 'he took some time to shed his teacher's mannerisms'. Under the heading of Bernac, and over the same writer's name, we find that his (Bernac's) art was 'very conscious and closely allied to the art of speech': the 'fastidiousness of delivery becomes dangerously close to affectation in his handling of German and English texts', though it may have had advantages with French. As Souzay, Bernac's pupil, became closely associated with German song, and if his teacher's influence remained so potent, then presumably Souzay was similarly regarded as suspect of affectation in his singing of Lieder. The pernicious influence of Bernac, according to Martin Cooper,

40

Souzay (right) with Dalton Baldwin

showed itself also in Souzay's 'almost too beautiful articulation of French texts' and in the alleged fact that 'his production and interpretation have never wholly lost a note of preciosity or self-consciousness'.

The mystery is that while these are the observations of a well-qualified and no doubt sincere writer, they awaken in this reader and listener no glimmer of recognition. Affectation seemed to me when I heard Bernac, and seems now when I listen to him on records, to be alien to his art as it is to Souzay's. Possibly Bernac's higher baritone (at times not unlike Hugues Cuénod's tenor) and his aptitude for the gaiety or apparent frivolity of some of some of Poulenc's songs might provoke such a reaction: perhaps it is the element of high camp that to Cooper amounted to affectation (as the posing of Wilde and the aesthetes had inflamed the flammable of an earlier generation). In other words it would have been something he didn't understand and didn't want to understand. But even so I find it hard to see that as a reaction to Souzay's art the criticisms have any validity at all.

In fact Souzay could have done with more of Bernac's flair. Comparing their recordings of Poulenc's *Métamorphoses* (Bernac with Poulenc in 1945, Souzay with Dalton Baldwin *c.* 1979), I find Bernac lighter and more nimble in the first song, better at the *très lié* of 'C'est ainsi que tu es' and

41

more gaily catching the light-foot rhythm of 'Paganini'. In the second song, incidentally, Bernac sings with great beauty of voice: this and the records he made pre-war, allowing for the difference between the two singers in tessitura or 'lie' of their voices, sound more like the young Souzay than does Souzay himself in his recording from the mid-1970s. Yet even comparing like with (relatively) like, Souzay of 1955 with Bernac in 1937, one finds a more open-hearted utterance in Bernac's way with Fauré's 'Prison', the fine setting of Verlaine's poem of the prisoner who yearns for freedom. The cry 'Mon Dieu, mon Dieu, la vie est là, simple et tranquille' releases its emotion, touchingly, in 'simple et tranquille'; and 'Qu'as-tu fais, voilà' brings tears into the voice – not an Italian tenor's tears but real emotion none the less. Souzay, by contrast, gives a measured, beautifully sung performance, but if emotion is there he is keeping it to himself.

Still, what a joy it was – and is – to hear him in his prime. His Lieder singing comes back now for that blessed quality so lightly brushed aside by the teachers and adjudicators, the beauty of tone and evenness of line. An early Schubert recital on a Decca LP opened with a performance of 'An die Lieder' that had authority and tenderness in all due proportion but was above all a blessing in sound, in lines such as a great cellist might draw (and you wouldn't find those people calling *that* meaningless). He was particularly well suited to Schumann – again among the early Deccas was a 'Schöne Wiege' full of pained sweetness and controlled passion. Not much of an opera singer, he nevertheless made some delightful solo recordings – of Mercutio's 'Queen Mab' for instance, or the haunting 'Legend' from Massenet's *Le Jongleur de Notre Dame*. He had a wide repertoire of songs, and gave a French tinge to many of them, such as Tchaikowsky's 'At the Ball' – a masterpiece of the musing imagination, with something very French in its intimacy, a touch that might almost have been learned from Yvonne Printemps. But of course it *is* French song to which we return, lovely things among them, as for instance, just recently discovered and published, a couple by Fauré from 1947, 'Mandoline' (elegant, courtly and not a bit 'precious' or 'self-conscious') and the charming 'Le plus doux chemin'.

In a procession of French baritones in their prime and in this period and repertoire – from Charles Panzéra, to Bernac, Souzay and Camille Maurane, and even on maybe to François le Roux and Félix Thierry, where all are artists, some with stronger conviction or insight than others, Souzay still takes the central place. It is partly that his voice has greater reserves of depth in it, and that this gives more centrality of voice-character. It has also to do with the range of recorded repertoire. But principally (remember we are referring to his prime) it is to do with sound.

The art of singing, even of French song, thrives best on the well-regulated production of a beautiful voice – whatever the merits of 'a perfect vowel'.

42

CHAPTER 9

Herbert Janssen

The record industry – or a twig of what we now have to specify as its 'classical' branch – has done so well by singers of the past that it would be ungrateful of us to cry 'shame' the moment an omission is spotted. But this is a surprising one. Herbert Janssen was widely regarded as having a place among the great artists of his time. He made excellent records, not so many as we could wish but certainly enough to make up a well-stocked double CD album. Patient search of the catalogues will find him represented in anthologies of songs by Schubert, Schumann, Brahms and Wolf, and of operas by Wagner. He has his place – and I should think so too – in *The Record of Singing*. But as far as I can discover, no recital disc, whether on CD or LP, has yet been devoted to him and his art; and on my own supposedly alphabetical recital-shelves nothing interposes between the tenor Jadlowker and soprano Jeritza.

The Record of Singing, that great leveller, places Janssen in the third of four monumental record albums, as a member of the inter-war German school, one of six baritones, all highly talented; and when represented as here by a single item, and that one of their best, all or any of them may seem *primus inter pares*. But Janssen is special. His expression and timbre were intensely personal; his technique is fascinating; his sensibility has a musical refinement, his tone a seriousness. Most of these baritones, as we hear them on records, are eminently sound, innocent of loosely vibrating notes or bulging phrases. Heinrich Schlusnus was one of the great exponents of bel canto, Gerhard Hüsch the model of a good all-rounder. Janssen, even in his prime, was probably a little more risky, but his singing went deeper, was of a richer, softer texture and had a greater capacity for both tenderness and anxiety.

His career covered roughly three decades, with phases corresponding. In the 1920s he sang mostly in Germany; the 1930s established him internationally; the 1940s were his American years. Give or take a little, it is on the middle period that his reputation now rests. He was a regular visitor to Covent Garden, singing in every international summer season from 1926 to 1939 and prominent in that famous generation of Wagnerian singers headed by Frida Leider, Lotte Lehmann, Lauritz Melchior and Friedrich Schorr. These also were the years of his successes at Bayreuth

43

and of his residence in Berlin as principal lyric baritone of the State Opera. His debut dates back to 1922 in his thirtieth year (of military age in 1914, he survived the full four years as an officer in the cavalry). In Berlin he sang in a wide range of parts, Italian and French as well as German, and became noted for his Italianate production. He is reported as saying that for best part of a year he practised daily the aria 'Il balen del suo sorriso' from *Il trovatore*, formidable in its range and tessitura, formative in its insistence on beauty of tone and a legato style.

Of that part of his repertoire London heard nothing: it did, however, enjoy the benefit of his study, which provided the technical basis for all his singing, the Wagnerian roles included. His Wolfram, Gunther and Kurwenal became legendary. Of those, the last aroused at one time objections from Ernest Newman, who wrote (*Sunday Times*, 9 May 1929) that 'Mr Herbert Janssen as Kurwenal was so manifestly miscast that it is hard to understand how such a mistake could have been made. This exceptionally fine artist, who excels in delicate shades of singing and acting, has neither the weight nor the roughness of voice for so blunt and rather crude an old dog as Kurwenal.' He must have come round to it, for two years later, almost to the day (3 May 1931) he was writing of Janssen, in a context of praise, 'turning that fine jeweller's art of his upon the music of Kurwenal'. If we can judge by recordings from the stages of Covent Garden and the Metropolitan, both judgements may be right, for Janssen sounds unlike his normal self as the Kurwenal of Act 1 but totally right for Act 3. Neville Cardus saw that same performance in 1931, writing in the *Manchester Guardian* of Janssen's part in it as 'one of the most movingly beautiful pieces of work I have ever known ... his singing and acting alike were wounding to the heart in Act 3'.

The references to delicacy may prompt a question about the suitability of his voice for a large house or for Wagner at all. Later, in the 1940s, when he sang at the Metropolitan as Wotan and Hans Sachs he was found deficient in power. At Covent Garden his heaviest role was the Dutchman, and the only complaint concerning volume in all his time there appears to have been raised in his first season with a remark that the voice, beautiful in itself, seemed not to free itself effectively from the throat. In the 1930 season the *Daily Telegraph*'s music critic notes 'his mezza voce is quite remarkable for its carrying power'. Of his Dutchman one observer remarked upon the skill with which he concealed the fact that the low Gs and A flats were not really in his voice; but no critics appear to have complained about lack of power.

In fact he was credited with bringing distinction to whatever he touched. With him, the Speaker in *Die Zauberflöte* 'stood out alone' (*Gramophone*, July 1939), and Cardus (*Manchester Guardian*, 3 May) found 'more wisdom in one syllable of Janssen's Speaker' than in all the pronouncements of the Sarastro. His Kothner in *Die Meistersinger* was a brilliant comic sketch. Telramund in *Lohengrin* had him darkening the

Janssen as Wolfram in *Tannhäuser*

tone 'without producing an ugly sound' (*The Times*, 16 May 1931). Newman in 1938 described his Dutchman as 'one of the truly great things of
the operatic stage of today; here is a sufferer who carries on his shoulders
not only his own but the whole world's woe'. 'Beckmesser' of *The Gramophone* (August 1937), in a survey of the Covent Garden season, selected
Janssen's Amfortas in *Parsifal* as a supreme example of the operatic art:
'He still stands immeasurably superior to other German baritones, tenors
and basses in vocal culture, and without sacrificing any beauty of tone he
conveys even more vividly than before the drained weariness of a man
racked by spiritual and physical suffering.'

'Beckmesser' was Walter Legge; and it is to him, as a producer of records
for His Master's Voice, that we owe the best part of Janssen's recordings
on commercial discs. As the record companies of more recent times have
not yet compiled and issued a Janssen recital, we will devise one for

45

ourselves. Restricting it for the time being to normal CD-length, we will allocate more than half to Lieder, as that important part of his work has not figured in this account: Schumann, Brahms and Strauss can occupy the first section, Wolf and Schubert the second.

The opening item shall be 'Widmung', the song of Schumann's that introduced the present writer to Janssen when the original 78rpm disc was still in the catalogue. Though the singing and Gerald Moore's playing are fine throughout, distinction – the Janssen touch – is felt in certain phrases. The 'linkage' at 'O du mein Grab' is one, and then the affectionate, easefully softened 'Du bist die Ruh, du bist der Frieden', with a subtly responsive modulation of tone, sensitive to the tenderly adjusted harmonies at 'du hebst mich liebend über mich'. That feeling for the character of a note as reconstituted by its harmonies is there in the other Schumann song too.

This is 'Die Lotosblume' in which, after the almost childlike narrative simplicity of its first verse, the second brings an enharmonic change that casts a magical light on the lotus and its love-affair with the moon. Janssen's is the very voice of the poet's fancy here, embodying the veiled softness of moonlight, the calm surface of water and petal, the timeless mystery of the scene. There is a technical wonder too, as the evenness of line and texture is supported at once by a secure breath control that does not deny the voice its natural, humanising degree of vibrato, and also by a mastery of enunciation that achieves perfect clarity and yet is assimilated smoothly into the singing-line.

The Brahms group would comprise 'Auf dem Kirchhofe', 'Wie bist du, meine Königin' and (unforgettably stamped with Janssen's vocal personality) 'Nicht mehr zu dir zu gehen'. For Richard Strauss we will limit ourselves to two, 'Allerseelen' and the most lovingly caressed 'Zueignung' ever.

Of all the singers recruited in the 1930s for the Hugo Wolf Society albums, Janssen was probably Walter Legge's own first choice. Later times have brought a fuller, more detailed understanding of the songs, and, in particular, Fischer-Dieskau's singing of the *Harfenspieler Lieder* has a deeper appreciation of their expressiveness: but to my ears Janssen's voice is still the finer instrument for them. These, with 'Komm, o Tod', 'Denk' es, o Seele' and the two Byron settings (*Vier Gedichte*) will suffice to represent his Wolf. For his Schubert, records offer less, and, fine as Gerhard Hüsch was, I still wish the singer chosen for the *Winterreise* of those years had been Janssen: not that he would necessarily have been more musical or have brought more specific insights, but that there was always something rare and personal about the very sound of his voice. We'll have two songs from *Schwanengesang*: 'Kriegers Ahnung' and the great challenge of 'Der Doppelgänger'.

Not much space now is left on our putative CD for opera. I'd include first some oddities such as Valentine's death scene in *Faust* and a duet from

Rigoletto with Lotte Schoene, examples of the early days in Berlin. Then, as a memento of his career at Bayreuth, the solos of Wolfram as recorded from the stage in 1930 are essential. Something of his Dutchman at Covent Garden in 1937 and as much as can be accommodated from the second Act of *Götterdämmerung* in 1938 will make up the rest.

In *The Gramophone*, July 1936, 'Beckmesser'-Legge wrote: 'His voice is of ravishing quality, he is musically and mechanically a faultless singer, and a magnificent actor ... Janssen, I make bold to say, is the greatest artist on the contemporary operatic stage.' Sometime early in this new millennium we should be able to open the record catalogues – or scan the database – and find that an enterprising producer has at last put together a recital to be found under this distinguished and still honoured name.

CHAPTER 10

Elisabeth Schumann

In Hugo Wolf's song 'Wie glänzt der helle Mond', an old woman looks up at the distant moon and thinks about the star of her own youth, which seems more distant still. The accompaniment glimmers high over the voice, and the singer softly, serenely contemplates Paradise, where soon she will sit veiled in silver, gazing upon her white fingers, while St Peter by the gate cobbles away at some old shoes. As the years went by, Elisabeth Schumann became increasingly fond of this song. It was a memorable item in her programmes, and sometimes one felt she even chose her dress with it in mind. The cream silk, silvered on shoulder and pocket, set off the greying hair, with its white streak up from the forehead, the eyes adding a further sparkle, the smile another radiance. The voice never sounded beyond *mezzo piano*, and Schumann's tones were pure candlelit silver. They recalled with touchingly frail beauty the youth now glinting, light-years away, in the night sky.

Yet, aptly as she sang this song of age, one could hardly think of her as becoming old. Her voice seemed to inhabit a perpetual springtime. Even when its bloom faded and its shine became dim, it told only of a May day that had clouded over. Her personality remains vivid in the memory as a delicious breeze on a sunshine day, full of gaiety and energy. One felt she might have said, along with Shakespeare's Beatrice, 'There was a star danced, and under that was I born.'

The danger for an artist who evokes such feelings and comparisons is that she will be thought of in the very terms Beatrice applies to herself, as one 'born to speak all mirth and no matter'. An English critic in 1926 characterised her as 'a mere fair-weather singer'. She shared with most light sopranos a limitation of colour range: a darkening of tone was foreign to the nature of the voice, and even to experiment risked sullying the airy brightness so essential to its being. The critic no doubt meant that Schumann's emotional range, like the palette of her colours, was small compared with, say, that of Lotte Lehmann in opera and Elena Gerhardt in Lieder. Even so, his criticism was mistaken. Her voice had tenderness and sorrow in its compass too, and the springtime gaiety was not just a passing prettiness but a strength. It was rather like G.K. Chesterton's discovery, as he drew with his piece of chalk from the South Downs, that white is not

48

Schumann as Sophie in *Der Rosenkavalier*

an absence of colour but, when applied to a piece of brown paper, a positive, valiant affirmation.

In her centenary year Schumann is still a living memory,[1] for she was active in concert work and teaching up to the time of her illness and death in 1952, not long before her sixty-fourth birthday. The time will come, however, when she has passed entirely into the musical encyclopaedias and the living history records of the gramophone. What the books will tell is that she was among the most admired singers of her age, enjoying a special success in the *soprano leggiero* opera roles of Mozart and the songs of Schubert and Richard Strauss, with whom she gave many recitals in Europe and the US, and who dedicated some of his songs to her. There: it will all go into a single sentence, carrying little more of the warm individuality than an epitaph cut in stone. Her name also will appear in the history of certain houses, notably the State Opera in Vienna and Covent Garden in London. In a library or second-hand bookshop, somebody from time to time will browsingly come upon a sentence that conveys an unusual warmth of feeling from the writer toward a singer. Victor Gollancz's

Journey Towards Music tells of Schumann's Sophie in *Der Rosenkavalier*: 'No one will ever forget the soar and leap of her voice at the presentation of the rose. Imagine silver as pure as young happiness and as true as steel, and you have an idea of it.' Or maybe it will be an obituary piece by Philip Hope-Wallace in a posthumous collection of his occasional writings called *Words and Music*: 'A supreme artist, she had the demure simplicity of a child with the radiant wit of the most highly civilised society.' Or leafing over the biography of the conductor Otto Klemperer, somebody will read of the soprano with whom he fell in troubled love, and on whose account shots were fired in the Hamburg opera house one night in 1913. More likely a record will be playing, perhaps of 'Heidenröslein' or 'Deh vieni, non tardar', and something about it will catch the ear of one new listener, who will say, 'Now that's a singer for *me*! Who was she?' So a new love affair will begin, and the memory will survive.

Mind, it will depend on the record. I don't think the early, pre-electrical discs will work the spell. There are disappointments here, and they derive from faults that were not going to disappear in later years. For instance, the Baroness's song from *Der Wildschütz* has a jolly way of half-sounding a note, the other half being a scoop or a semi-staccato that makes a speech point rather than a proper singing note. It was this kind of practice, along with the slight build and playful manner, that prompted the judgement many will have found offensive in Michael Scott's *The Record of Singing*, Vol. 2. Throughout her records, he feels, 'We are all too conscious of the winsome ways of the soubrette.' Her achievement, he concludes, was one 'of personality, like that of a *diseuse*'. Admirers should not rise to the bait with instant apoplexy, for the art of the *diseuse*, 'a talent to amuse', is not altogether to be despised. Moreover, the judgement is supported by some acute technical analysis, as well as a number of quotations, which may on balance have a belittling effect, but which have to be valued since they are taken from comments by contemporaries. There are also critical notes on the records, and these can be readily tested in the course of any Schumann recital to which we might treat ourselves on an occasion such as this centenary month.

For myself, the programme begins with the quintet from *Die Meistersinger*. This recording, so fine in nuance and detail, derives its strength from her. 'Hell und laut' (clear and loud) are among Eva's words, and in just such a way her voice rings out as the ensemble swells in volume. No doubt she is placed forward of the others, who include Lauritz Melchior and Friedrich Schorr, but Eva is the centre, the focal point of the group, and her prominence is justified. Even so, there is little sense in the recording that she needs any special consideration, for the voice seems to carry of itself. Reverting to the critical analysis of Schumann's method, one notes how finely sustained these notoriously testing phrases are – no suggestion of shallow breathing or unsupported tone here. Scott remarks that 'By the time she was forty, her voice was no more than a wisp of tone.' That would

SHAKESPEARE MEMORIAL THEATRE
STRATFORD-UPON-AVON

General Manager: HENRY TÖSSELL
Reception Secretary: ALICE CROWHURST
Assistant Manager: BRUCE ORGAN

RECITAL by

ELISABETH SCHUMANN

ACCOMPANIST: HUBERT GREENSLADE

Programme

DEH VIENI ! (MARRIAGE OF FIGARO) ...	Mozart
DAS VEILCHEN ...	
SHE NEVER TOLD HER LOVE	Haydn
SAILOR'S SONG ...	
GEHIMES ...	Schubert
NACHT UND TRÄUME	
DER JUNGLING AN DER QUELLE	
DIE FORELLE ...	
RUHE SUSSLIEBCHEN ...	Brahms
THERESE ...	
WIE BIST DU MEINE KÖNIGIN	
SCHWALBE SAG' MIR AN	
IN DEM SCHATTEN MEINER LOCKEN ...	Hugo Wolf
IHR JUNGEN LEUTE ...	
WIE GLANZT DER HELLE MOND ...	
FUSSREISE ...	

Sunday, 8th September, 1946

At 8 p.m.

have been in 1928; but this recording was made in 1931, the sixth 'take' of the session. She also had sung the role at Covent Garden the previous year, when there were no complaints about a lack of carrying power. One remembers Gollancz's 'true as steel' comparison, and I also recall that one of the gallery habitués at Covent Garden in those years mentioned how small the voice of the accomplished Adele Kern sounded in 1933 to ears that had been accustomed to Elisabeth Schumann.

That, however, was in Schumann's famous role of Sophie. Our record programme would have to include 'Wie himmlische, nicht irdische', where the high B is so beautifully placed and the phrase, though deliciously floated, does not dissolve into some incorporeal loveliness but remains eager and impulsive. Marcel Prawy, historian of the Vienna Opera, wrote that 'For all its tenuousness ... it filled every corner of the house', and this was true as late as 1937. No doubt we normally would be listening to it in the studio recording of 1933, but there are also excerpts from two performances at the Vienna State Opera, one in 1936, one in 1937, with differing casts but having Schumann as Sophie in both. Here, far from being a 'wisp' and a mere emanation of personality, the voice holds its own in trio and duet – sounding if anything finer than in the studios.

Central to her opera repertory was Mozart, and it's here that the criticisms in *The Record of Singing* become most severe: 'The incessant slithering and sliding, pecking and twittering, the lack of a solid legato, assume a greater prominence than they would have in the opera house or concert hall with the artist's physical presence to distract us.' Strong words, but the records are at hand, and we can judge for ourselves. 'L'amerò, sarò costante' from *Il rè pastore*: an occasional slither, maybe a twitter or two. 'Venite, inginocchiatevi' from *Le nozze di Figaro*: yes, a slide and a peck every now and then. But 'incessant'? On the contrary, the majority of notes are taken cleanly and held firmly for their full value. As we move on to 'Voi che sapete', the complaints become absurd. Clear, bright tone, well-bound phrases, judicious shading, a sure feeling for rubato – enjoyment restores a sense of proportion.

Schumann was not without faults, and they show up in Mozart, as in Bach and Handel. For my own part, I would be content now to move on to Lieder and perhaps end up with some operetta. But we'll take another Mozart record first – 'Vedrai, carino' from *Don Giovanni*. Not a slither, a slide, a peck, a twitter, but a tenderness that is never mawkish, expressed with an unaffected simplicity that is never insensitive. As for her physical presence, no, it is no longer there, alas, 'to distract us'. I fancy, though, that you do not need to have seen her in order to see her now. Voices with character carry a physical image. Glance at a photograph, as a record of Elisabeth Schumann is playing, and you see her clearly enough. The star of youth that had become so distant to the old woman of Hugo Wolf's song is quite close after all, and the voice shines with the radiance of its owner, in the year of her centenary, as it did when she was a loved, honoured figure in the musical life of her time.

[1] This chapter was published originally in *Opera News*, Dec. 1988 and reprinted in *Voices: Singers and Critics* (1992). It has been slightly shortened and otherwise emended.

CHAPTER 11

Lilli and Lotte Lehmann

At the start of her career it sometimes had to be explained that the Lehmann announced for that evening's performance was not Lilli but Lotte. Not that it could have taken anybody very long to tell the difference. With forty years between them, Lilli was old enough to be Lotte's mother if not her grandmother (there was in fact no family relationship at all). She was hardly likely, in 1914, to be singing Susanna, Micaëla or Mignon, and once either of them had uttered a note they could not possibly have been mistaken one for the other. As to looks … Yet even that amounted to little compared with the difference in personality. Lotte was charming, Lilli was stately. Lilli was respected; Lotte was loved.[1]

Even so, in a way which diminishes all these points of difference, they were alike: both had a greatness which in their own time appeared to many to place them beyond the competitive reach of contemporaries in their field; and most of those who went as far as that would take a further step and add that no one has ever surpassed them since. Lilli's Isolde, Brünnhilde, Donna Anna and Norma as heard in the 1890s formed critical touchstones for the next century. Lotte's Marschallin and Sieglinde, as known and cherished in the interwar years, became icons; and any soprano who made even half a success in those roles after the Second World War had to face the fact that somewhere in the house would be old-timers (not necessarily so old either) who would be saying 'But of course she's not Lotte'.

One great role – great in itself and in its importance in their respective careers – they had in common: that of Leonore in *Fidelio*. Lilli graduated to the part (having first sung the light lyric role of Marzelline) in 1885 at the Vienna State Opera, repeating it in many seasons there till 1910. In 1887 she sang it in New York and London, making a great impression with Mapleson's company at Her Majesty's. She seems, however, not to have found a chronicler to give life to the impression such as Lotte had for her Leonore at Salzburg in 1935. The performances were conducted by Toscanini, and for Vincent Sheean (*First and Last Love*, Gollancz 1957) they remained among the experiences of a lifetime. He recalled that Toscanini would often go out of his way to reject an already acclaimed singer in favour of one picked by himself from the ranks. 'In the case of Lehmann he was swayed not by her fame as Leonore but by his own ardent admiration, which on one occasion, I was told, led him to declare at the end of a difficult passage in rehearsal: "You are the greatest artist in the world".' There were moments of ecstasy – the beginning of 'Ich folg' dem innern Triebe' and 'O namenlose Freude', for instance. 'Every note of her voice conveyed the meaning of the part', and that included the spoken words; words such as 'kühl' and 'schwül' had what he remembered as 'a slow tenderness'. There were imperfections, but the incandescence of conductor and soprano made them insignificant.

This warmth towards Lotte on the part of that particular writer – his book is dedicated to her and he became a personal friend – might be suspect if it were not so typical. Similarly, writing of Lilli in the *New York Sun* on 8 December 1928, the veteran music critic W.J. Henderson may be indulging an old man's fondness for the rose-tints of memory. He too was on personal terms with the singer, whom he recalls meeting in Berlin some twenty years earlier. He asked after her holiday arrangements and was told that she was scheduled first to give three performances. 'What will you sing?' he asked. 'She smiled a demure smile and answered, "Violetta"'. Demure smiles were not normally in her line, but they are perhaps not unbecoming in a prima donna about to confide that she is booked for *La traviata* at the age of sixty. When he wrote his tribute to her in the *Sun* she had just celebrated her eightieth birthday and Henderson's mind went back to 1885 when she made her New York debut (as Carmen!). Then, more especially, he recalled a performance of *Tristan und Isolde* in 1899: 'the greatest ever given in the Metropolitan', he thought, 'possibly the greatest given anywhere'. Years later, in her drawing room in the Grünewald, he asked whether she too remembered that evening: 'Yes,' she said, 'it was the ideal *Tristan* of my life.'

We must not, I think, permit ourselves that little smile and lift of the eyebrows that come so readily when old men tell their dreams. Over the years these great occasions – the *Tristan* of 1899, the *Fidelio* of 1935 – acquire a glow in the recollection, yet the experiences were real enough. Their occurrence is one of the reasons why opera houses are still full: people go in the hope that tonight might be one of the occasions. And if a Lehmann were in the cast, a Lotte or a Lilli, there would be a fair chance.

Nor should we suppose that the old men, or their younger selves, were deaf to the faults or limitations of these singers they so admired. For WJH, the 1890s constituted the Met's Golden Age right enough, with Lilli Lehmann as one of its prime adornments; but as he heard her night after night he recognised the flaws. Her Marguerite in the *Faust* of 1887 was 'far from perfect ... the attack of her high notes being conducted on a method of cautious approach which was inartistic and wearisome'. In *Aida* on 16 January 1890 'she seemed to have considerable difficulty in controlling her voice, and her *mezza voce* effects were not what she intended them

Lilli Lehmann

to be'. Even the famous Norma, revived for her on 28 February of that same year, is heard through this critic's ears without the protective layer of legend upon it. The audience may have been 'fairly carried away' but: 'It must be said that Fr. Lehmann took many of the elaborate ornamental passages at a very moderate tempo and sang them with evident labour, thus depriving them of much of that brilliance which the smooth, mellow, pliable Italian voices impart to them.'

Now this needs noting, partly because it comes from the heart of the 'Golden Age' and makes a damaging observation on one of its most prized trophies. It is often held up as a thing of wonder that Lilli could be not only a great singer of the heroic Wagnerian roles but also an accomplished coloratura, a Violetta and Constanze, a Queen in both *Die Zauberflöte* and *Les Huguenots*, and earlier even a Gilda, Dinorah and Rosina. We know from recordings made when she was nearly sixty, that her virtuosity in florid music was indeed very considerable. We also know that while these recordings excite in us great admiration they do not leave us entirely happy. In 'attack' she can be clean as a whistle one moment then coming-up-from-under the next. Her fondness for a glottal 'launch' must surely have been ruinous; and in fact a ruin, albeit a noble and often beautiful one, is what we find. The declamatory passages in the solos of Donna Anna

55

Lotte Lehmann

and Leonore almost pitifully find the indomitable spirit undermined from within by a frailty of middle-register notes which any singing-teacher would know to be an inevitable result of working the chest-voice too hard and too high. Yet Lilli was herself a teacher of the highest repute, and it was known that she aimed at nothing short of perfection.

In some respects the deterioration of her voice recalls that of Callas's – except that with Lilli, at a far more advanced age, there is no hint of incipient wobble. But these two great sopranos have in common a proud history of versatility, Callas forsaking the heroic roles (Isolde and Brünnhilde included) for 'bel canto', while Lilli (as far as the main emphasis of her career was concerned) did the reverse. Both went from one extreme to another, whether we are thinking of volume or range. Both were dauntless workers, compulsive perfectionists, Callas in her acting, Lilli in her singing (Emma Calvé reported with awe that she would practise for three hours even on performance-days). And both paid a heavy price for this much-vaunted versatility. They were also women whose stage appearances, in their different ways, inspired a conviction of greatness.

Lotte had her greatness too, but the extremes to which she aspired (and can you have greatness entirely in moderation?) were kinder to the voice, being neither those of power nor of range. She was a great Sieglinde, and that is a strenuous role. She sang a lot of Richard Strauss, who is by no means so considerate to the soprano voice as is often supposed. The role of Fidelio almost certainly wants more of heroic tone than she had to give, and yet she was a great Leonore. Turandot, which she sang in Vienna (their first) in 1926, suited her not at all and she gave it up. But generally she undertook what was right for her and her voice lasted well. She retired from opera in 1946 and gave song recitals for a few more years till reaching the age of sixty-three. She then taught, wrote, painted and lived. It was a sensibly-regulated career.

In other respects, 'sensibly-regulated' is a cold phrase to use about Lotte Lehmann, whose genius lay in something else. Almost any of her records make it clear: she was an artist of generous impulse and one with a spirit as radiant, warm and full-bodied as the voice which gave it utterance. And if there remains any doubt, the written records do more than dispel it. Typical of the devotion she inspired is the memoir in Neville Cardus's *Full Score* (Cassell, 1970). He recalls her on stage, summoning to mind moments in *Die Walküre*: 'the ecstasy of Sieglinde's cry as the door of Hunding's hut swung open, revealing to her and Siegmund the moonlit spring night ... The rapture of Lehmann's voice, the gush in her throat, caught one's breath and, indeed, caught her own.' That may have been in Vienna or in London: in both cities she was probably the most dearly loved singer of all in those years between the two world wars.

They are not to be forgotten, these unrelated Lehmanns. Utterly unalike in character or 'image', they were as one in devotion to their calling and their achievement of greatness within it.

[1] To Lilli is attributed opera's severest snub. Lilian Nordica was one of New York's most admired sopranos and she wished to visit Lehmann and pay her respects. The glacial response allegedly was: 'I am accepting no pupils this season.' Of Lotte, a story was told me by a London taxi-driver, Alf Levy, who in the 1950s picked up a fare whom he was to drive to an hotel where a friend would be waiting. The friend emerged and the cabby almost fell to his knees. 'Madame Lehmann!' he said. 'You recognise me!' exclaimed the friend, for she was indeed the famous singer, who had not appeared in London since 1938. 'Madame Lehmann,' he said, 'give me *Die Walküre*, I can hear every note of your Sieglinde. Give me *Der Rosenkavalier*, the Marschallin is you.' Smiles all round.

CHAPTER 12

Selma Kurz

'There's a long long trill a-winding', as just possibly they used to say in Vienna on nights when Kurz was singing. There were more authentic jokes about the *lang* and the *kurz* of it, for Mme Short had the longest trill in memory. Her favourite trick was to saunter round the stage or stroll the whole breadth of it trilling all the way as the Page in *Un ballo in maschera*. Caruso, appearing as a guest-artist, would take an imaginary pair of scissors from his pocket, wink at the audience, and snip. On one occasion (but this was in London) a less complaisant conductor is said to have brought down his baton in mid-trill or cadenza, thereby inaugurating the modern age of opera. Toscanini would have approved, but the audience may have reflected that an imaginative cadenza or even a wondrous trill is more musical than a loud, abrupt and common orchestral chord.

Kurz did indeed make poetry out of her cadenzas. Time and again on records one hears the aria through and finds oneself sitting up to listen more intently as the cadenza starts. There is nothing inartistic in this: she did not interpolate inappropriately (no trills for Mimì or cadenzas for Cio-cio-san), and in Donizetti, Meyerbeer and so forth the open place at the end of an aria, duly filled in by a capable singer, is part of the architecture. All depends on how it is done. Sometimes she will sing little but what is written, as in the very lovely 1923 recording of 'Ah, non credea mirarti' from *La sonnambula* (the penultimate high G, conventionally added in 1911, being sensibly deleted here). The effect is not one of gratuitous showmanship but of drawing us in towards the character, the girl whose sad aria it is. For those few seconds (25 in this instance) her voice, which is herself, is on its own, the scale descending like the hopes, that have momentarily revived, but only with the added sadness of a brief chromaticism, settling down with resigned finality on the quiet keynote. This is the legitimate business of opera, and of music, and not the 'mere' display of a beautiful voice.

In other cadenzas the treatment is more expansive. The Queen's aria in *Les Huguenots*, 'O beau pays' ('O vago suol' in Kurz's Italian version), has a fairly elaborate written cadenza, which Kurz follows to the end and to which she then adds. As she sings it, the whole cadenza is extremely beautiful and serves an expressive purpose; but most lovely of all are those

final additions, an upward arpeggio in staccato, two gentle scale-like progressions, rapidly ascending and descending, another and higher flight, then a final sequence with a prolonged trill on the F sharp and home to the keynote. That may *read* like a classic example of the soprano practising her exercises in public, but it does not sound so. The aria's nostalgia is taken up in the dreamy echo-sequences at the start of the

written cadenza. It intensifies with the conflict of major and minor impli-
cations as the sixth note of the scale is flattened, restored to pitch and
flattened again. The dream ('Oh, qual piacer di sognar') reaches the height
of its wishfulness with the high B natural and fades with the descending
scale. Then, with the extra figures, the feelings take a more imaginative
turn, flying first upwards and away, then fluttering more wildly like wings
against the bars of a cage, and finally, with the perfection of that long high
trill on the 'incomplete' leading-note, comes a point at which the vision of
a distant homeland is held before the mind's eye and brought to its rest in
the keynote where for a moment the dream is fulfilled.

Each of the singers in these volumes has something special: with Kurz
it is the gift to make the cadenza speak. Or perhaps that needs re-wording
for it may seem to equate meaning with speech, and the very point is that
words are not the sole conveyors of meaning. It is not surprising that two
of Kurz's best recordings – the 'Lockruf', or 'Siren Call', from Goldmark's
Die Königin von Saba, and the partly unaccompanied 'Saper vorreste' from
Un ballo in maschera – are either wholly or partly sung as *vocalises*;
characteristic too that she should sometimes have included vocal exercises
by Concone in her concert programmes. I would love to have heard them:
she was the high mistress of wordless eloquence.

A meticulously trained singer, she numbered Jean de Reszke and
Mathilde Marchesi among her mentors. The real work seems to have been
done by Johannes Ress (teacher also of Leo Slezak), and certainly the
outcome was much more typical of the German school than of any other.
Hers was the gently rounded tone which for its high notes turns to the
head voice rather than aiming at a more penetrative brilliance. She could
swell a note to an enveloping fullness, but the Cs and D flats are rarely
taken at full volume, and on those exceptional occasions the tone tends to
harden and lose resonance. For the most part, she sang well within her
capabilities, and no doubt the preservation of a flawless purity owed much
to that. She had an ideally even scale, in which she could progress
note-by-note, in diatonic or chromatic mode, with never a disturbance of
smoothness and precision.

Hers was a substantial career shortened by illness. She started as a
mezzo, with Carmen, Azucena and Fidès (in *Le Prophète*) in her repertoire.
Her debut-role at Hamburg in 1895 was Mignon, which remained a
favourite for life. This, with the *Tannhäuser* Elisabeth, Agathe in *Der
Freischütz*, Werther's Charlotte, Mozart's Cherubino and even Sieglinde
in *Die Walküre* were all among her early roles, moderate in tessitura and
calling for lyric warmth and reserves of power rather than any special
brilliance in fioritura or high-notes. She came to the Vienna State Opera
(then the Court) in 1899, two years after the momentous appointment of
Gustav Mahler. It was Mahler who recognised the potential coloratura
soprano in Kurz, and in his ensemble he had need of one. Erwin Stein, in
his memoir of the period (*Opera*, 1953), recalls her as a 'brilliant' Queen of

the Night and a 'very accomplished' Constanze in *Die Entführung*, but above all he tells of the sense of mission which spread through the whole company. None of the easy-going Viennese ways were to be brought into the opera house: the tyranny was absolute and yet, rather marvellously, the musical tempo was not. Mahler was not a Toscanini. Robert Heger, himself a conductor at Vienna in later years, recalled that Mahler would conduct in a way that sometimes seemed to have no tempo but a 'seemingly indeterminate rhythm' (see Eduard Kravitt: *The Lied*, Yale 1996). In the manner of late romanticism, it seems that the conductor enforced his control and then used it to provide conditions for creative freedom. Kurz must have learned and benefited, for the essential quality of her singing combined technical discipline with a freedom that can sound almost improvisatory.

In Mahler's time she sang over thirty roles in the house. They included 'coloratura' parts such as Rosina, Lucia and Lakmé, but she was also the theatre's first Mimì and Butterfly. In *Les Contes d'Hoffmann* she began by singing only the doll, Olympia, but later took all three roles in the same evening. In 1911 she was their Tatiana and Sophie, and in 1916 'created' the Zerbinetta of the revised *Ariadne auf Naxos*. From 1921 onwards she suffered from increasingly poor health though remaining active both at home and abroad. Her daughter was the distinguished singer Desi Halban

61

who devotedly kept her memory alive: in the *Record Collector* (Vol. 13, number 3) she gives 1929 as the year of Kurz's last operatic appearance, and recounts that she sang at a private baptism not long before her death in 1933.

At the opera house, a gentle, rather soulful, portrait of her standing by the piano still has its place in the gallery. Vienna was the centre of her life and art, so much so that one almost forgets she had a career abroad. She was also a favourite in Paris and Warsaw, and was part of some illustrious seasons at Monte Carlo and Covent Garden. Londoners welcomed her in 1904, when some of the music critics clearly saw her as an alternative to Melba, remarking how *Rigoletto* suddenly seemed to have acquired new dramatic life. She came to have a fondness for England (particularly enjoying, so it was said, trips to Southend and Margate), and evidently she brought her trill along with her. *Musical Opinion*'s critic at *Les Huguenots* noted 'a marvellous shake, not as in the case of Oscar [in *Un ballo in maschera*] of abnormal duration, but swelling out to a wonderful volume of tone'. Several critics commented on her effective acting, and at least one on her tendency to sing sharp. That appears to have been unremarked when she returned, years later, in 1924. She made a strong impression as a poignant yet strong-willed Violetta, and the *Daily Telegraph* was quite surprised to find 'the dear old opera emerging as music drama'.

In the course of writing this chapter I found myself at a recital in London sitting next to a colleague whose appearance belied his years. He told me about his first *Ring*, Walter conducting, Leider, Lehmann, Melchior, Schorr heading the cast. That was in 1924. I enquired whether by any chance he had heard Selma Kurz. 'Oh yes,' he said. '*Traviata* and *Bohème*.' And then he paused, for much less time than it takes a computer, to search for an evening 76 years in the past. '*Warm*,' he said.

CHAPTER 13

Frida Leider

'But you should have heard Leider.' It was a kind of litany at Covent Garden after the war. If those corridors only could speak, they would give back an echo of that sentence, sighed, muttered or declaimed, which clung to the walls throughout the long Wagner intermissions. It commonly is said to be boring, this compulsive nostalgia of old-timers. I myself never have found it so, for it prompts the most eager of questions: 'Ah, what was she like?' The boredom, or rather the disappointment, usually arises out of the answer. 'Oh, she was marvellous, incomparable. I'll never forget her.' And then of course it becomes evident that they *have* forgotten her, because they can remember nothing to speak of.

This is a common experience, whoever the singer. As it happens, the admirers of Frida Leider are more helpful than most: they can recall Brünnhilde's 'Alles weiss ich,' the gestures, the waving of Isolde's scarf signal, 'Er sah mir in die Augen.' Then their own eyes will fix momentarily on a figure standing on a darkened stage in 1938, and yes, they can see her and perhaps even hear something. But the magic, the spell, the irreplaceable individuality? It eludes capture, slips away beyond words.

For some, Leider *was* those years; or rather, with Lotte Lehmann, it was she more than any other artist whose voice and presence gave regular, dependable distinction to the summer seasons, those few concentrated weeks when London was the home of international opera, relished all the more keenly for its long absence. Leider and Lehmann both came to the house first in 1924, the year that also brought Elisabeth Schumann, Maria Olczewska, Lauritz Melchior, Friedrich Schorr and Bruno Walter. She returned in every international season save the last. Leider was an honoured artist throughout the world but at Covent Garden she was adored. If we can believe the critics, she had her limitations too, some of them shown up almost cruelly when Kirsten Flagstad arrived with a voice that truly *was* incomparable. But if we believe them when they find fault, we must also credit their praise; for the most part it glowed.

There is one account of her debut, as Isolde, that brings Leider before us with uncommon vividness. This is by Dyneley Hussey, whose article in the *Saturday Review* (17 May 1924) was headed simply 'A Great Isolde'. He says he had gone to the opera without expectations; at least, he had expected little of the Tristan (the veteran Jacques Urlus, who gave more than that little), less of the Brangäne (Ernestine Färber-Strasse, who redeemed her first Act by singing gloriously in the second), and the Isolde was unknown. Walter conducted, and Hussey stressed his importance more by implication than analysis, for when Karl Alwin conducted in his place the miracle was achieved of making even the loveliest passages uninteresting. But it was on account of the new soprano that the evening proved unforgettable: 'It was the magic spell woven by the hands of the Isolde about the rapture of her face and the loveliness of her voice.' This became one of those rare occasions when 'The cup of one's ideal overflowed with the excess of beauty.' In passing, it might be noted that he described the exhilaration as being a great *dramatic* experience. (One of the more irritating commonplaces purveyed by opera tattlers is the notion that there *were* no dramatic experiences in the opera house before Callas.) When Hussey listed the qualities that made the new Isolde 'the woman of Wagner's imagination', he put 'great actress' first, then 'great singer', finally 'great beauty'. That last aspect might not have presented itself so readily as the others, for the photographs of Leider's Isolde, though striking, are less clearly beautiful. Hussey saw the beauty as 'of an unusual type, with something in it of the primitive'. The face was always alive, 'the continual interpreter of her innermost emotions. Conflicting ideas passed across it like the shadow of clouds upon a sunlit world – love curdling to hatred, the ecstasy of reconciliation and, in the last Act, a terrible pity which burnt upon one's brain its almost unendurable beauty.' Still more remarkable were the hands: 'When Isolde was beaten in spirit, they hung limp and dejected; at her decision the wrist became, of a sudden, steel.' All honour, then, to the artist – and some honour too to the critic who communicates his experience so vividly.

It is more difficult to share a *voice* in words, but to some extent Hussey does that too. 'Her voice is pure in quality, and she uses it, as only great singers can, like an instrument for the registration of every subtle inflection in the words and music.' To tell the truth, that's not quite what I want to know: these subtle inflections are not the monopoly of great singers, and I want to hear about her, at first hand, as a singer. Hussey tells us a little by way of disagreement with his colleague Percy Scholes of the *Observer*. Scholes had written of himself as 'very definitely with the strong-minded minority in the house that refused to acclaim Frida Leider as one of the great Isoldes. Her voice in *forte* is somewhat harsh ... her singing in certain passages lacks smoothness ... and she is a tremolist. It is a long time since any performance produced so divided an opinion in the audience.' People hear voices differently: one listener's 'harshness' is another's 'incisiveness', and the singer whose 'vibrancy' excites you is your neighbour's 'tremolist'. Hussey clearly was nonplussed by Scholes's reaction – 'some trick played by the imp of acoustics', perhaps. He gives his own version as follows: 'Where I was sitting, her voice sounded sweet and round, except when

In the Berlin Tiergarten

dramatic expression demanded a hard tone, as in the commands to Brangäne; and there was never, to my ear, a tremolo in the ordinary, bad sense of the word. Sometimes the notes thrilled with emotion; but it was done purposely, just as [Elena] Gerhardt will set her tone quivering upon one important word in a song.'

That critical exchange helps us now to listen through the records to a voice on-stage. Scholes's 'tremolist' does seem absurd, for in so much other singing (think of the *Fidelio* aria) there is no firmer voice on records. But, as it were, out of the corner of my ear, I can hear what prompted his judgement. Hussey's 'thrilled with emotion' is very close to my own appre-

65

hension of the voice on records, and there is no doubt that the vibrato, when brought into play, is part of the thrill. But while it may seem impertinent of one who heard neither singer in the flesh to question this critic's comparison with Gerhardt, I fancy that when Hussey introduces the great Lieder singer to reinforce his point about Leider as an artist, he is confusing the sound picture of her as a singer. Leider's vibrato is faster and more even than Gerhardt's, and though it serves an artistic purpose it is not to achieve a special effect on a particular word. On records, and to my ears, it is far from anything I would describe as 'tremolo', but I can imagine that at Covent Garden it could be obtrusive to a listener whose temperament was not responsive to the thrill of experience in the opera house. Hussey loved it; Scholes was happier in the concert hall.

In some degree this double hearing persisted throughout Leider's years at Covent Garden. She was indeed a loved, highly respected, virtually indispensable artist, but the sum total of her reviews conveys a sense that one could not say to the time machine 'Take me to the opera house when Leider was singing' and be confident of hearing entirely what one hoped for. Phrases like 'a little tired', 'not quite in best form', 'troubled by the high notes' recur frequently. Herman Klein, writing in *The Gramophone*, found the famous 1926 *Don Giovanni* disappointing, partly because of Leider, 'whose dramatic forces were for once on a higher plane than her vocal artistry – notably as to "Non mi dir", where her phrasing and coloratura left just a little to be desired'. I take that to be the mild demurring of a gentleman critic who could have been more harmfully specific had he chosen. 'Non mi dir' is not among Leider's recordings, but she recorded 'Or sai chi l'onore' twice, both times magnificently. Still, Klein is unlikely to have found fault without cause: he too was an admirer, and only the previous year he had pronounced on Leider's Isolde that 'No more inspiring singer of this part has been heard since the famous Milka Ternina.' Just as there are those Latin sentences implying the answer 'Yes' or 'No,' so do such statements imply the comment 'Wow!'

There was another view, expressed by the somewhat cussed but always interesting Kaikhosru Sorabji, who held that 'she is not really a dramatic soprano at all, but a lyric soprano who has missed her true vocation'. Her records lend this opinion some support. They include a 'Vissi d'arte' and 'D'amor sull' ali rosee' that are not only among Leider's best but also among the best of all recorded performances of those arias. In *Il trovatore* her fluency, trills and high notes seem made for such music; the tone is fine in its definition as well as its purity, and she holds the line firm and even. Her Tosca is aristocratic, with the dignity of pure if intensified lyricism. Or one might think of her Act I *Trovatore* aria, with its shortened cabaletta deft in its staccatos, nimble in scale work; or the Countess' 'Porgi, amor' in *Le nozze di Figaro*, slender and graceful; or Armide's 'Ah, si la liberté', so tender in manner, so human in its nobility. It is doubtful whether an experienced listener brought in to hear these 'blind' would

jump to it that this was the voice of a born Isolde and Brünnhilde. And when we turn then to the Wagner recordings, it is this same lyric-dramatic voice that we hear, not one that has transfigured itself into something big especially for the heroic repertory.

Yet this, I believe, is one of the reasons why she is special in these roles: she sings them as a lyric soprano intensified. It is this compound of lyricism and tension, of straight tone and vibrancy, that distinguishes her records. For her effect in the theatre we turn to the critics – to Hussey, to W.J. Henderson for her relatively short time at the Met, where she exercised 'the indescribable magic of genuineness', and to Ernest Newman recalling her greatest role: 'Frida Leider's Isolde showed us a brain so possessed with the part that the body, down to the smallest movement, had a kind of spiritual eloquence of its own.' So when the litany 'You should have heard Leider' is chanted (the voices, alas, thinning out now), we can almost take courage and reply that indeed we have done and continue to do so. Certainly the records, the critics and a little imagination preserve 'the magic, the spell, the irreplaceable individuality' well enough for us to know them and to treasure them accordingly.

CHAPTER 14

Lauritz Melchior

There is probably nothing that the collector of old records likes more than
to have a friend or neighbour drop by and listen to half-an-hour's records
during the course of which something will inevitably provoke the cry: 'My
oh my! They're not made like that any more! Tell me, will you, where are
their likes today?' Sometimes, if the devil is in him, the collector can play
devil's advocate and answer: 'Well now, they're here for instance … and
here … and here.' He may then take down enough records from his other,
more modern shelves to show that the art of singing is not entirely dead
after all. But at one point at least his advocacy will face an impasse, and
that is when the question of Wagnerian tenors arises. The collector who
plays to his acquiescent neighbour the Forging Song of Siegfried or the
Rome Narration of Tannhäuser as sung by Lauritz Melchior cannot turn
to those more modern shelves for a counterpart here. None exists. Melchior remains what he was in his lifetime, Wagner tenor supreme; and as
the years go by his standing among the century's singers only increases.

It increases, for one thing, because records preserve the best of him.
Though not a bad actor, he was not normally a great one either, and his
bulky figure, however dignified in movement, remained stolidly unroman-
tic. He could be inaccurate, especially in ensemble. He was apt, particularly in later years, to press ahead of the beat, and a listener would
sometimes feel cheated of the full value of the sung notes because of a way
he had of closing in too quickly on the consonants. In his best years, the
1920s and 1930s, he was often criticised for these and other shortcomings,
while the kind of glowing admiration one would have expected him to
evoke is comparatively rare among the critics. He hardly increased his
reputation among musicians by going into films in later years; he also
continued to sing in public just that bit too long. These are matters which
time will dim. What it will bring out more and more clearly is the glory of
the voice and, more remarkably, the sensitivity of his art at its best.

He was to some extent taken for granted. Even now, when we look back
to those inter-war Wagner nights at Covent Garden and the Metropolitan,
and indeed most of the great opera houses of the world, the presence of
Melchior in the cast lists seems an inevitability. We feel that he was
'necessary'; and yet in fact he was, as the philosophers say, highly 'contin-

gent'. There might well have been no Melchior in those casts at all, and all
we might then have known of him would have been as a baritone based in
Copenhagen and Scandinavia, singing an admired Wolfram or Iago, perhaps as far afield as Berlin and crowning his career, say, with a powerful
Amfortas in one of the pre-war Bayreuth festivals. That this was not so

owed much to the intervention at a crucial stage of two individuals, one an American singer, the other an English novelist.

The singer, who had become known as Madame Charles Cahier (originally Sarah Jane Walker), urged the young baritone to start thinking tenorwards. This was somewhere around 1916 after he had been singing baritone roles at the Royal Opera in Copenhagen for three years. His voice had shown promise at an early age and serious vocal studies began in 1908 when he was eighteen. His debut at the Royal Opera was as Silvio in *Pagliacci*, and roles that followed included Germont *père* in *Traviata* (which he had already sung while touring the smaller houses with the Zwicki Company) and di Luna in *Trovatore*. It was in this opera, again on tour, that he met Madame Cahier. A pupil of Jean de Reszke and a singer of considerable status, having sung, for instance, in the first performance of *Das Lied von der Erde*, she became a famous teacher and was later to have an important influence on the career of Marian Anderson. In Melchior she clearly heard a tenor in the making, and he returned to Copenhagen to study under the admirable Danish tenor Vilhelm Herold whose own singing career had just come to an end. Working hard on the voice, he emerged on October 9 1918 to make his début as a tenor – and as Tannhäuser, no less.

The following year brought him to London, where the second decisive influence came into his life. He sang at a Promenade Concert on 23 September, and in the audience was Hugh Walpole, who noted: 'the joy of the evening was a Danish tenor, Melchior – quite superb. Just the voice for me.' He wrote to the singer, met him over lunch and formed with him one of the friendships of his life. He found Melchior 'a great child, but very simple, most modest, with a splendid sense of humour'. During the following weeks he heard him sing again and now became convinced that he had the makings of not just a good singer (he was already that) but a great one. When next year he visited Melchior in Denmark he felt that his countrymen underrated him: 'I see no one who really appreciates it. However they will one day.' Back in England he took Melchior down to Cornwall with him, where he created a sensation singing in Polperro! In London he sang at Marlborough House for Queen Alexandra who made appreciative comments but (Walpole suspected) was probably deaf. Walpole dedicated his novel *The Young Enchanted* to Melchior and in 1922 arranged lessons for him with Victor Beigel which were to make him 'the greatest Wagner tenor in the world'. When Melchior was called to Vienna, Walpole went with him and from there on to Munich where the great Anna von Mildenburg agreed to coach him, prophesying that he would soon 'have the world at his feet'. Walpole also saw to it that he took lessons in German, and eventually, in 1923, there came the great reward of all this, for Melchior's first recital in Munich was such a success that he was engaged for the Bayreuth Festival of 1924. In the vital twelve months up to the Festival Walpole supported him financially so that he could thoroughly master *The Ring*, and in

Melchior's awards and decorations included the Commander Cross of the Danish Flag, Chevalier Légion d'Honneur, Order of Saxe-Coburg, and Honorary Auxiliary Fireman of New York City

particular the role of Siegmund in which he was to make his debut at Covent Garden as well. In Bayreuth he was also to sing Parsifal: 'Never have I heard such singing,' wrote Walpole. 'Everyone in the boxes near me was crying.' Siegfried was to follow next year and by 1925 Walpole had the satisfaction of knowing that 'he is recognised by everyone now as the greatest Heldentenor in the world'.

1924 was indeed the *annus mirabilis*. Melchior's association with Bayreuth which started then continued every year till 1931; and at Covent Garden he appeared in every season from 1926 to 1939. It was also the successes of this year that drew him to the attention of other countries, notably the United States where he appeared first in 1926 at the Metropolitan, remaining there till 1950.

It was in the 1927 season that he first impressed the critics as he had impressed Walpole: the Parsifal of 17 May 'astonished us all by the quality of his performance'. 1928 brought his Tannhäuser to London, but according to the *Musical Times* he 'only awoke to an intelligent, sensitive style

71

in the third Act'. Of his Siegfried they complained that he 'bellowed intolerably in the last Act', and they added 'his more taurine utterances are simply not musical at all'. He sang his first London Tristan the next year, also his elder Siegfried in *Götterdämmerung*, and this time the *Musical Times* grudgingly admitted that there was no one better. *The Times* praised his Siegfried in 1930 for its 'genuinely expressive singing', and in *Götterdämmerung* he gave 'a finely rounded performance, always singing well ... but never as well as in his final lyrical relation of his own history'. The most lively, formidable and influential of all the London critics of those years was Ernest Newman of the *Sunday Times*, and he continued to complain till the 1931 *Tristan und Isolde*, when he concluded that all previous estimates would have to be revised: 'His more powerful tones are as brilliant as ever, but he now employs them with more poetic discretion ... His Tristan on Tuesday was not only extremely dignified: it had a curious spiritual quality about it even in the moments of greatest frenzy.'

1931 was also the year when he appears to have become a properly recognised and valued part of the establishment in New York. Performances in which he did not appear were notably inferior to those in which he did, and in 1932, with Leider, Olczewska and Schorr also in the cast, the Metropolitan put on a *Tristan* that recalled 'the fabulous days before the war', with Melchior showing more 'vocal finish and depth of feeling' than ever before. This improvement continued, so that in 1936, this time with Flagstad as his Isolde, Melchior received the ultimate accolade from Henderson, who reported of the performance on 24 December that he had just heard 'the best Tristan the Metropolitan has known since Jean de Reszke'.

He left the company in 1950 after disagreements with Rudolf Bing, which did not stop him singing elsewhere. As late as 1963 he was heard at a concert in New York, fifty years after his operatic debut. And still he had ten years to live. It was a full life, in keeping with the large composition of the man. There was a good deal of body about Melchior, and a good deal of jovial, easy-going humanity, which perhaps cost him something in artistic stature and respect. But what remains now are the recordings, not all of them Wagnerian. There are songs, both ardent and delicate. The famous aria from *L'Africaine* is thrilling in sheer power and beautiful in its lyricism. His Otello solos in German are deeply felt and sung with marvellous control and one remarkable and largely unacknowledged thing about records is that they are pure spirit. The physical bulk, the appetite, the thirst, the joking and buffoonery are all refined away. What remains is a voice and a soul: the voice utterly individual and irreplaceable, the soul always alive, ardent, tender, romantic. Hugh Walpole said Melchior would be acknowledged as 'the greatest living Heldentenor'. He might have gone further, for, faults and all, he has proved himself Heldentenor of the century.

CHAPTER 15

Ben Heppner and Jacques Urlus

Lauritz Melchior was indeed Wagnerian Heldentenor *in excelsis*, and yet the operas in which he was reckoned to be so indispensable have been given countless times, in effect dispensing with him. Not all of those performances can have been irredeemably spoilt by the substitution, and some of the tenors, in certain respects, may even have been preferable. With Siegfried Jerusalem as his nearest successor, the best in the immediate post-war period was Wolfgang Windgassen, a singer remembered now with affection as man and musician, his voice an instrument of great beauty till it grew tired and worn. The man for vocal excitement was Ernst Kozub, posthumously famous as 'our tenor' in John Culshaw's *Ring Resounding*. Decca's recording team pinned their hopes on him as a potential Siegfried till they realised that not in a month of Sundays was he going to learn the part. But they were right to hope: his cries of 'Wälse!' still ring in the memory, resonant and dauntless, the very essence of *Heldentenorismus*. Vickers was an incomparably intense Siegmund, Tristan and Parsifal. Peter Seiffert had one of the most vibrant Italianate voices in the business. René Kollo was a Lohengrin whose voice shone like the silver of his armour. Alberto Remedios in the English National Opera's pioneering *Ring* was scrupulous, clean-cut and expressive. Gösta Winbergh in *Die Meistersinger* brought lyric grace to Walther's often gracelessly sung music, and James King was ever reliable. It seems that, hard-up as we consider ourselves to have been in the second half, or post-Melchior era of the century, we have not really done so badly.

And then in recent years has come Ben Heppner. He had one clear and immediate distinction, that his voice was fit for Wagner but that it was to be Wagner via a cautious and circuitous route. He has been a tenor of steady growth and without the usual baritonal foundations. Beginning with a light lyric voice, spinning a reputedly pretty line in Mozart, he was encouraged by his teacher to look towards the *spinto* repertoire. This essentially meant Italian opera, though when he started winning prizes and making the opera establishment aware of him it was soon made clear that the German repertoire was what interested them. He took things slowly and wisely, allowing two years to elapse before making his major operatic debut in 1989 as Lohengrin with the Stockholm Opera. A secon-

Jacques Urlus as Siegfried

Ben Heppner

dary role in *Tannhäuser* and then a first Walther in *Die Meistersinger* (repeated in 1990) showed where his career was tending, and also that it was one to take seriously. In the meantime he kept a watchful eye on developments and guarded against premature specialisation. He diversified with Czech opera (Dvořák's *Rusalka* and *Dimitrij*, and Janáček's *Jenufa*), Mozart (*La clemenza di Tito* at Salzburg), Puccini (*Turandot* at Covent Garden), Tchaikowsky (*Queen of Spades* at the Metropolitan) and Britten (*Peter Grimes* and the *War Requiem*). In all of this – and there was much more – probably most important was the determination to keep contact with Italian opera, to keep the voice high for as long as possible, and to encourage its natural lyricism.

Very carefully he limited his association with Wagner to the roles he knew were good for his voice, and resisting the calls to Tannhäuser, Tristan, Parsifal, Siegmund and Siegfried. In particular he refused to sing Siegmund, he of the low tessitura and first tempter of upwardly-mobile baritones. His approach to Tristan was similarly cautious, almost stealthy, performing first separate Acts, and then singing the part on stage first in Seattle, letting the Metropolitan wait another two seasons till the part was well and truly in his system. He himself has fought shy of the description 'Heldentenor', aware of the expectations it arouses and the

DE WAGNERVEREENIGING N.V.

DONDERDAG 19 EN ZATERDAG 21 NOVEMBER 1931

DES AVONDS TE HALF ZEVEN URE IN

DEN STADSSCHOUWBURG TE AMSTERDAM

RICHARD WAGNER

TRISTAN UND ISOLDE

HANDLUNG IN DREI AUFZÜGEN

PERSONEN:

ISOLDE	HENNY TRUNDT
TRISTAN	JACQUES URLUS
KÖNIG MARKE	JOSEF VON MANOWARDA
KURWENAL	FRITZ KRENN
BRANGÄNE	LYDIA KINDERMANN
HIRT und Junger Seemann	CARL SEYDEL
MELOT	JOACHIM SATTLER
STEUERMANN	HANS KOMREGG

Schiffsvolk, Ritter und Knappen.

dangers it incurs. He nevertheless consolidated himself in the Helden-tenor's wider repertory, with Florestan in *Fidelio*, Samson in *Samson et Dalila* and the Emperor in *Die Frau ohne Schatten*. He has still only one foot in Melchior-territory, and yet is probably nearest already to achieving the status.

Reverting then to the earlier years of the century, to Melchior's prede-cessors and his contemporaries, we find little evidence of a much greater profusion of talent. Nearest to him in his own time was probably Max Lorenz, who began well but seems to have developed into a vocally coarse representative of a school we do not want to see revived. The Yorkshire tenor Walter Widdop (Vol. 2, Ch. 8) was sometimes spoken of as capable of putting all to shame, but he lacked the opportunities and still needed a lot of coaching in stagecraft and the German language. Franz Völker was a fine Lohengrin, Gotthelf Pistor an inspired Parsifal, Fritz Wolff a successful Walther. Before that, Johannes Sembach sang pleasingly for the Metropolitan, Heinrich Knote ably and enduringly in Germany, and Giuseppe Borgatti brought the welcome touch of an Italian voice to his Tristan and Siegfried at La Scala. There were others (Leo Slezak a hugely admired Lohengrin, Tannhäuser and Walther though not taking those further steps into the danger-zone), few of them leaving behind much that one wants to listen to twice on gramophone records. The exception to this is the Dutchman, Jacques Urlus. In the first decades of the century (and of the gramophone), he pre-eminently appeals as a Heldentenor who sang musically and whom it is still a pleasure to hear.

Like Heppner (and indeed Melchior in his capacity as Heldentenor) he started late: he was 27 at his debut in 1894, compared with Melchior at 28 in 1918 when he emerged from re-training and Heppner 32 at the start of his career as dramatic tenor in 1988. Like them, he approached the heavy repertoire with care: he sang small roles first, graduated to Max in *Der Freischütz*, and kept up a fair variety of lyrical roles in French opera and Italian. Even so, he was a marked man, for, then as now, a tenor with the voice for Wagner found himself resolutely channelled in that direction, so that by the turn of the century he had sung all the major Wagnerian roles save Parsifal. With Leipzig as his base, he gained a considerable reputation leading to engagements abroad, including an American debut in 1912 with a call to the Metropolitan the following year. His debut in *Tristan und Isolde* was unhappy as any in the house's story. It seems that shortly after his arrival in New York he caught cold and, with no cover or understudy available, just about managed to get through Act 1. In the second Act his voice went entirely and, while Toscanini showed the sympathetic side of his nature and Johanna Gadski sang the Love duet with herself, Urlus turned his back to the audience and wept. In spite of all, the opera continued, and the sick-bed scene of Act 3 was mimed with painful authenticity. Then, four nights later, he appeared as Siegfried and triumphed. Experienced critics reported that this was the best since Jean de Reszke: they liked his voice, the expressiveness of his singing and the 'youth, freshness and vigour of spirit' that characterised his impersonation. The particular terms of W.J. Henderson's praise provide a cue for reflection.

Henderson lights immediately on two words: 'quality' and 'legato'. Urlus, he said, 'does not shatter his phrases with the brittle staccato so long authorised by Cosima Wagner but now gradually losing its vogue in Germany. Mr Urlus is that rare thing, a musical tenor and his musical intelligence shows itself in his treatment of the melodic line and his use of nuance.' It is precisely this combination of virtues that so distinguishes his records. He made many, from 1902 to 1927. Taking a few more or less at random – the 'Bildnis' aria from *Die Zauberflöte*, the 'Paradis' in *L'Africaine*, 'Rachel' from *La Juive*, Rienzi's prayer, Lohengrin's narration, then Siegfried's – I find myself impressed afresh by the 'singerliness' of it all:

76

perhaps there is something slightly old-fashioned in this careful production, but what virtues in the fluid style and evenness of line! Nor does he
nurture these at the expense of a more dramatic or lively delivery: Siegfried's story of the 'mürrischer Zwerg' is lightly pointed, a glint of humour
in the tone before sweetening for the wood-bird. He also recorded Otello's
death, dramatic without dramatics, deeply moving, not least through
fidelity to the score. And the two solos recorded electrically at the age of
60: for some reason I had remembered them as sounding old, yet in fact
they are wonderful in voice as well as in stylistic mastery, with the prayer,
'O Souverain', from *Le Cid* a most moving coda to this long recording
career.

Heppner also impressed from the first as a singer: that is, as a producer
of beautiful sound. Other strengths can be added but this is what distinguishes both of these tenors in the first place. Heppner seems to be well
aware of this priority in the choices he makes, not simply in the way he
guides his path towards its eventual confrontation with the heaviest roles,
but in keeping the upper part of his voice trim and Italianate. The
recording he made of Italian arias showed limitations of temperament but
the singing was admirable. With both of these tenors some of their
strength in Wagner must be derived from the wider musical experience.
Heppner is also a song-recitalist and has worked in modern opera (it was
his lead-role in Maxwell-Davies's *The Lighthouse* that proved the first
significant turning-point in his career). His most recent recording is of *Das
Lied von der Erde*, and this was a great favourite of Urlus's too, along with
Das klagende Lied and the *Lieder eines fahrenden Gesellen*. Urlus was also
a famous Evangelist in the *St Matthew Passion*. I don't quite see Heppner
following in that line – and if that is one contrast between the two, here is
another. Look up 'Heppner, Ben' in the record catalogue and there he is,
with nine operas, five solo recitals and various bits and pieces (such as
Beethoven's Ninth). Under 'Urlus, Jacques' are two items, both of them
tucked away in anthologies. There used to be excellent recitals on LP
(Rubini, Rococo, Club 99), and certainly there is no lack of material. More
of it, I imagine, is available in the USA than the UK: somebody will have
to have a word with Mr Marston.

CHAPTER 16

Jessye Norman and
Leontyne Price

In one of his *Letter from America* broadcasts some years ago, Alistair Cooke told a story involving Leontyne Price. How it arose I cannot now recall, but his main subject may have been the time it took for public opinion, or for the habits of mind among the public, to catch up with changes in law and institutions regarding matters of race and colour. Even in the northern states and among educated people, prejudices and their attendant customs remained. Only whites had been allowed to sing at the Metropolitan Opera, for instance, until Rudolf Bing in 1955 invited the great Marian Anderson to join the company for performances of *Un ballo in maschera*. And yet black singers, if sufficiently well-known and 'respectable', might be asked to perform at private functions, their terms of engagement normally being a fee 'and coffee'. Years after the colour-bar had been lifted at the old Met, and when Leontyne Price had become prima donna, probably of the new, she was asked by some hostess high in the ranks of New York 'Society' how much they paid her per performance. The woman would not have dreamt of asking such a question of a white professional, but habits of thought and speech had not moved with the times. The singer answered the hostess's question. The sum she quoted was a large one, impressive even to the wife of a millionaire. And after a pause, summing up her best Mississippi accent, she added: 'And coffee.'

I met her to speak with only once. She told of her interest in Queen Elizabeth I and of the pleasure she took in historical visits while in England. A dignified woman, not so much reticent as careful and restrained in speech; she spoke softly and amiably, but might draw the line firmly (I felt) if friendliness turned to familiarity. She had, after all, two dignities to uphold: that of First Lady of the great national opera house, and that of an honoured inheritor. When Marian Anderson had been at last invited to the Met it was too late – too late, that is, for her voice. Her debut as Ulrica the fortune-teller in *Un ballo* was followed by a few further performances but nothing more. The inheritance fell to Leontyne Price. In 1955 her operatic career proper had just begun (previously she had been singing in a famous touring production of *Porgy and Bess*, her single

Leontyne Price as Amelia in *Un ballo in maschera*

appearance at the Met having been in a 'Jamboree' concert in which she sang 'Summertime'). In the following years she made a name for herself in San Francisco and Chicago, London, Vienna and Salzburg. The seal was set on 27 January 1961, when the New York house heard her in opera for the first time and recognised instantly that a singer of the first rank had arrived. Her role was the *Trovatore* Leonora, one which tests practically every aspect of a soprano's art. She gave two more performances and followed up with Aida, which was to remain essentially hers till she retired from the company twenty-four years later.

This was a role she had previously sung in London (she was soon to be too expensive for us). If I say that she was a *vertical* Aida, that may seem an odd way of putting it and may need some explanation. She and the palm trees, which in those days were still permitted in Act 3 to grow on the banks of the Nile, were as one: emblems of the atmosphere and dignity of the opera from this point onwards. Her voice seemed tall, like her physical presence. Unlike so many Aida-voices, hers was not a broad, heroic sound; it had (so to speak) no fat in the middle. Its characteristic beauty lay in the upper range, and its quality was essentially lyrical. Accordingly she was not, as I remember it, one of those who dominate the ensemble of Act 2 with the sword-blade clarity of an Eva Turner or the broader power of a Gwynneth Jones; and it was the Nile scene and particularly the great solo that left a memory of having been the Aida of one's hitherto unrealised ideal. We have had other fine Aida voices since – and particularly, not so long after Price, Martina Arroyo, then in her opulent prime. But for the third Act at least, none ever again quite matched this Aida whose voice aspired towards the night sky with the easy dignity of a column of smoke that rises on an evening when the wind has dropped and the air is still warm.

'Smoky' is a word that has been used of Price's voice before now, but in a different sense. 'Dusky' is her own term: 'I do have a dusky quality in my voice which is, I think, sensual. The sound is what I recorded Carmen with' (*Gramophone*, November 1996). That was a Carmen for the 1960s, the permissive age of the beautiful people, smoke in the air which also tinkled with the bells of the flower-powered, inviting to a sensual paradise potent as the cassia blossom hurled at Don José and treasured in his prison cell. She murmurs a lazy Habanera, the chorus swaying dreamily under its spell, and as the Act moves towards its fateful conclusion she breathes, in recitative, the words 'Le charme opère'. Once out of the spell of the sixties' naive sensuality, the dusky murmurs seem to have lost some of their charm (and Karajan's slow tempi become a drag). But the real trouble is that the 'smoke' in the voice permeates beyond Seville and its ramparts. It also thickens. Later recordings, such as that of the Tel Aviv recital of 1980, show the quality stripped of metaphor – not 'smoky' or 'dusky' but breathy.

It has to be added that the truthfulness of the impression given by records may itself be debatable. Leontyne Price appeared last in London for a public interview in St John's, Smith Square, where recordings were played from a newly released edition on compact disc. The reproduction, installed by the company, must have been regarded as the best money could buy, but the sound of the voice as heard there (sometimes breathy, sometimes metallic) in no way corresponded to the sound recalled from Covent Garden and the Albert Hall. Indeed, after the Albert Hall concert of 1968, some comments on records written when the experience was still recent show that there existed a disparity between what one heard on records even of the late 1960s and the beautifully delicate, refined tone of the voice 'live'. She sang then, twice, Adriana Lecouvreur's air about the handmaiden of art, and the memory is vivid to this day of the voice rising, very pure and silvery, a gentle sheen to it, a lovely element in a perform-

80

Jessye Norman

ance which held the audience in that special kind of silence which testifies to the 'Genio creator' at work.

Any disparity between the Jessye Norman of records and of 'live' experience is of a different kind. In beauty and fullness of tone her recordings do her pretty fair justice – except that always the sheer *quality* of a great voice stands out from the multitude more clearly in live perform-ance. Here it is the physical presence, or lack of it, that makes the difference. We are always warned not to say anything about size in connection with Jessye Norman, but size is part of the truth: the amplitude of voice and person go together. In recital there can be a quite extraordi-nary warmth which could not have been generated except by some genuine glories of singing but which is then intensified by the presence of a woman who seems to embody a broad, generous humanity. At a London concert in 1993 when I had no personal cause to feel very warm towards her (she having rejected a programme note I had written in favour of one by my French colleague, M. Tubeuf), she won total admiration in a programme which moved from Schumann to Strauss, then Messiaen (*Poèmes pour Mi*) to Schoenberg (*Brettl Lieder*). She was generous with encores too, and the concert culminated in a spiritual, 'Sion's walls', which even those monu-ments of heavenly splendour could hardly have surpassed.

81

If records tell a different story here, it is in another way and also in difference one with another. For one thing, when less under the personal sway and at liberty to hear an item again or play it as sung by another artist, one may find that the mastery of so wide a repertoire does after all have its limitations. A recital with James Levine at Salzburg in 1990 recently released on disc includes six items from Wolf's *Spanish Songbook*, and something felt to be lacking urges one to find out what the experts do. So back to Schwarzkopf and Fischer-Dieskau, and (as we find) to altogether fuller, more meaningful performances, the Liebestod of 'Bedeckt mich mit Blumen' now a secret which the singer hugs to herself while recalling the sweet torment, or even in the feverish 'Bitt' ihn, o Mutter', where Norman enacts the song quite powerfully, but where as soon as a really attentive listening-process begins one hears how (for instance) Schwarzkopf points the sense of the verb 'zielen' – 'beg that boy no more to *aim* at me'. Or in French song: everything sounds fine – lovely tone, sensitive lights-and-shades – but it's a different story when the comparisons start: with (say) Madeleine Grey in Ravel's *Hebrew Songs*, or Croiza in Duparc's 'L'invitation au voyage', or Yvonne Printemps in Poulenc's 'Les chemins de l'amour'. The other side of the record (in a metaphorical sense) is that in some instances, where in a facile way Norman has been judged out of order, her achievements can be in fact quite remarkable. Two cases in point are her recordings of *Das Lied von der Erde* and *Bluebeard's Castle*: criticisms which were quick to call them bland do not hold when one comes to listen in detail and without preconceptions.

Jessye Norman has had the most glorious, large-scale soprano voice of the age. When she sang Strauss's *Four Last Songs* in public one could hear for the first time how they must have sounded when Flagstad sang them at the premiere – or how a slightly younger Flagstad, who could cope more readily with 'Frühling', might have sounded. At a concert in Covent Garden she gave as an encore Delilah's 'Mon coeur s'ouvre': in one sense it was absurd for at that *adagio* or *lento* a second verse was hardly thinkable, but it was also unforgettably wonderful on account of the seemingly endless splendours of beautifully phrased melodic line, a perfectly placed high B flat appearing at the end to arise out of this mezzo-soprano (or even contralto) richness.

She came to the Metropolitan in 1983, two years before Leontyne Price's final appearances there. How far it would be correct to see a succession here can hardly be judged at this distance. But these two sopranos, at their best, have given to their times – the stages and halls they have graced, but also the 'image' of the singer in their age – a certain magnitude. Especially it is fitting and right, even if ironically so, that out of the race which for so long was excluded as of inferior status should come the two singers who in their time have done most to fill that stage with a sense of majesty.

CHAPTER 17

Zinka Milanov, Mario Del Monaco and Leonard Warren

As philosophers have probably observed from time immemorial, every-thing has cause but not everything has reason. The cause why these three singers have never been what I think of as 'mine' will soon be plain to see. The reasons are another matter: under suspicion from the start and only mildly to be probed in this chapter.

Each of the singers has an image. In my mind, and in brief, Milanov is velvet, Del Monaco a wall, Warren a square. The velvet is purplish, part of it a little crumpled. The wall is not of aged mossy stone with plants growing in its crevices, but the kind which people have in mind when they say that something is like banging your head against it. The square is massive, a thing of wonder but not of curiosity: it seems all open to the eye and therefore not to invite exploration.

Another image surfaces now, and may explain why the three bring themselves to mind in alliance. This is of a curtain-call at the Met where they hold hands and bow, perhaps after a performance of *Andrea Chénier*. I'm not certain whether this is imaginary or the memory of a photograph seen at some time in the past, but there is an atmosphere about it, an evocation of time, place and excitement. Quite probably at various points in the performance, if one had been there, a wish might have crossed the mind that Milanov's voice had a firmer grip, that Del Monaco would respond instead of just stating or announcing. But the occasion would have been a real night-at-the-opera, and satisfied clients would have struggled into their coats, looked around for their programmes and observed to one another 'Some night, heh?' 'Some night'.

Perhaps attitudes are coloured by the fact that those particular nights (the ones envisaged by that image of the curtain-call) were not part of our operatic provision in Britain. Warren never sang here, and the others did so but rarely. Milanov was highly regarded at Covent Garden on account of her Tosca but memory of the *Trovatore* Leonora is dim till halfway through. She gave us little cause to match sound with reputation till the ensemble at the end of Act 2. Then the fourth Act aria and its recitative were everything we hoped they would be, and she left a fine taste of her

83

best quality in the final scene with the ascending phrase 'Prima che d'altri vivere', which had its soul already in heaven. Even with this limited acquaintance it was very clear that Milanov was a singer who at best could be a great part of a great night at the opera. Yet at the same time her appearances confirmed a feeling gained from records that hers was, so to speak, a selective voice, producing celestial effects at one point and letting others go short of real satisfaction.

The famous studio recording of *Aida* with Björling shows this from the start. The first impression is of an uneven, almost squally production, but then with the high note on 'pavento' comes such loveliness as makes all well again. A similar process occurs in 'Ritorna vincitor' and the duet with Amneris. As in *Trovatore* with 'D'amor sull' ali rosee', the time of her greatness in *Aida* arrives with 'O patria mia'. Beautiful in every way – tone, phrasing, inflections, the *dolcissimo*, the *sfumate* – this has a perfect matching of aria and voice: I suppose of all voices in the world this is the one that best befits the warm night air, the nostalgic song borne on the scented breezes to a distant homeland. Some unfocussed phrases reappear in the duet with Amonasro, but again all is loveliness in her 'Là tra foreste vergine' as, finally, in the Tomb scene. Milanov was then nearly fifty years old and the preservation of her voice is wonderful indeed; but the recording remains a fair example because, if one goes back to the start of her career at the Metropolitan, to the 1937 *Gioconda* with Martinelli, the same pattern emerges – passages of the utmost loveliness, in the fine lyric-dramatic manner, interspersed with others where the focus blurs and the 'grip' loosens.

Milanov's limitations as an actress (she was known as 'la donna immo-bile') matter little now, and did not greatly affect my own share of pleasure and incompleteness at Covent Garden. The expressiveness of her singing was limited too, though less severely; and certainly she was an artist of infinite subtlety compared to Mario Del Monaco. He also was a rare visitor to Covent Garden (attracting all the more interest when he did come, however), and I heard him only in *Otello*. This was in 1962 in some impressive performances under Solti, once with Gobbi as Iago, once with Otakar Kraus. I had rather expected that Del Monaco's stentorian tones would marginilise Kraus whereas in fact, from a seat far back in the house, it was Gobbi who more nearly went under in the Oath duet, while the Czech, a resident member of the company, had a harder, more penetrative tone. Del Monaco impressed with the solid dignity of his voice and pres-ence, and also with his honourably scrupulous reading of the part; but on both occasions (again as remembered) he scarcely ever caught the heart or engaged the brain until the last Act. The scene with Desdemona and then the death brought out a deeper, broader tone that achieved nobility.

One of those performances has survived on records, care-of the pirates, and presents a truly magnificent account of the opera. Del Monaco's 'Esultate' is marvellous in its command, clean and unforced in its power,

Zinka Milanov as Leonora in *La forza del destino*

the unquestionable voice of authority. His reappearance with 'Abasso le spade' has the same ring: the authentic Otello voice. He does not make a public address out of the Love duet any more than he will do later of the soliloquy. This he takes well with *voce soffocata* and even the piano markings duly observed. In Act 2 he sometimes moves ahead of the beat

85

Mario Del Monaco as Otello

Leonard Warren as Amonasro in *Aida*

(he always liked to take it fast from 'Tu! indietro!' onwards), but he gives notes their full value in declamation and is incisive in diction as in tone. Yet until the last scene, or what remains after Desdemona's murder, he makes us feel Otello's anger and determination but not his pain. Otello needs to have some admixture of pain in his voice in almost everything he sings bar the 'Esultate': even before Iago's poison has been injected he is a man whose unexpected happiness makes him fearful. Del Monaco's is a straight-up-and-down chap, and though the intensity of the last scene leaves a poignant memory, the 'wall' is still there, even in this nobly impressive achievement.

The baritone voice that could in its own time stand beside Del Monaco's power and brilliance was Leonard Warren's. Its resources were phenomenal. In an early, pirated 'live' recording of *Simon Boccanegra* he sings the secondary but important role of Paolo in a cast headed by Tibbett, Rethberg, Martinelli and Pinza. None of these could be called lightweight, yet the clear impression is that the 28-year-old newcomer has the biggest voice among them. In terms of 'size', that is: quality is more doubtful, as he is recognisably 'modern' among these veterans in his possession of something else they did not have – the relative lack of a precise and steady focus. This does seem to have been a feature, if an intermittent one, of his early singing, and though records from the 1940s show it to have been very largely corrected, it still emerges, and towards the end of his tragically curtailed life begins to manifest itself in a slowing and broadening of vibrations, which could become a 'beat'. He still, at the end of his career, could astonish with both power and quietness, cutting-edge and mellow covering, low notes and high.

His upper range was always so remarkable it almost ceased to astonish; it is said that he would sometimes use the second half of 'Che gelida manina', top C and all, for warming-up and might even sing 'Di quella pira' in the original key if he felt like it. The original complaint about separated registers (baritone and tenor) was met by exercises that smoothed the transition. Similarly, objections that his singing of Verdi had everything except style lost force when he began studying in mid-career with Giuseppe De Luca. He also learned to sing intimately; and though charm was not readily in his gift he evidently knew how to bestow it on the audiences of his Russian tour in 1958, where they clamoured for 'The Way to Colorado', alias the gently hillbilly 'Colorado Trail'.

Warren was among the supremely gifted and conscientious singers of his time. His death on stage just as about to sing 'Egli è salvo' in *La forza del destino* was not so sensational as genuinely grievous, and grieved. The date, 4 March 1960, lives in Metropolitan history, and Warren, dying, like Caruso, at the age of 48, never knew the regress of the down-turning parabola.

As with the others, Milanov and Del Monaco, there are reasons why he never became one of 'my' singers. But it is time to face the cause. In retrospect I think it was simply that these three singers took the places, chronologically, of three who *were* 'mine': Ponselle, Martinelli and Tibbett. The cause is not one I can admire, nor do the reasons justify exclusion. I now find much to admire and even cherish in all of them. But in relative terms (that is, in straight comparisons) I still find the reasons valid. Ultimately the difference lies in artistic imagination. Ponselle in records from *La forza*, Martinelli in his *Otello*, Tibbett as Boccanegra, for example: vocally, over the whole spectrum of the performances the earlier generation may not be superior, but in creative artistry they command a scope (depth, intensity, individuality) that is beyond the range of their successors.

87

CHAPTER 18

Renato Bruson and
Sherrill Milnes

In these brief studies each singer has been the centre of attention as an individual, interesting perhaps as representing a trend or a characteristic, but rarely offered for consideration primarily within the context of a national school or tradition. In Chapter 8 the view was opened a little to consider the baritone Gérard Souzay in relation to others in his line, and it may be opportune to do something similar now with two more baritones, an Italian and an American. At the same time I have in mind to narrow the sights in musical reference and to take a more detailed look at the two artists in a particular work.

Bruson was probably the best Italian baritone of his generation and Milnes the best American; both have an honourable place in a distinguished line. The Italian line goes back much further in time (though as the years pass, the differential becomes less, at least as a statistic). The term 'baritono' (meaning originally 'deep-sounding') is known to date from the fifteenth century but came into usage as distinct from 'basso' early in the nineteenth. At the turn of that century into the twentieth, the 'Verdi baritone' was well-established though records suggest that the high-ranging yet full-bodied type we came to know first through singers such as Titta Ruffo and Pasquale Amato may have been a fairly new breed. The American line is commonly thought to start with Lawrence Tibbett in the 1920s, though at the same time others, such as John Charles Thomas, were beginning to make a name for themselves, which renders it unlikely that they were entirely first generation. Certainly by mid-century 'the American baritone' was a well-recognised species, and the leading exponents were probably not inferior to their contemporaries in Italy.

The most powerful baritone of that generation was Leonard Warren (see the previous chapter), while Robert Merrill (Vol. I, Ch. 47) was commendable as any in respect of the good production of a beautiful voice; and if it were argued that they were a more doubtful proposition when it came to style a ready answer could be that so were most of the modern Italians. The Italian baritones of that generation were headed by Gobbi, Bechi, Taddei, Silveri, Mascherini: there were fine voices and effective

88

Renato Bruson as Falstaff

actors (Gobbi in a class of his own) but probably none would be advanced as a model of style in a way that Battistini, De Luca, Stracciari, Amato, Scotti and Stabile might have been in earlier days. The Italian school of baritones was even then, by mid-century, in decline. For a while, until his lamentable illness and death in 1967, Ettore Bastianini held the prime position. His was a voice in the authentic tradition and he produced it in accordance with tried Italian methods; but stylistically he not merely lacked distinction but gives the impression on records (which include live performances) of singing as though without an idea in his head. More imaginative and characterful was Rolando Panerai, more powerful and exciting for a while were Giangiacomo Guelfi and Matteo Manuguerra, but it was Piero Cappuccilli who by general consent became Italy's principal baritone following the decline and retirement of Tito Gobbi. Bruson, six years younger than Cappuccilli, inherited the position perhaps ten years later.

Cappuccilli was a remarkably able singer, with solid tone, ample range and power and exceptional breath-control; yet, in its tone and expression, his singing rarely fired the imagination or lodged in the memory. Bruson came on the scene as something unusual – a modern baritone with a special aptness for the lyrical music of Donizetti and early Verdi. He also had quite the most beautiful voice. On his first appearance in Britain at Covent Garden in 1976 this voice made an immediately strong impression: it glowed. For some years, the opulence of his tone increased, and in this respect outclassed his nearest rival among Italian contemporaries, Leo Nucci. They sang together in *Falstaff*, with Bruson taking the name-part and Nucci as Ford; in their scene in Act 2, Nucci's tone, which at that time would have withstood almost any other comparison, sounded less than golden. Bruson's was probably the most opulently beautiful Italian baritone voice of my own 'live' experience: that is, roughly, of all those within half a century. Yet at the same time the demands of roles such as Falstaff and Scarpia upon this lyrical voice brought a loosening of the originally reliable firmness. His more recent recordings in the 1990s have shown the process accelerating, and his initial distinction, as a lyric baritone of the De Luca type, seems almost to have been effaced.

Bruson rose in a period of decline among Italian baritones, and probably of Italian singing generally; Milnes came to be the leading American baritone at a time when the fortunes and achievements of American singers had never been so high. He is Bruson's senior by one year (born in 1935) but came to international prominence at an earlier age. Too young to have had Tibbett as his living model or reference-point (as Merrill did), he nevertheless benefited from that inheritance. Irving Kolodin, chronicler of the Metropolitan's history and critic of the *Saturday Review*, saw him as extending the distinguished line directly from Tibbett and Warren. Overtaking some of the intermediate generation, such as Cornell McNeill, he became paired in status on stage and recordings with Placido Domingo, rather as some years previously Merrill had been with Jussi Björling. On the opening night of the Metropolitan's season in 1970 he sang in *Ernani* and in 1979 in *Otello*; this was the decade of his pre-eminence and vocal prime. In as far as he has a successor it must be Thomas Hampson (Ch. 45), though there are more differences there, I would say, than between Milnes and his own predecessors.

Hampson has not, as far as I know, sung Verdi's Macbeth but if he did, there would be the general expectation of a highly intelligent performance. I'm not sure that the *expectation* would have been as high when Milnes set out to record the part, but certainly it is what he achieved. Now, Bruson is commonly thought of as a particularly intelligent singer among Italians, but, taking the role of Macbeth as an example, or perhaps as an index, of what is meant by intelligent singing in Italian opera I cannot see that the native Italian comes within hailing distance of the American. And though it would be foolish to suppose that wide conclusions could be drawn from this single example, the comparison may be suggestive.

90

Let us follow the role through in the singers' respective recordings, Milnes's made in 1976 and conducted by Riccardo Muti, Bruson's in 1983 under Giuseppe Sinopoli. Macbeth enters with the Italian version of 'So foul and fair a day I have not seen'. Bruson states it; Milnes points the paradox ('bello'). When Macbeth sees the witches, Bruson is authoritative but not surprised; Milnes is startled. After the prophecies, Macbeth ('Due vaticini') thinks them over, Bruson with due privacy and seriousness, but not (apparently) troubled by them. Yet the force of the prophecy (says the libretto) is such as to make his hair stand on end: he recognises and fears the temptation, a deeply worried man. Bruson is not totally unaffected by the experience, but the anxious perplexity which Milnes gets into his voice at 'Ma perchè sento' has no counterpart; nor has Bruson 'seen', as Milnes has, that 'la man rapace' ('the grasping hand') has a latent violence which the voice can legitimately bring out with emphasis, effectively contrasted with the legato of 'Alla corona che m'offre il fato'. That is: if Fate smoothes the way to the crown – *legato* – there is no need for the hand – *sforzando* – to force the issue.

In the scene of the dagger-soliloquy and murder, Bruson appropriately contrasts *piano* and *forte*, for instance in the repeated 'intendo' as he assures Lady Macbeth that he understands what is afoot, but Milnes uses the repetition to steel himself into decisiveness. When Bruson sees the imaginary dagger he expresses due horror ('Orrendo imago'), but with Milnes's sharp intake of breath we *see* the thing: suddenly it's there. 'Sulla metà del mondo' ('Now o'er the one-half world'): Bruson softens his voice, but it is Milnes who communicates the sense of horror crawling over his skin. Then, when the murder is done, Milnes sings 'Tutto è finito' as a lament, where Bruson impresses with his softness but is not (as is Milnes) a man who knows that in the last few minutes all life has changed.

A photograph in the booklet with the LP set shows Bruson in the recording session acting intensely, a hand outstretched and spectacled eyes wide, like one who has seen a ghost – as Macbeth has done in the banquet scene. There is no doubt of his sincerity, but it doesn't really work like that. For instance, a key to Macbeth's disturbed mentality in that scene is the murderer's report that Banquo's son has survived. 'Cielo!' exclaims Bruson in his opera singer's voice, but Milnes makes it more like an involuntary gasp and we know how shaken he is. As he pulls himself together to face the company after the first sight of Banquo's ghost, Bruson duly begs pardon ('Ciascun mi perdoni'), but Milnes's voice, pathetically limp, is that of a man still recovering from an ordeal. And at the end of the scene ('Sangue a me', 'It will have blood') Bruson is quite rightly hushed and so is Milnes, but Milnes's hush is internal. The tension is still within, and gradually it takes a new turn: again he steels his voice as Macbeth steels his will.

Macbeth's visit to the witches and the final scene follow the same pattern: with Bruson, a sincerely apprehended generality, with Milnes, an

Sherrill Milnes

intelligently perceived specific. The individual instance must not be pressed too far, but I would say there is a certain representative force in these comparisons, especially with regard to this aspect of the Italian school. For instance, the comparison might have been made with the previous Italian Macbeth on records, Cappuccilli, and then the contrast would have been even more marked. If Gobbi had recorded the role, that, no doubt, would have produced a very different result; but Gobbi was a dramatic genius and not representative. Both Milnes and Bruson, I would say, *are* representative.

Both, it goes without saying, have, or had, exceptional voices. Milnes's, as I remember it in the house, was better the closer you were to the stage, but it gave good value throughout the range and was often thrilling at the top. Bruson's tone could be overwhelmingly beautiful. I don't know that Milnes's was distinctively 'an American voice'; Bruson's was certainly Italian. But behind the voice and the singing-style is a culture, involving attitudes and habits of mind. The two Macbeths, I would say, are more than two individual baritones.

CHAPTER 19

Jose Carreras and Miguel Fleta

Singing from the Soul is the title of Carreras's autobiography. 'Soul' – that abused, unsubstantiated, necessary word – is what comes to mind when listening sympathetically to Fleta. With Carreras, certainly since his great illness, the voice has functioned under severe limitations. With Fleta, even in his prime, taste and technique imposed limitations different in kind from Carreras's but comparable in degree. In both, some quality that is beyond voice, and even beyond what we think of as musicianship, exercises a fascination and evokes a response which seems to call upon the immemorial word to account for it. Fleta was the tenor-hero of his country in the first half of the century as Carreras has been in the second. Is the 'soul' that we intuitively posit in some way a national possession? Have these voices, these arts and 'souls', any demonstrably shared characteristic that might in turn be redefined as Spanish? I doubt it, but perhaps we shall see.

First, who was Miguel Fleta? Such is fame that even readers of this book, with their given interest in singers and singing, may find the name no more than vaguely familiar. He is remembered in the history books primarily for having 'created' the role of Calaf, the Unknown Prince in Puccini's *Turandot*. That was in 1926 after at least three famous Italian tenors (Gigli, Lauri-Volpi and Martinelli) had been named. But Fleta's real identity was as a popular icon, the operatic counterpart of some great matador, and one whose vocal exploits would be applauded in much the same way. The held high-notes, their long diminuendo and carry-over into the next phrase, may not have appealed to the tastefully erudite, but they still brought the house down. Fleta-nights in Spain became pop-concerts in atmosphere if not in repertoire. He sang his role in the opera, Don José or Canio or the Duke in *Rigoletto* for instance, and then, still in costume and with a piano trundled on to the stage, songs and arias by request might follow till singer and audience were exhausted and he was borne shoulder-high back to his hotel. He enjoyed comparable popularity in South America, though rather less in New York, and he never sang publicly in London. Several of his recordings became best-sellers, particularly the song called 'Ay ay ay' which accompanied him everywhere.

Miguel Fleta as Don José in *Carmen*

Excessively prodigal of his gifts, often at the expense of his health, he declined and died, in 1938, at the age of 39.[1]

Carreras, as we know, came very near to death when he was just one year older. In 1987 leukemia was diagnosed, his case being complicated by the necessity of using the patient's own bone-marrow for transplant (they took it out, cleaned it and put it back in again, but the process was a great deal more complicated and painful than that might suggest). Even then there remained the danger of rejection: the odds were against his survival and still more strongly against the likelihood of a return to the stage. He could, in other words, well have been a 'singer of the century' whose career had lasted just about as long as Fleta's. How would they then have compared?

94

José Carreras

Carreras, again like Fleta, had a brilliant early career. As boy and man he has been one of those lucky people who know their own mind. It seems he knew his from the age of six, when he saw *The Great Caruso* at the local cinema and found next day that he had memorised the arias. From morn to night he sang them, for months on end, in his strong boy's alto; and when he won the part of the boy in Falla's *El retablo del Maese Pedro* it seemed quite natural that the twelve-year-old should be making his operatic debut at Spain's foremost opera house, the Liceu. In the years that followed, there grew a shared conviction that he was born to sing. Powerful support arrived when Montserrat Caballé heard him and recognised his talent as he sang his role of Flavio, the confidant, in her own first *Norma*. This was in 1970 and was followed by his first leading role, as Gennaro to Caballé's Lucrezia Borgia. He also won outright the coveted first prize of the international Verdi competition at Parma, which led to performances at their opera house with its notoriously formidable audience. No favours were expected for a Spaniard, but evidently they knew a good singer when they heard one, and after the first 'bravo' all went well. So indeed did his rapid succession of debuts in Madrid, London (at the

95

Festival Hall), New York (with the City Opera), Vienna and Milan. Within five years he had gained a position which most would regard as the top of the profession. If confirmation were needed, it came promptly with his invitation from Karajan to sing Verdi's *Requiem* and *Don Carlos* at Salzburg.

By the end of that year, 1976, Carreras was thirty. Fleta, born, like him, in December, reached thirty in 1928. He had made his operatic debut when two years younger than Carreras at the time of his. By 1917, when not yet twenty, his voice and style had developed sufficiently for him to be recognised as a cut above the other singers in a prestigious 'jota' competition (which nevertheless he did not win). He also attracted the attention of a teacher who eventually became his wife. With her he left Spain for Italy, made an immediate impression and was engaged by the composer Riccardo Zandonai for performances of his *Francesca da Rimini*. The hero, Paolo, was his debut-role, conducted by Zandonai himself who in 1922 engaged him for the world-premiere at Rome of his *Giulietta e Romeo*. In 1920 he became a favourite at the Volksoper in Vienna. Prague and Budapest, Monte Carlo and Venice also heard him before his return to Spain for a sensational debut in Madrid. It was on this night, in a performance of *Carmen* before a half-empty house (like Tetrazzini in London) that the Fleta legend was born. Many at that time were convinced that his was the finest tenor voice in the world.

South America became his second kingdom, and in 1923 he sang for a season at the Metropolitan in New York. The record companies, eager for new tenors after the death of Caruso, spread his name still more widely, and when he was chosen for the premiere of *Turandot* at La Scala a greater honour could scarcely have been in anyone's power to bestow. Like Carreras in 1976 he could feel that he had arrived at the summit: the difference was that, while Carreras stayed there, Fleta's fortunes waned. Carreras had another twelve years before tragedy struck, and from it, as we know, he was to emerge for what was virtually a second career. Fleta reached this critical point in 1928, both vocally and personally. Thereafter his name carried him through tours of Europe, South America and even the Far East, and though he sometimes recaptured his old form the great days were over. He returned to Spain, soon to be in the throes of its civil war. Somewhat pathetically he would appear everywhere in falangist uniform but by then was yesterday's man and a sick one at that. He became seriously ill in 1937 and, unlike Carreras, did not recover.

A casual listener to Fleta's records might remark simply: 'Fine voice, sad case.' Expanding on that, it might mean: 'Yes, this is a voice of unusual quality, richly beautiful in the middle range, bright and valiant up top. Flexible and many-shaded, it can excite with both gentleness and force. Yet one moment I'm loving it and the next I'm not. At one moment he is all youthful grace and beauty; at another, either the vibrations will loosen or the tone will so to speak tighten into a scowl. Great material: I'd like to stay longer, but life is too short and I'll move on to a tenor I can be sure of, young Carreras for instance.' Of the young Carreras this same listener might have remarked merely: 'That's the one for me: marvellous.' Meaning: 'This is the sound of a tenor voice which, like the other, is of exceptionally fine quality, but is a unity with no distractions such as registers (upper or middle) or vibrations (tight or loose); it conveys emotion that does not run to excess, has a good span of phrase but not such as deliberately draws attention to itself. And although this appreciation may appear to have a lot of negatives in it, the enjoyment is totally positive.'

Perhaps the hypothetical listener is not so casual after all, but it's a listener who does not want to linger. Fleta invites lingering. Personally, I have spent a lifetime trying to avoid him, for my first record of his (a badly arranged Brahms waltz and the Aubade from *Le Roi d'Ys*) seemed a poor thing. But I return, and do in fact linger: over his 'O paradiso', 'Celeste Aida' and zarzuelas for instance. Playing the young Carreras ('Quando le sere', the last scene of *Lucia di Lammermoor* and 'E lucevan le stelle' came to hand) has certainly yielded enjoyment, but not much of it revolves in the head afterwards. In his middle-period Carreras grew thicker in the upper middle notes, the treacherous *passaggio*, a process which is so dangerous and likely to forfeit elegance, as I think it did. When he survived his illness and returned first to the concert platform I shared in the general rejoicing but hoped that he would build this second career on new foundations. Perhaps that was not possible; still, it was discouraging to find that one of the first things he did was to add to his repertoire the still heavier and 'thicker' role of Samson. Yet hearing him again in recital only a few nights ago was a moving experience. That he could hold his audience so compellingly with such limitations of range and repertoire is testimony to the personality and spirit, but also to a kind of fascination with what the voice can still do. He is not a poet of the voice as Fleta's records show him to have been, but there's a flame and always has been, from those early Verdi operas he recorded in his freshest youth, through all his touchingly acted Don Josés, to the encore-song he addressed to the balcony the other evening. Whatever the special gift is, 'soul' is not a bad word for it, and it unites these two Spanish tenors across the gap of the generations. Whether the 'soul', or any other feature of their art, is peculiarly Spanish, we are, I'm afraid, no nearer to finding out – except that, if it were, I think we might have noticed.

[1] The year of Fleta's birth is given as 1897 in most reference books. In notes for a compact disc on the Preiser label, Clemens Höslinger describes this as one of the many myths that have grown up around Fleta's name, and gives 1893 as the date of birth. More recently, Fleta's grandson, pointing out that the essential documents were destroyed in the Civil War, has given 1898, which is the date accepted here.

CHAPTER 20

Claudia Muzio

In its operatic usage, 'diva' is a silly word, indicative, at any rate, of silly attitudes: but if justification were sought for it in reference to one singer of the twentieth century, that should be Muzio. In the opera houses of North and South America she was admired often to the point of worship. In private life she was dignified and withdrawn; a widely held belief was that she had indeed no private life but was devoted wholly to her work. On stage she transcended the status of prima donna; she was the great tragedienne, the Duse of the lyric theatre. In legend, she was 'the divine Claudia', 'la divina'.

'La storia mia è breve.' Born into the business (she was the daughter of a stage director at the San Carlo, Covent Garden and the Metropolitan), she made her debut in 1910 at the age of 20, and scored a notable success in her first, and last, London season in 1914. She joined the Metropolitan in 1916, singing with Caruso, as she did on the opening night of the following season in *Aida*. Chicago and San Francisco became her head-quarters for another decade, with the high temple of Muzism in Buenos Aires. When she returned to Italy it was with the aura of divinity and, all too soon, a weak heart. In 1936, aged 47, she died.

The conditions of a mystique were already in place. At the Metropolitan, where she had been absent for twelve years, she reappeared in 1934 in her famous role of Violetta in *La traviata*: not only had her art matured but her name had acquired the magic of nostalgia. Rather similarly with the record-buying public: whereas most of the great singers chose to perpetuate their art with the Victor company or its associate HMV, Muzio recorded for the less accessible Pathé and Edison, till her totally unanticipated return in 1932 with a series for Italian Columbia. This had the inspired surprise of a miracle: the records caught and brought to renewed notice a singer who was clearly special, a true candidate for greatness. It needed only her death for them to be revered as holy relics, which, in a sense, they were.

These were on 78rpm discs, and in the course of time were withdrawn from circulation, their critical status, if anything, enhanced. When the LP era launched its *Great Recordings of the Century* series, Muzio was one of the first singers chosen, along with Chaliapin and Melba, for a solo recital.

A fine selection from the Columbia series was edited by Desmond Shawe-Taylor, and Muzio's exalted place in the hierarchy was confirmed for another generation. Then came Michael Scott and his *Record of Singing*.

In the second volume of the books which together with their corresponding record albums constitute the most important work of their kind – a history matching word to sound – the author subjected Muzio to a revaluation. In many respects, the critique is fair and well-balanced. His writing nevertheless caused offence where he knew it would (he admitted in an interview to having taken the opportunity of settling a few old scores): which of course does not of itself invalidate his criticisms. As far as I know, these have never been faced up to in print, so perhaps that should be done now. He begins with the most famous of all Muzio's records, the 'Addio del passato' from the last Act of *La traviata*.

First to be criticised is the spoken reading of the letter, written to a mortally sick woman by the father of her estranged lover. This, says Scott, is 'most dramatic and done after the fashion of a tragedy queen in deepest *parlando*'. He contrasts it with Callas's way, as shown in live recordings, pitching the speaking-voice so that when she starts to sing there is no abrupt 'changing of gears'. It would, I think, commonly be found that if Muzio is played immediately after Callas the immediate effect is some- what comical, as it would be in moving from a modern 'naturalistic' Shakespearean actor to someone of the school of Henry Irving or even (and this is more apt) to John Gielgud, who (like Irving for that matter) was once himself thought modern. But Muzio's reading, granted such an historical adjustment on the listener's part, cannot quite be written-off as the stylised routine of a 'tragedy queen'. 'She takes a letter from her bosom and reads' says the stage-direction; but of course it is not 'a letter' and she is not, in the normal sense of the word, reading. It is the centre of her life at present; she has read it countless times already and knows every word of it. More truly it is, in her heart, a poem or sacred text. This is what prompts Muzio's incantatory style and which (granted the historical change of style in dramatic performance) justifies it. Scott says that Muzio does not 'let the voice rise and fall in line with the melodic cadence'. Again, it is true that the first phrases are centred, almost trancelike, on a monotone pitched around D flat, just as the accompanying music is fixed in the key of G flat; but shortly after the sad modulation, with the naturalised D in its melodic line, the voice rises. This is in response to the message of hope (her lover will return – 'egli a voi tornerà' – and beg forgiveness). These are the most cherished words in the letter but also the most heart-breaking. That she is indeed 'in tune' with the music is clear from that, and then, still more unquestionably, from a point remarked upon by Shawe-Taylor in his notes for the LP: that on the long syllable of the word 'curatevi' ('Get well') Muzio 'allows her speaking-voice to rest for an instant on the note B flat, thus making a passing effect of harmony with the accompanying *tremolando*'. As for the 'gear-change' with Muzio's introduction of the singing-voice on the word 'Attendo', Michael Scott's observation is valid, but not necessarily so the comment which follows: 'it sounds as if someone else had started to sing'. At best, that exaggerates; at worst it is a point-scoring remark, because in truth the voice changes no more then does the music. The sad-sweet indulgence is over. The last spoken words, 'E tardi' (literally 'It is late' but carrying the sense of 'Too late') break into the mood of the *tremolando* strings and melodic reminis-

100

Muzio as Violetta in *La traviata*

cence with the finality of a book slammed shut. The change from speaking to singing-voice responds to the change of mood and mode.

Turning to the aria, Scott remarks that Muzio 'equates the symptoms of her own heart condition with those of Violetta's consumption, thus turning the breathlessness to dramatic advantage'. Many listeners will have had similar thoughts and have been moved by them. They will also have been moved by the many shades of tone by which this troubled heart expresses its conflict of resignation and urgent hope: and that too could be thought to merit the critic's appreciative comment. But Scott has now only faults to find. 'The high As,' he writes, 'she lets go with something like a yelp.' Of the three high As, the second is elided and leads directly to a series of descending notes. No yelp there. The first stays on pitch and is sung so as to express a flushed, heightened emotional state. It is the third, the last note sung, which suggests the word 'yelp' – and it would surely not do so to anybody listening with even a modicum of imaginative sympathy. It betrays the lack of critical integrity as does the remark 'We should hardly be surprised if Violetta expired before the end.' And this, we note, is in a context accusing Muzio of exaggeration.

Other faults are found with this and with other records, but the *Traviata* solo, with which Muzio is so closely associated, will serve the

101

present purpose which is not so much to confute the critic as to test the singer's art in the light of his criticisms. It gains in the process.

To her contemporaries Muzio was often greatness itself. Most accounts note limitations, but they appear to have been thought incidental. Colleagues, including the sopranos, admired and regarded her as in a class apart. Most of Lanfranco Rasponi's 'last prima donnas' (Gollancz, 1984) speak of her: 'perhaps the artist who made the most unforgettable impression on me of all' (Eva Turner), 'a fragility in her voice, despite its strength, that was ever so deeply moving' (Gilda della Rizza), 'with Muzio, you suffered agonies with her heroines' (Gina Cigna), 'Muzio, who was my idol' (Maria Caniglia), 'Muzio was a case apart: you cannot classify her for in the end you had been so emotionally destroyed by the performances, you did not even know anymore what kind of an instrument she had' (Lucrezia Bori). Some of them recall particularly the *Traviata* solo mentioned above. Rosa Ponselle (*A Singer's Life*, Doubleday, 1982) recalls: 'Muzio's was a darkly coloured *spinto* voice that throbbed with feeling. Lauri-Volpi once wrote of the "tears and sighs" inherent in her voice, and of the "restrained interior fire" of her personality. No scene in *La traviata* more embodied these qualities than her Letter Scene, "Addio del passato". Fortunately for posterity, the Columbia company recorded her singing it at the very end of her life. It remains one of the finest of all *Traviata* recordings.' Lauri-Volpi in *Voci parallele* (Bongiovanni, 1977 edition) remembers especially her 'voce soavissima' in 'Casta diva' and 'D'amor sull' ali rosee': the voice, he wrote, had natural limitations despite which it gained an unsuspected resonance enabling her to confront the 'inhuman tessitura' of Turandot, the superhuman range of Norma, the humanity of Santuzza, the submissive devotion of Desdemona. Her singing, he said, had a depth of sensibility and musical culture invested with the spirit of her personality.

Such tributes were paid by those who heard her. Soul, spirit and personality are their constant terms of reference. Since then, those elusive records of hers on Pathé and Edison have been collected and edited in complete editions on compact disc. What they do is to add evidence of the beauty and skill of her singing, as singing: the loveliness of her voice and the accomplishment of its usage. Her place in the real 'record of singing' remains assured.

CHAPTER 21

Pasquale Amato

'A song of tender memories' was the long-familiar English translation (Fred Weatherly's) of 'Un nido di memorie' in the Prologue to *Pagliacci*. But of course 'Un nido' means 'a nest', and when Amato sings the phrase that is exactly what it is. It is as though he holds it in his hands with a loving care for the fragile, patiently wrought creation; then, as the phrase continues, the emotion deepens and swells in his voice as it is related ('in fondo a l'anima cantava un giorno') to the composer's own moment of creative inspiration. Amato's Victor recording of the Prologue is a master-class throughout, but this particular passage has the very soul of the artist in it. His voice is strong and darkly dramatic, but here he lightens it, sweetening in response to the orchestral direction *dolce con canto*. The 'cradling' is done through *portamento*, the carrying of the voice over, not in a straight line but a curve, upwards to 'nido', downwards to 'memorie'. Modern singers are so schooled in 'cleanness' and literalism that such a style is foreign to them (I once heard Martinelli, who sang many times with Amato, trying to teach a young baritone to do it this way, but there was no instinctive feeling there and the result was grotesque). And Amato is not 'taking liberties'; he is, in fact, scrupulous in respect for the score, as in his exact observance of the *marcato* lines over the first syllables of 'cantava un giorno'. He is a musician-singer of rare sensitivity and imagination, and never more so (hear the indrawn, restrained emotion of 'E voi, piuttosto') than when astride this famous warhorse, so often used for blatant display and crude effect.

Amato was born into the Italy of *verismo*. He was a young teenager when *Pagliacci* had its premiere in 1892, and at the very start of his career in 1900, which also saw the first *Tosca*. This, the 'new' music, quickly entered his repertoire, and his voice, tense and vibrant, with brilliant high notes, answered its needs. But he was also, and perhaps primarily, a Verdi baritone. He made his debut at Naples in *La traviata* and went on in his first season there at the Teatro Bellini to sing in *Aida* and *Un ballo in maschera*. *Ernani*, *Il trovatore* and *La forza del destino* followed, and soon *Rigoletto*, which in those early years he also sang at Prague and Odessa. In South America, under Toscanini, he added the role of Ford in *Falstaff*, the title-role coming his way in 1912. He was also an Iago, and a very fine one, if his recording of the 'Credo' is anything to go by.

103

To Mr. Ben Franklin in kind remembrance Pasquale Amato New York April 1915

That record illustrates very well the concentration and incisiveness of tone that made his voice, as we hear it now, such an apt instrument for the baritone-villains. There is a hardness of will-power present in the timbre itself, a quality which in turn disassociates him in our minds from the music of Germont in *La traviata* though that was one of his most

Comitato Esecutivo per le Feste Commemorative del 1911 in Roma

TEATRO COSTANZI

Lunedì 12 Giugno 1911, ore 9 pom.

(fuori abbonamento)

PRIMA RAPPRESENTAZIONE

dell'opera in 3 atti

(dal dramma di DAVID BELASCO) di Guelfo Civinini e Carlo Zangariol

La fanciulla del West

Musica di **GIACOMO PUCCINI**

(Proprietà G. RICORDI e C.)

NUOVISSIMA PER L'ITALIA

PERSONAGGI

Minnie	.	. Burzio Eugenia
Jack Rance, sceriffo	.	. Amato Pasquale
Dick Johnson (Ramerrez)	.	. Bassi Amedeo
Nick, cameriere della « Polka »	.	. Cilla Luigi
Ashby, agente della Compagnia di trasporti Wells Fargo.		Challis Benedetto
Sonora		Blanchart Ramon
Trin		Paltrinieri Giordano
Sid		Perini Giuseppe
Bello	minatori	Reschiglian Vincenzo
Harry		Sala Giuseppe
Joe		Pini Corsi Gaetano
Happy		Pulcini Attilio
Larkens		Angelini Fornari Rodolfo
Billy Jackrablit, indiano pellirosse		. Tavecchia Luigi
Wowkle, la donna indiana di Billy	.	. Leveroni Elvira
Jake Wallace cantastorie girovago	.	. Mardones Josè
Josè Castro, meticcio della banda di Ramerrez	.	. Sandrini Eugenio
Un postiglione	.	. Gbidini Riccardo

Uomini del campo.

Ai piedi delle Montagne delle nubi (Cloudy-Mountains), in California. - Un campo di minatori, nei giorni della febbre dell'oro, 1849-1850.

Maestro Concertatore e Direttore d'Orchestra :

ARTURO TOSCANINI

Maestro del Coro: **G. B. ZORZATO**

The first performance of *La fanciulla del West* in Italy

successful roles. The aria, 'Di Provenza', with its generous D flat major melody wants a roundness of tone such as Amato's contemporary Giuseppe de Luca pre-eminently bestowed upon it; and on the key-note, the D flat itself, we specially miss that comfortable centrality, sensing there and at the end of the *Rigoletto* solo, a certain reserve, if not exactly a tightness, of production. Yet granted that it is in some way 'the wrong voice', Amato's is a touchingly sympathetic performance, solicitous in feeling, restrained yet poignant in its appeal. In Rigoletto's plea to the courtiers, the sighed 'Ahimè' comes as to confirm the sense of defeat that is so pervasive once the energy of denunciation has run its course. Again, the voice-character may not seem entirely right for the role, which it certainly is for Di Luna in *Il trovatore* and Amonasro in *Aida*: one of the most dramatically potent achievements in the whole range of pre-electrical recordings is Amato's withering declamation of the curse 'Non sei mia figlia! Dei Faraoni tu sei la schiava!'

His masterpiece as a Verdi singer in the studios is nevertheless the great aria 'Eri tu' from *Un ballo in maschera*. He recorded it twice, first in 1909 for Fonotipia and then five years later for Victor. Generally, his earlier recordings bring the rapid vibrato into greater, and sometimes exaggerated, prominence, but in this solo, the similarities are more striking than any differences, and it is remarkable that two performances so alike and widely separated in time can sound so deeply and 'immediately' felt. The Victor recording was made just a week after the fourth performance of the opera in a new production at the Metropolitan. Toscanini conducted, with Caruso, Destinn, Amato, Hempel and Matzenauer in the leading roles. In a busy season, which had already heard him in the opening-night *Gioconda*, then *Lucia di Lammermoor*, *Pagliacci*, *Aida*, *La Bohème* and the American premiere of *L'amore dei tre re*, Amato was at the height of his powers and his career. The 'Eri tu' has a fused mastery of technique and expression. The characterisation is of a man whose sense of loss and hurt runs deep and is nobly borne. The sadness of betrayal ('l'amico tuo primo') does not at this stage efface tender memories. The words 'E finita' have the conviction of real, present, development, and only with the realisation of hatred ('l'odio') does a savage spirit break through the dignity and restraint. Correspondingly fine are the *legato*, the breadth of phrase and variety of colour, the care over judiciously placed high notes which (as on the high G of 'brillava') are still allowed full licence to ring out and thrill.

There are other fine records in this Victor series, among them a dazzling 'Largo al factotum', a tensely dramatised duet from *La forza del destino* with Caruso, a *Te Deum* scene from *Tosca* impassioned, menacing and suave. But the opera which most regularly preserves Amato's name in the history-books is of course not there at all. 'Of course' because in one of the most notorious of missed opportunities in gramophone-history, no recordings were made of music from *La fanciulla del West* by the leading artists of the world-première – no 'Ch'ella mi creda libero' from Caruso, no 'Laggiù nel Soledad' from Destinn, no 'Minnie, dalla mia casa' from Amato, let alone the duets which are so exciting and galling to think of. It appears the publishers, Ricordi, feared that the sales of the vocal score would slump if the principal numbers could be heard on records; it all seems highly misguided whatever the explanation. Inwardly one can, I think, hear Amato as Jack Rance, ideal in that intently vibrant, emotionally involved yet restrained manner of his.

He should have taken part in another Puccini premiere, one which could have brought him a still greater personal satisfaction. The role of Michele in *Il tabarro* might have been made for him (and quite possibly was), but when *Trittico* was given its world premiere at the Met in December 1918, Amato was off sick. His illness was a serious one, resulting in the loss of a kidney, and a decline in his vocal powers seems to have dated from this time. He took up the role in *Tabarro* a year later, and also sang in the New York premiere of Leoncavallo's *Zazà*, but by early 1921 he was being phased out, and when the roster was announced for the next season his name was absent. In its place was that of Titta Ruffo.

At the age of 43, Amato would normally have expected at least another decade of singing, and indeed he did continue till 1934 though with varying success. From Berlin, Vienna and Paris in 1924, came reports of him in poor vocal condition; there was also the rather sad story of unsuccessful attempts to find sufficient work in Italy to make his home there. On his return to the USA, he taught in New York and later joined Alfredo Salmaggi's newly formed opera company at the Hippodrome. In the opening season, 1933, he sang in the first-night *Aida*, *Pagliacci*, *La forza del destino*, *Tosca*, *Otello* and *Un ballo in maschera*; in 1934 he was also named artistic director. From 1935 until his death seven years later, he taught as head of the Opera department in the University of Louisiana. The tenor Lauri-Volpi in his book *Voci parallele* gives a picture of him as a likeable, vulnerable man; genial ('un viso cordiale, aperto e sorridente') but highly-strung and miserable about the perceived deterioration of his voice in the early 1920s. That, evidently, was real enough, and yet the last records he made, a series for Homocord in 1924, remain impressive, and at the Hippodrome he was still cheered to the echo.

It had been, after all, a great career. There were the glittering occasions – the opening nights with Caruso at the Met, the *Fanciulla* première, the earlier acclaim at La Scala. But underlying those, and giving him more substance in terms of musical value, is the sense that he could be relied upon in a broader field. In Italy, for instance, he was the leading Wagnerian baritone of the day, and at the Met learned to sing his Kurwenal and Amfortas in German. When Walter Damrosch's opera *Cyrano de Bergerac* was given at the Met – in somewhat dubious English – Amato was chosen for the title role. He was the Met's first Prince Igor and the Scala's first Golaud in *Pelléas et Mélisande*. More than that, he remains now, through his records, a touchstone and an archetype. More still, he is a flavour, distinctive and personal, a singer whose way with familiar phrases stirs in the memory when other men sing them: 'un nido di memorie' in himself.

CHAPTER 22

Riccardo Stracciari

When Herman Klein – old man of awesome memory and magisterial utterance – was writing his survey of 'Some Columbia Celebrities' (*The Gramophone*, October 1926), he came to the name of Riccardo Stracciari and paused. As all of us brought up 'in the old days' will remember, the light-blue Columbia catalogue included no biographical section but did allow itself, very selectively, to add after an artist's name a brief descriptive phrase. Stracciari was termed 'one of the World's few Great Grand Opera Baritones', and it was in front of this that Herman Klein had paused. He hum'd and ha'd, stroked his handsome white moustache, and wrote. 'Allowing the "few" to be correct, I will not be critical enough to deny the justice of considering Stracciari amongst the elect, provided he does not object to being judged by that standard. His voice records well, and he is unquestionably a sound artist, as I have often declared when writing about his work; but beyond that I do not feel inclined to go.'

What they managed to get away with in those days! Klein will allow Stracciari a place 'amongst the elect' but obviously thinks he isn't really up to it: the best that can be said for him is that he is 'sound'. Wherein lies the soundness and what constitute the deficiencies are left to be guessed at, for 'beyond that I do not feel inclined to go'. This blocks the way both to a higher evaluation and to further critical discussion. Listeners, however, will surely want to go further, probably in several directions at once.

'Sound', it is clear, won't do. For the most part, Stracciari rises well above mere soundness, while sometimes and in some respects he sinks below it. For instance, there is one anthology on compact disc which opens with his 1917 recording of Valentin's air in *Faust*. A modern listener, coming upon this and its singer for the first time, would be most unlikely to find it 'sound'. The introduction, 'O sainte médaille', is omitted and the cavatina, sung in Italian, opens with the famous melody ('Even bravest heart may swell' in the old English translation) calling surely for a true legato. Now if this means a 'binding' of notes within an evenly-voiced phrase, Stracciari's treatment of the opening lines is not legato, but more a sequence of individual notes, or what is sometimes referred to as 'hairpin legato', where the notes have each a small but disturbing swell. The modern listener will then be surprised to find that Stracciari ducks the

108

Stracciari as Rigoletto

first high G, though that was common practice in those times and it is merely a detail. What will probably limit enjoyment more pervasively is something in the voice-production for which the usual term was 'throaty' but which I think is more truly the 'nasalità del toscano' (or 'Tuscan's nasality') observed in Stracciari by the tenor Lauri-Volpi. At any rate, there is enough in all of this for the ordinary listener to look dubiously at the critic's judicially awarded allowance of 'soundness'.

So one also pauses, with Klein, to hesitate over the Columbia catalogue's accolade of 'one of the World's few Great Grand Opera Baritones'. But of course the *Faust* aria is not yet over: the middle section is still to come, and that tells a different tale. The aria follows the simple ABA form: roughly meaning 'I don't want to leave you but I think I ought to go but I still don't want to leave you'. The B section welcomes the manly challenge of battle as the music quickens and the vocal line becomes more florid, emphatic in manner and high in *tessitura*. Now, at a *forte*, the voice is free and brilliant in its resonance; moreover, this is a passage quite frequently pummelled or hammered (*martellato*), and Stracciari here produces a model of singing, which is vigorous yet essentially legato in style. Then, at the repeat of the opening melody, so far from avoiding the high Gs, he takes them with thrilling security and with an exciting ring in the voice. 'Sound' is a weasel-word for this.

If the record company had been more specific and qualified Stracciari as one of the few great Verdi baritones, it would have been nearer the mark. He was by no means limited in repertoire, but the centre of his excellence was certainly in Verdi. The 'Di Provenza' (*Traviata*) of that 1917 series introduces some quite different aspects of his art. As 'pure' singing there is much to admire – the scrupulously observed light *appoggiature*, or grace-notes, the clean 'take' of the high Fs, the complete adequacy (rare in high Italian baritones) of his low notes. There is also a vivid and emotionally affecting characterisation. In this appeal of father to son the tone is immediately established as one of gentle solicitude. With the second verse a more personal feeling finds restrained expression, and its urgency then grows, incorporating the cadenza and intensifying it for a clear dramatic purpose. Thomas Hampson's singing of the aria (see p. 224) intensifies further, making the appeal more spontaneous and practical; but of all the 'old' baritones who anticipated this kind of treatment Stracciari is an outstanding example.

He was a famous Rigoletto, and at the age of fifty-five recorded the role complete: a fine demonstration (among other things) of what 'the Verdi baritone', the term itself, means. He has no problem at all with the *tessitura*, and even at such an age gives the impression that he could, if need be, sing the part half-a-tone higher – which is sometimes said to be a necessary condition of singing it at all. He also made exemplary recordings of solos in *Nabucco*, and it is worth pausing a moment over the two arias from *Un ballo in maschera*. These, again from 1917, capture the very

110

Stracciari as Napoleon in *Madame Sans-Gêne*

essence of the lyric-dramatic art. More than most of his contemporaries, he gives these set-pieces life as within their context, and more than later generations he endows them with vocal graces. 'Alla vita che t'arride', Renato's warning along the lines of Rosencrantz's 'Never alone did the King sigh but with a general groan', is allowed time to register; more importantly, the written phrases are like bones that put on flesh, with all those refinements of *portamento*, phrase-over, *rubato* and *tenuti* that so naturally belong to it. The cadenza is a marvellously fluent flourish, the culminative point of the argument's urgency, its high notes confirming a sense that what we are hearing is a performance as it might be from the youth of Battistini, who at best was the supreme master of such things. At his own best, Stracciari's art reaches backwards and forwards in time, and he becomes a figure very central to the tradition.

His repertoire extended well beyond Verdi – the role he sang most often (said to amount to some 900 performances) was Rossini's Figaro, and he also sang in Wagner (*Lohengrin* and *Tannhäuser*), Strauss (*Feuersnot*) and verismo (*Tosca, Pagliacci*). And he was vocally long-lived, making his last appearance in opera in *La traviata* when nearly seventy. Even after that he was heard occasionally for a few more years in concerts, while becoming also a noted teacher (Boris Christoff among his pupils), enjoying his cards and billiards, and (possibly as a result!) dying in 1955 amid what Lauri-Volpi described as 'tribulations and straitened circumstances'.

It had been a distinguished and honourable career, if not quite as brilliant as befitted 'one of the World's few Great Grand Opera Baritones'. He was valued at La Scala during a few seasons after his debut there in 1904 and then again in the second Toscanini era in the 1920s. He remained a regular visitor to the Colòn and other South American houses from 1901 to 1928. And he did sing at Covent Garden and the Metropolitan, though without making quite the mark he would have hoped for. One souvenir of his time in the States was the warm regard of Rosa Ponselle, who more than sixty years later recalled her concerts with him in conversations with James Drake (see *A Singer's Life*, 1982). She thought of his voice as 'a shower of diamonds'. It is not a bad phrase to keep in mind when listening to his records, especially the brilliant 'Largo al factotum'. Perhaps a quotation from the *Corriere della sera* (14 February 1923) may also help to fix him and his ebullient Figaro in the mind: 'No anxieties about him, either in voice or action. Besides, the voice is still as we have long known it: easy, flexible, resonant, well provided with the agility to traverse the whole baritonal range. His acting is expressive, always spontaneous and suiting itself to the character.' On this occasion, apparently, the Milanese audience cheered and cheered. A happy account of what was no doubt a delightful performance.

I still prefer Ponselle's memory and her turn of phrase: 'Brilliant and penetrating, alternately dark and light ... brilliant, just brilliant ... like a shower of diamonds.'

CHAPTER 23

Beniamino Gigli

One of the most delightful of reports by a music critic is the account Neville Cardus wrote for the *Manchester Guardian* of a concert by Gigli in London in 1935. He arrived late, to find Gigli singing 'Plaisir d'amour': 'and by his soft phrases, light as the lightest and mellowest viola, he was transforming the Albert Hall into an intimate music-room: we felt the flavour of antique airs and graces from a world lightened by the sunshine of old Florence'. It reminds me that I too heard Gigli at the Albert Hall, but that was 17 years later. He was then over 60, and a world war had intervened, during the course of which reports reached us that he was dead. (Somewhere among my school books is a Latin grammar with the words 'Gigli is dead' inscribed on one of its pages.) He sang 'Plaisir d'amour' in this concert too, and though there was not on that occasion a compatriot of his to murmur appreciatively, as on Cardus's evening, 'Bella, bella, bella', it was, as I remember, followed by a communal sigh of contentment. He followed it with Des Grieux's 'Dream Song' from *Manon*, and such was the personal quality of his singing that it seemed we were hearing the very voice that had become so familiar to us from the recording he made back in 1931 when he was in his prime, and (as far as the popular vote was concerned) beyond question the world's favourite tenor.

But that was it: *vox populi* was not necessarily *vox critici*. In as far as the general public wanted to hear an Italian tenor, it was Beniamino Gigli they wanted to hear. The critical consensus was by no means so sure. When he first sang in London at Covent Garden in 1930 there were indeed headlines such as 'The Great New Tenor' and 'New Tenor Triumphs'. The opera which introduced him was *Andrea Chénier*, and Philip Page in the *Evening Standard* wrote: 'He was immediately and emphatically (everything about this opera is emphatic) a success.' The *Evening News* called him 'the best Italian tenor since Martinelli' who had last sung at the house in 1919. 'Gigli's voice is marvellously steady, rich in tone and flowing in its impassioned delivery,' said the *Daily Express*: 'It seemed last night the perfect Italian operatic voice, robust yet refined.' He also inspired immediate confidence: one of the most judicious of London's critics, Richard Capell, wrote that 'After a little of him one had the comfortable feeling that all his notes were going to be genuine coins from the mint, and they were.' Others were less happy.

A critic from those days whose reactions to the singers he heard have the ring of truth and perception is *Musical Opinion*'s 'Figaro' (A.P. Hatton). 'His voice is best in its middle register and undoubtedly it has uncommon virtues, such as roundness and steadiness, the suggestion of great strength in reserve, a solid backing of breath control, and undoubted resonance.' But, 'Gigli's voice seems to me to lack the essential fire and passion of the great Italian tenors.' He noted faults of style, such as 'the gulp', and, later, in *Tosca*, the way he had of making his listeners 'all too conscious ... that he was Mr Gigli, the celebrated Italian tenor and not Mario Cavaradossi'. But it was Ernest Newman, most potent of the critics, who in the *Sunday Times* gave the most disenchanted and yet attentive reports. Perhaps in a grumpy mood because he so disliked the opera itself, Newman recalled having heard Gigli with pleasure at the Metropolitan in New York some five years earlier: 'The voice now seems to have become more powerful in parts, but at the same time harder and coarser.' He then noted that he had three 'planes' of singing and that these were 'for the greater part of the time isolated from each other; there is none of that graduation between them, and still less of that subtle shading of the line of a phrase, that are the marks of first-class singing'.

The 'isolation' or distinctness of 'planes' is something I remember from the Albert Hall concert of 1952. It was further emphasised by the positions, the physical stance, he adopted for singing loud notes and soft. In quiet singing he stood relaxed with head up and slightly back; for a loud passage he braced himself like a fighter, with legs apart and lowered head. Thus, in 'O paradiso', which was his brave opening number, the first half was (basically) in the first position, the second in the second. It is often difficult to say when a tenor's head voice becomes a falsetto, and one was well aware of that uncertainty very often when Gigli sang in those later years. It might be said that the very fact of an uncertainty shows how skilful he was in such usage, but certainly the isolation of 'planes', observed by Newman in 1930, became more noticeable as the years went by.

If he was not a favourite with the connoisseurs, this would be so almost by definition: the connoisseur is one who 'knows' better than the masses, and since the masses liked Gigli above all others, the connoisseur had to know better (Cardus was remarkably independent of cultism in showing his straightforward pleasure in the Albert Hall concert). On more valid grounds, the criticisms had to do with taste, both in music and in manners. Thus it was natural for Peter Pears as a young man working with a madrigal group, the New English Singers, to note in his diary: 'Surely the sharper one's taste, the more pure one's artistic performance ... Personality is a different thing from Artistry. Gigli is Personality. Schumann [the soprano Elisabeth Schumann] Artistry?' Partly the objections arose from another matter of taste, an antipathy to overt emotion. Gigli was always

114

good at crying, and one critic noted in this 1930 season that he indulged in 'sobbing tricks' even in Act I of *La traviata* 'before any milk had been spilt'. But years later, in an obituary note (*Opera*, February 1958), another English critic, Philip Hope-Wallace, was to admit all these points ('to the end of his long and wonderful career he was capable of introducing a spontaneous gush of vulgarity into any otherwise flawless piece of vocali-

Gigli as Mylio in *Le Roi d'Ys*

sation') and still conclude that 'to accuse him of lack of taste was to miss the point, like complaining of a rose that it is too red'.

This 'long and wonderful career', we remind ourselves, had very humble origins. As Gigli wrote in the opening sentence of his autobiography (London 1957): 'I was born with a voice and very little else: no money, no influence, no other talents.' The son of a cobbler in Recanati, a small town where the only glimpses of a higher culture were found in the churches, he sang from the earliest age he could remember. As a small boy he found that people would ask him for a song, and they never had to ask twice. Singing was his element, as natural to him as breathing and almost as necessary. It remained so throughout life, so much so that it became one of the grounds on which his rival, Giacomo Lauri-Volpi, would reproach him. The man would sing from balconies, in town-squares, to gallery-queues, and with all those records of his playing over the radio all day long, there was no getting away from him: the well-educated, almost patrician, Lauri-Volpi found it insufferable. But Gigli was not seeking publicity in

116

such matters. It is true that he wanted to reach the public, but the act of singing was simply fundamental to his being. It had always been so, ever since those earliest days when, as an errand-boy for his father, he sang to the carpenter and 'there among the wood shavings, the chisels and the dust' won his first applause.

His gift was of course prodigious – for nothing less would the Rome Academy have waived its rule about proficiency in piano playing. And if he was prodigal in its use he also exercised a sure instinct for its preservation. He nurtured a lyric repertoire (*La traviata, Manon, La Bohème* and so forth) that extended in the direction of the *spinto* (literally the 'pushed' tenor) with *Andrea Chénier* and his debut role of Enzo Grimaldi in *La Gioconda*. Like Caruso, he sang *Lohengrin* at an early stage in his career (the first time was at Rio de Janeiro in 1920), but unlike his predecessor kept it in his repertoire, giving more than 30 performances in all, the last being as late as 1948 at Lisbon. He added the heavier roles in Verdi judiciously, with *La forza del destino* in 1933, *Aida* in 1937, and *Il trovatore* in 1939. He never attempted *Otello*, though in a film called *Mamma* he can be heard singing excerpts.

One result of this evenly measured development was the marvellously preserved voice heard in that Albert Hall recital of 1952. Shortly afterwards his sheer stamina declined, yet on that occasion it was as though he could have sung all night – and he nearly did. In the printed programme were arias from *L'Africaine, La forza del destino, Luisa Miller* and *Pagliacci*: encores included 'Una furtiva lagrima', 'La donna è mobile', 'Che gelida manina' and 'Nessun dorma'. Among the songs were Mozart's 'The Violet' and Rachmaninov's 'In the silence of the night' (both in Italian), the latter sung with beautifully placed headnotes. Quite new to me at the time was the free-for-all when it came to encores, when all of Italy-in-London vied with each other in shouts of 'Santa Lucia!', 'Sorrento!', 'Mamma!' My own joy, I remember, knew no bounds when he produced for final encore-songs the two in which, on a record with a rose-red label, I first heard him: 'Maria Mari' and a saucy tarantella called 'Quanno a femmena vo'. I would swear to it that by this late stage in the evening the voice of the 62-year-old tenor was the very same as the one which rang out so brilliantly through the crackly shellac of the 1925 recordings. I had a train to catch and so for me the evening could not end as it should have done, and as it did for Neville Cardus back in 1935: 'After the concert the Soho cafés were ecstatic. Waiters went about their work throwing their voices up and down with a magnificent recklessness. Not every waiter had been able to get away from his labours to hear Gigli. But it was enough for them all that Gigli had delighted us. They shared in his triumph; they were proud to be sons of Italy with him, and happy to cast huge smiles at us and to be of the same human family, all linked together by praise of Gigli.'

CHAPTER 24

Mirella Freni

Few singers of comparable celebrity have come through so unscathed as Freni from a career that has lasted so long, developed so boldly and been so much in the spotlight. Throughout the early years she was everybody's favourite, with a voice and stage-presence pretty as the sound of her name. She gained in experience, wisely at first and if eventually less so it was Herbert von Karajan who got the blame. Growing steadily in stature as an artist, she continued to develop, experimenting with repertoire and re-emerging as a beloved veteran. She has remained the romantic heroine, rather as Magda Olivero did (though not yet at her astonishing age), singing Adriana or Fedora or whatever, still the centre of attraction – and still attractive.

She has been praised for many qualities – the beauty of her singing and the charm, sincerity, pathos and sheer professionalism of her acting – and all such praise has been well deserved. But for present purposes I want to concentrate on one particular feature of the voice: this is a purity of tone, which one might compare to glass if 'glass' did not give the adjective 'glassy', suggesting coldness. There has never been anything cold about Freni's singing, but her tone has been gloriously free from that admixture of wear or breathiness or surface-scratch or metallic tinkle that enters so many fine voices and corrupts even from an early age. And as with good glass in a good light, it shines. One hesitates, perhaps, over the use of the present tense; yet when heard last (not that many years ago) the voice seemed to have aged in other respects but relatively little in this.

So it is the young Freni, and that original shining purity, that I want to remember now. She came to us in Britain in 1960, as charming a Zerlina and Susanna as ever was seen and heard. But it was her Nannetta in *Falstaff* that enchanted most. The Fenton of that production was Luigi Alva, then still sounding as we hear him in his early recordings, and together they were the ideal young lovers. In fact that is how they seemed – not just a good Nannetta and a good Fenton in Verdi's *Falstaff*, but the very embodiment (in their presences certainly but principally in their voices) of young love. Most readers will have known times in the opera house when the thought has occurred: 'Have I ever heard anything better, of its kind, than this? *Can* there be anything better?' It was so up in the

Freni with Nicolai Ghiaurov in *Don Carlos*

gods at Covent Garden all those years ago as the two young singers graced the stage, weaving in and out among their elders. Verdi so clearly loves them himself, these lovers he endows with such tender lyricism amongst the slap-bang and clatter of the busy world. They are the sweetening in what, despite its humour, might otherwise be an acerbic comedy. More

119

than that (as in *The Tempest* or *Gianni Schicchi*): the whole world may indeed be a joke, but if Fenton cannot love Nannetta, if Miranda cannot love Ferdinand and if Lauretta and Rinuccio cannot love each other, what a sour joke it is. It was this lovely casting of Freni and Alva that made so much difference. Never had the love-call, 'Bocca baciata non perde ventura' sounded more gracefully amorous, and certainly never had Nannetta's response, 'Anzi rinnova come la luna', risen more blissfully to its high-note which holds out on a moonlit thread the prospect of eternal love.

No wonder, perhaps, about the youthfulness of sound and appearance, for this Nannetta (she was born in 1935 and the performances took place in 1961) was still in her mid-twenties. Everybody foretold stardom and many happy returns without necessarily realising that eventful years lay behind her even then. It was said that she had sung 'Sempre libera' in public at the age of ten and that Gigli had advised retirement for some years to come. Singing was in the family, her great-aunt being one Valentina Bartolomeo formerly of La Scala and remembered now as the Tosca and Aida of early (pre-electrical) complete recordings. There is also more to this 'Sempre libera' story, for in it she was accompanied by Leone Magiera, then aged eleven. He became her first husband (Nicolai Ghiaurov is her second), and their marriage put a two-year closure on her career. Perhaps it was as well: she had made her début as Micaëla at the age of twenty and was still only twenty-two when she began again, immediately consolidating her position by winning first prize at the international competition in Vercelli. She followed this with successes abroad, in the Holland Festival of 1960 catching the experienced ear of Leo Riemens who reported to *Opera* magazine from houses that filled immediately at the announcement of her name: she had become an instant public favourite. In Wiesbaden she 'placed the listener under a complete spell' with her Liù in *Turandot*; and, said the critic, 'she seems to be at the beginning of a great career'. In England she was hailed as that rare bird, an Italian who knows how to sing Mozart. Then, on return to Italy, she showed, at the Piccola Scala, that she could be a highly accomplished Handelian too. The Piccola could of course be as far towards the great Scala that a small-voiced singer might get, but Freni was not one of those. This was a voice with unusual fullness of tone: she was to the typical soubrette as Sutherland was to the average coloratura. Early in 1963 she made the decisive debut of her career. The historic house was treated to a new production of *La Bohème*; the producer was Zeffirelli, the conductor Karajan and Freni was generally agreed to be the Mimì of a communal dream.

As Massenet's Manon ruefully concedes, 'Nous n'aurons pas toujours vingt ans'. Yet, amazingly, Freni's Mimì has survived, spanning the decades. 1980 brought her back to Covent Garden in the part, and still the crystalline purity remained along with the seeming-youthfulness of her stage-presence. Another ten years passed and still 'she looks the part' was

Freni as Cio-cio-san in *Madama Butterfly*

the report from Rome, where Mimì's 'Ma quando vien lo sgelo' sent shivering those mysterious waves that tingle down the spine at such moments.

Another wonder of the later years, not the long survival of another old role but the acquisition of a new, was the Tatiana of *Eugene Onegin* which she learned to sing in Russian and was the first non-Russian to sing at the Bolshoi. The role was a clever choice, for she carried the audience with her in Acts 1 and 2 through sheer affection and their willingness to invoke the 'considering' clause; and then in the third Act her transformation into the older woman was an utterly convincing reality.

All the same, I don't think I want to hear all of this on records. If Freni retained one part of the youthful voice, its purity, she lost something in terms of youthful steadiness. Recording shows up unkindly what we will not call a wobble, perhaps not even a beat; but whatever the apt term, it is certainly not 'steady' or 'firm' or 'even'. The *verismo* collection and the dramatic Verdi arias recorded in the later years from mid-1980s onwards have their characteristic strengths of tone and expression, but the vibrations have loosened, and even when the notes hold firm they give notice that at any time the voice may spread.

So as we look back to the middle years of her career, it does seem that when the old heads were shaking doubtfully about *Don Carlos* and *Otello* in the early 1970s and then more emphatically at the very mention of the word 'Aida' in 1979 they were not being fearful without cause. On the whole, Freni's was a well-paced career. She had her set-back in 1964 when her first *Traviata* became the object of institutional thuggery at La Scala, but a progression from Micaëla to Aida over a period of twenty years may not seem ill-judged. The performances themselves suggested, as did *Opera*'s critic reporting from Salzburg, that the casting of *Aida* was 'completely justified'. It probably was so as far as the present audiences were concerned, and the singer herself may have thought no harm had been done. And perhaps none had, but in all such cases it may take time for the effects to be known, and even then they act insidiously in a process the cause of which can be hard to identify. The fullness of Freni's lyrical voice carried its dangers from the start. Gigli's advice against premature exposure was well-justified on account of the plausibility of a successful public appearance at too early an age. Similarly the voice that so impressed Lord Harewood when he heard her at the Metropolitan in 1966 ran a risk even by giving the glorious feeling, as he said, that there was nothing she could not do. Many who heard her during the 1970s told how wonderfully the voice was expanding; nevertheless it was at about this time that her records began to show a less welcome development in that the voice became very slightly, but progressively, less steady. Unlike her contemporary Renata Scotto (born in 1933) she pulled back after the Aidas, and her admirers breathed more freely. Not all of the new roles which followed proved suitable, but Manon Lescaut brought new triumphs, and her Tatiana won the matured respect due to an artist whose enduring charm has gained depth and assured mastery.

All the same, it is to the early records I personally return. And since the clear glass of ever-replenishable youth is to be the great and distinctive pleasure, then the earlier the better. Thus, I take the earlier *Butterfly* of 1974 under Karajan rather than the later (1987, Sinopoli), and even the first *Bohème* (1964, Schippers) rather than the second (1972, Karajan). From 1969 comes the enchanting *L'amico Fritz*, the name-part happily filled by her fellow-Modenese and colleague of many years, Luciano Pavarotti, then a stripling of 34. Collections of arias from the 1960s recall her luminous Marguerite in *Faust* (the voice shining as though in reflection of all those jewels) and her Micaëla (whose solo would often be the bright centre of the whole evening's *Carmen*). I would even go back to that World Record Club recital which introduced her to many of us and which ended with Nannetta's 'Sul fil d'un soffio etesio' with its smiling portamento and crystal-clear high As. But that is it: Freni the human crystal. The glass is lit by human warmth, and the warmth irradiates the clearest glass.

CHAPTER 25

Edita Gruberova

My generation (and therefore subsequent ones) missed Tetrazzini, and not many are left who can tell at first hand of her successors, Dal Monte and Pagliughi. But we heard Gruberova. She came nearest, I fancy, to recapturing the *gaiety* of coloratura. Where Callas conferred a richer humanity, and Sutherland a fuller tone, Gruberova brought back the light. Without quite the Italians' penetration, she has the shine. She has showered the sparks so that one blinks as when a room is suddenly lit with a glitter of chandeliers. And like Tetrazzini she has had a sense of the fun of it: her Zerbinetta in *Ariadne auf Naxos*, brilliant almost beyond belief, was also marvellous as a great comic creation, coloratura itself being part of the comedy.

She mastered the famous solo with such completeness that it seemed she could devote all her energies to acting. At Covent Garden she found herself in the toils of a tiresomely hyperactive production, but her vitality came from within. She used the scales as arguments; the high notes were like points nonchalantly scored in some rhetorical debate. She made comedy out of the sheer length of it, and at moments when an end seemed in sight she would be off again, tirelessly illustrative of her prescripts for the 'grossmächtige Prinzessin', the nominal prima donna who of course has to stay silent while this creature from a lower art-world makes glittering rings round her. It was a performance that could have fallen into the bad ways of the production itself, but was not overplayed and now remains in the mind as a delight for the eyes as well as a wonder for the ears: a masterpiece of operatic art.

The career in which performances such as this were a recurrent culmination began in her native Bratislava. She made her debut as Rosina in *Il barbiere di Siviglia* at the age of twenty-one, and sang in the provinces for a further two years. As usual, this was time well spent, gaining experience, learning repertoire and occasionally extending it in unexpected directions as when she appeared as a Slovak Eliza Doolittle in *My Fair Lady*. It also led to a contract with the Vienna State Opera. Her debut-role as a guest-artist in 1970 was the highly coveted one of the Queen of Night in *Die Zauberflöte*. Then, on becoming a member of the company and no great favourite of the Director, she was moved to the sidelines, with Barbarina

123

rather than Susanna in *Le nozze di Figaro*, and (what must have been hard for an already experienced Violetta to accept) the role of Flora in *La traviata*. The big chance came when she auditioned for Karl Böhm who was to conduct a new production of *Ariadne auf Naxos* the following year. She sang Zerbinetta's solo and won the part. Life at the top began with her first-night success.

In *Opera* magazine, Vienna's encyclopaedic critic Joseph Wechsberg wrote of her performance in November 1976, saying that the public success of the opera had come to depend on her. It was, he said, 'a magnificent *tour de force* that did not appear as such': the singer, he explained, 'is young and does not know the meaning of fear'. She polished off the fiendish runs while powdering her nose, and if Dr Böhm had not grown impatient of the cheers that followed her solo 'the standees might be cheering still'.

The triumph of Gruberova's Zerbinetta in Vienna was like Sutherland's in London as Lucia: the excitement had to do with beauty of tone and proficiency of technique no doubt, but also with what for these particular roles was an exceptional volume. Both opera houses were accustomed to neat and pretty but small-voiced coloraturas. The Zerbinetta of highest expectations had been Rita Streich, a lovely singer to be sure but, as we discovered when she sang the part at Glyndebourne, by no means so ample or pure of tone as she sounded on records. Gruberova, like Sutherland, was of a larger vocal build, and she combined this (and at the time of writing still does so) with a rare purity, nothing stringy about the tone, and even now with no signs of wear upon the surface. She also impressed with the rare ability to invest her coloratura-roles, where appropriate, with dramatic weight while still preserving the brightness. Thus, Beate Kayser reviewing the Munich *Zauberflöte* for *Opera*, reported 'glittering coloratura cascades which she also charged with dramatic intensity', and at Salzburg Charles Osborne noted 'a glittering menace'. Her singing has been, in fact, expressive over a much wider emotional range than that, and in this respect her records provide plentiful evidence.

Yet they certainly do not flatter her. Sometimes they have an unkind habit of exaggerating faults and reducing the superiority which in the flesh is clearly established by a pure tone over one that is in some way adulterated. With Gruberova, the records catch an occasional unsteadiness which in the opera house is noticeable only if consciously listened out for. In a recital of coloratura arias on EMI the loss of precise focus is always intermittent but frequent enough to be a nuisance. In Lakmé's Bell song it occurs only when the voice is under increased pressure late in the solo; in Lucia's Mad scene the first line is firm, the second not quite, and so on. Occasionally intonation causes a twinge, as at the start of Juliette's waltz-song. And the sheer brightness, and a quality of timbre which some hear as a whine, can become wearing (it does so, I find, in Semiramide's 'Bel raggio', included in the same recital). I am also sure that in the flesh

all of these would seem so incidental and peripheral that they would affect enjoyment and unprejudiced critical judgment very little.

On the positive side, records show a strength of imagination and a warmth of feeling that written comments often neglect. Her *Lucia di Lammermoor* of 1991 under Bonynge finds her vividly narrating the ghost-story, with the trills as little shudders of thrilled horror. In Act 2, the confession 'Ad altr'uom giurai mia fè' is a subtle compound of reluc-

125

Gruberova and Agnes Baltsa in *I Capuleti e i Montecchi*

tance and determination. 'La mia condanna ho scritto' is the moving prelude to Lucia's madness, and when the famous scene begins it introduces a child, simple, girlish and virginal. Her 'Alfin son tua' is murmured in a ghostly pianissimo.

Always she gives a sense of imaginative engagement, in this role as in everything else. Her repertoire has extended well beyond that of most coloratura specialists and involves her in genuinely distinctive characterisation. Her Agathe in the aria from *Der Freischütz*, for instance, is the village maiden and quite different in voice-character from the Countess Almaviva whose aria she has just sung in this recital. Her record of Glauce's aria in *Medea*, souvenir of a major early success in Vienna, finds her responsive to the urgencies, anxieties and eventually the confidence of its triumphant ending. In Mozart's great concert aria for Alceste, *Popolo di Tessaglia* ('the best I have written in my life' he called it) the voice is compassionate and grief-laden before going on to the *allegro* with its fearsome runs, triplets and Gs in alt. In the song repertoire too she can be found remarkably sensitive and individual in her approach. She can establish – as many opera singers seem unable to do – a private world, so that Schubert's 'Im Frühling' is all internal, and genuinely *addressed* to the self ('nein, armes Herz'). She has also the gift of a real smile in the voice, so that the end of that same song ('den ganzen Sommer lang') has a lovely sense of a hugged inner happiness.

Best of all in the Lieder repertoire is her Strauss. Most obviously well-suited are the Brentano settings op. 68 with their evocations, in 'Amor', of Zerbinetta and in 'Ich wollt' ein Strausslein binden' of a satirically accumulated lushness as in parts of *Der Rosenkavalier*. A fuller range of mood and expression is met in a chronological selection of songs recorded in 1990 with the pianist Friedrich Haider. This begins with 'Rothe Rosen' (1883), Gruberova settling beautifully into the intimacy of Lieder-singing, sensitive to the developing subdued excitement from the dreamy mood of its opening to the rapt quietness of the close. In 'Die Nacht' she catches the initial hush and then with the naturally bright shine of her voice moderated to gentleness she mirrors the poetic images of silver taken from the stream and gold from the copper roof of the cathedral. The recital follows through (a delicious 'Junghexenlied' on the way) to the post-humously discovered 'Malven' (1948) where she is ideally steady and light of tone, introducing no alien sophistication into this touching simplicity.

The records, then, will demonstrate to posterity a supreme virtuoso and a sensitive artist in a wider musical field, but they will need to be supplemented by the testimony of those who heard her 'in the flesh' and in her prime. I personally have never heard a more dazzling performance than her Zerbinetta. I have never heard a purer tone than when she sang Giulietta in *I Capuleti e i Montecchi* at Covent Garden, nor come upon a more delightful confluence of two pure streams of tone than in her duets with the Romeo of Agnes Baltsa. As for her prime, she was probably past that when I heard her most recently, in a duet-recital with another mezzo, Vesselina Kasarova. There was a little too much fussy shading, especially when they came to 'Mira, o Norma', but their *Tancredi* duet was a triumph, the voices evenly matched in freshness if not in years. That was in 1999 and the date alone (Gruberova was born in 1946) suggested that the prime years of the voice were over. A recording might reveal something of that but to the audience on that night at the Théâtre des Champs-Elysées it was simply a time for rejoicing in the purity and flexibility of both of these voices. And perhaps a few old heads were marvelling at this 'veteran' soprano and wondering what voice in their time has *shone* with such purity in its beam of light ... since Tetrazzini.

CHAPTER 26

Ivan Kozlovsky

If a visitor says 'Astonish me' – meaning 'Come on now, all these old singers of yours, all those scratchy old records, I couldn't listen to them unless there was something really miraculous, so show me' – then you know that they are not going to be satisfied merely by hearing the wonderful purity of Melba or even the miraculous richness of Caruso. They want a dazzler, and one that does not facilitate the riposte: 'Yes, but when you can have June Anderson or Nathalie Dessay or Ruth Ann Swenson *and* modern recording ....' Of course, the choice of a tenor may risk a similar objection ('Chris Merritt, Rockwell Blake ...'), but that would be harder to sustain. This is not really a game or a debating-point, and an ear for technique as a means to vocal poetry will soon discover that Fernando De Lucia's singing is of quite a different order from that of such representatives of modern times as those. In its different way so is the art of the Latvian tenor, Herman Jadlowker. But probably the most astonishing of all is the Ukrainian, Ivan Kozlovsky, born in 1900 and singing throughout most of his 93 years of life.

First, for the shortly-to-be-astounded visitor, a selection of five records might be made, each of them from a different decade, 1930 to 1979. To an amazing degree, conditions of recording apart, they might all originate in a single session. If the voice aged at all in tone, as it must have done, records impress essentially not with difference but with continuity. The texture seems never to have loosened or dried; the high notes are still plentifully available without any thinning of the voice's main body; the line is as flexible at 60, the movement as fluent. Volume is harder to determine but appears also to have remained fairly constant, while the breath-control never wavers.

He was a prolific recording artist and had an immense repertoire. He was constantly adding new material to his concert programmes, and he drew on the full resources of Russian and Western music up to but (as far as I know) not including atonalism. The five records from as many decades might, for instance, include solos by Bach, Rossini, Schumann, Mussorgsky and Britten. All of these he makes his own: he seems to have sung nothing without absorbing it so thoroughly that the performance becomes a personal expression, a newly-created compound, a musical transubstantiation.

128

Postcard showing Kozlovsky in concert and in the roles of Vladimir
(*Prince Igor*), Lenski (*Eugene Onegin*) and Alfredo (*La traviata*)

Sometimes this will take quite a mild form. He sings some of Bach's
Geistlicher Lieder, shading the phrases but preserving their essential
simplicity. Beethoven's 'Ich liebe dich' ('Zärtliche Liebe') has a charming
lightness and impetuosity, a smiling intimacy of address that refreshes

and renews it. Schubert's 'Der Jüngling an die Quelle' is delicate, with finely contained passion and the beloved name 'Luise' murmured as a deliciously private indulgence. 'Le Temps des lilas' from Chausson's *Poème de l'amour et de la mer* evokes the most sensitive of tone-colouring: the sadness felt through an unbroken singing-line as it lingers nostalgically, swells and retracts. The restraint of means is remarkable in a singer who also astonishes by excess.

He is very fond of slow tempi. His 'Che gelida manina' is allowed the luxury of two sides in the original recording, with long-held high-notes and prolonged cadences. In the Serenade from *Pagliacci* he lengthens and abbreviates notes at will in a way that would infuriate most modern conductors and probably most of his own time too. Yet the charge of indulgence is facile: the song in context is a ditty improvised by the *commedia del'arte* Arlecchino, who wheedles and cajoles, holding on to his high notes because they are his pride and joy and symbols of macho prowess. There is excess, but the drama is not affronted, though the conductor's beat may be.

To a remarkable extent the excesses of individual solos settle down easily enough in the context of the complete operas. Kozlovsky recorded in a greater variety of these than any other tenor of his time: *Il barbiere di Siviglia, La Bohème, Boris Godunov, The Demon, Dubrovsky, Eugene Onegin, Faust, Halka, Katerina* (by Arkas), *Lohengrin, Madama Butterfly, Mozart and Salieri, Natalka Poltavka* (Lysenk), *Orphée et Eurydice, Prince Igor, Rigoletto, Roméo et Juliette, Rusalka* (Dargomizhsky), *Sadko, The Snow Maiden, La traviata, Werther.*[1] The last of these is an interesting example as well as being a most moving performance. It was made with the Moscow Radio Orchestra under Dron most probably in 1940 and, like everything else in Kozlovsky's repertoire, in Russian. He spins most of his solos out to what in isolation would seem inordinate length; but, as we find, it is in keeping with the overall style of performance, Charlotte's Letter scene (for instance) taken at a speed that matches (say) that of Werther's Invocation to Nature.

This is an exquisite piece of singing, its introductory phrases establishing Werther's character as the romantic poet of dreams, idyllic in the softness of his high-notes as the image of an earthly paradise takes flight in his mind. The first duet brings a lovely and imaginative moment as Kozlovsky holds the exclamation, the 'O', like one taking a mental photograph to be preserved for ever ('O spectacle idéal d'amour et d'innocence'). Kozlovsky does the character of Werther a great service: he brings out, more fully I think than any other, the dreamer and idealist and minimises the element of self-pity. His sorrow is real, and the opening of the second Act brings a new note of wildness and desperation, but he doesn't whine. His singing of Ossian's poem takes its mood from the opening line 'Pourquoi me réveiller?': it clings, romantically, to the dream. The slow tempo is itself dreamlike: all the extremes here are consistent with the charac-

130

Kozlovsky as Lenski in *Eugene Onegin*

terisation. The dream itself and the wild exultation following are the self-induced states-of-being of a man who from the moment of his entry in this scene we feel to be very close to madness. 'Pale, almost fainting' says the stage-direction as he stands in the doorway, and never has that moment, I think, been so vivid and harrowing on records. In the fourth Act the directions read 'de plus en plus halluciné' and again Kozlovsky, with his pale, other-worldly tone, discovers the dying man's voice most convincingly in his own, his 'Là-bas dans la cimetière' still without sobs or self-pity, almost objective as the fulfilment of the romantic poet's identity.

The whole performance is a curious mixture of the idiomatic and unorthodox. But of course the doxy which is 'ortho' in this instance is the one established in our minds by modern performances and recordings, which find their model of authenticity in the 1935 recording of the opera with Georges Thill and Ninon Vallin. Finely sung as that is, it nevertheless presents a sanitised and fundamentally unimaginative view of the

131

opera. Russian performance either preserved an earlier tradition or simply based its view of the opera on the contemporary response to Goethe's original, and in that sense this recording is more authentic and orthodox. Kozlovsky, particularly, was a tenor very close in style to the 'old-fashioned' De Lucia, mentioned at the beginning of this chapter. Though modern in his role of musician-singer who extends his repertoire and explores, he was stylistically an anachronism. Compared in Russia to their most admired tenor of the previous generation, Leonid Sobinov, he sounds to us, on records, like the more controversial and imaginative Dmitri Smirnov (see Vol. 1 Ch. 48), who in the 1920s sang in a way that confronted the orthodoxies of that time. Kozlovsky could never have sung in the West under the ruling conductors as he did in Russia, and even there the licence permitted him was granted only because he *was* Kozlovsky.

The only tenor of his generation (two years younger) who enjoyed a comparable status was Sergei Lemeshev, on whom there is an interesting page in Lord Harewood's memoirs, *The Tongs and the Bones* (London, 1981). Lemeshev's name appeared outside the Bolshoi in larger letters than the opera itself, which was *Eugene Onegin*. It was in the second Act, with the solo 'Vashem domye' that something extraordinary happened. Lemeshev sang 'in long, wonderfully expressive phrases' very slowly, with much *rubato*, 'in a bygone style' which, says the author, was 'beautiful and grandiose in a way ... I shall never forget and probably never again hear'. I imagine that a Kozlovsky night would be very similar.

Of the two singers, Lemeshev seems to have had the sweeter voice and he impresses deeply on records; but Kozlovsky is the more amazing. If that hypothetical visitor, looking to be astonished, requires still more, there is plenty available. Start now with the Simpleton in *Boris Godunov* and reinforce the record with the film, unforgettable in the scene of Boris's confrontation in St Basil's Square. Then for the dramatic force within this lyric tenor try the intense and tireless 'Field Marshal', last of Mussorgsky's *Songs and Dances of Death*. For some totally unexpected variety, not to be missed is his recording of Britten's *Serenade for Tenor and Horn* with its Tennyson russified and realised with vivid imagination. Then – but purely for astonishment – it might be time for the outrageous 'Ecco ridente in cielo', the Count's cavatina in *Il barbiere di Siviglia*, in the course of which come three cadenzas, each more outrageously astonishing than the last.

[1] As listed in the admirable discography by Tom Peel, *Record Collector* Vol. 44 no. 3. A complete *Fidelio* is mentioned hypothetically.

CHAPTER 27

Antonina Nezhdanova

Sergei Levik, invaluable chronicler of Russian operatic life in his time,[1] tells of an educative disappointment. He went to hear a new Juliette in Gounod's opera, and, as he says, 'felt a lack of something'. At first he could not think what it was, for the singer's technique seemed flawless, the happiness and grief of the character were felt, and the voice struck him as being one of exceptional beauty. Also there was this characteristic which he came to think of as the key to it all, the quality of simplicity. He summoned up remembrance of Juliettes past, from Emilia Bobravaya, a coloratura soprano of dizzying virtuosity but none too good on the matter of intonation, to Maria Galvany, the Spanish pyrotechnician whose displays illuminated most of the major Russian towns when she appeared there as guest-artist. And then, when Levik looked back on his younger self, so sure in his opinions and so critical of all that failed to meet his expectations, he saw that it was the expectations themselves that were at fault. This Juliette had indeed been different from her predecessors. They had sought to dazzle and had even permitted themselves the little smile of complicity with the audience in the recognition of how brilliant they were being. They were not Juliette, and this woman was. She had exercised superb technical skill but without self-consciousness, the attitudinising and ostentation that, for him, had virtually become part of the show. She had all the accomplishments, but the distinction of her performance – and cause of his initial disappointment – was her simplicity.

Antonina Nezhdanova was soon to be known as the finest of Russian sopranos. Levik himself set one singer apart from all the others: this was Felia Litvinne, soprano of a more dramatic type, a prime influence in establishing Wagner with the Russian public, and an artist whose voice (it seems) became the character she was singing. Nezhdanova was of quite a different type as to voice and repertoire: her single Wagnerian role was Elsa in *Lohengrin*, and that was probably the heaviest part she sang. But she too gave herself to the music and the role. The voice 'was of a rare beauty and warmth', Levik reported, and every sound was expressive, so that she too joined the ranks of those 'set apart'. At the end of his chapter, he asks himself why it was that those two, Litvinne and Nezhdanova, so different from each other, were also so different from the other sopranos.

Perhaps, he says, it was because their art somehow defied analysis into separate elements: it was all one, whole and indivisible.

For us in these later years, a further contrast arises: not between these eminent singers and their contemporaries but between the two of them. For the greatness of Litvinne we feel much more dependent on the written word; about Nezhdanova we need no persuasion. It is curious, a rather touching anomaly, that Litvinne herself had such faith in the power of her recordings to present her to posterity: 'Ci-gît Félie Litvinne', she said, indicating the gramophone and her discs, made between 1902 and 1908. Recent transfers to compact disc have indeed made them much more accessible, in all senses, for the originals are both rare and 'difficult'. Her large voice did not lend itself readily to the process, and the sound (style as well as timbre) does not make her easy listening. But while Litvinne remains somewhat doubtfully represented by her records, Nezhdanova was a natural for the business, and hers (except the very late ones) are a joy. Of course it is good to have from Levik and others testimony to her effectiveness on stage and in the concert halls, but in a way different from many of the famous women who recorded in the early days of 'pre-electrics', we feel that she is being truly caught, and in her prime.

Juliette's waltz, 'Je veux vivre dans ce rêve', was among the solos recorded in 1906, when we hear her voice at its freshest. This presumably was the sound Levik heard at the Bolshoi first in 1903, and its directness answers to his description. Taken fast, though not with the breathless urgency of Melba's record of 1904, the song is eager, joyful and young. The feeling of simplicity lies in that. But to us I daresay, the pleasure of it is found not so much in character as in 'pure' singing: the voice is blissfully even and free, and the technical brilliances are accomplished with the ease and accuracy of a singer thoroughly secure and confident in her training. The scales, staccatos, trills and high notes are exhilaratingly in place, and yes, as we reflect, they do have an innocence about them – it's the song of a girl for whom life has suddenly burst into flower and the sun is shining.

That this should be so is the more remarkable for the fact that the singer was by no means a girl at the time: she had been a late starter and was not a young girl in these early years of her career. Born in 1873, she had been attracted to music from the start, but seems to have tried her hand at almost everything before settling to her vocation as a singer. As a youngster, she went from painting to dancing to teaching and to medicine. She sang with choirs and sometimes as soloist in the homes of the well-to-do. Sometimes an opera company or a celebrated singer would come to Odessa, and she would go to hear them, probably knowing in her heart right from the beginning that this was what she wanted to do. Well-connected people heard her and teachers took an interest. It was the usual story, but rather late in resolving itself. She was unlucky in a love affair, lucky in finding an Italian teacher whose school was of the traditional type rather than of the new *verismo*. The Moscow Conservatory

Nezhdanova as Manon

broadened her musicianship, the teacher took her with him on a visit to Italy, and in 1902 she was ready for an audition with the Bolshoi. Before becoming a member of the company she was the object of attempted body-snatching by the rival St Petersburg company but had the strength and good sense to resist. She did, however, make an unofficial debut at the Bolshoi as Constanze in *Die Entführung aus dem Serail* and made a notable success of it. A few days later she stepped in for an indisposed colleague in *A Life for the Tsar* – and *her* life, as a top-ranking professional singer, began at once.

But she was, by then, in her thirtieth year, or near to be. There are always two ways of looking at this: at 23 or 24 there remain six or seven years of that vocal freshness which is precious in all voices but most of all in lyric sopranos, and yet on the other hand a later start should mean that the vocal cords are stronger and the feelings more mature. It is also true that a more durable career may result in the end. Nezhdanova was certainly a survivor. She celebrated thirty years at the Bolshoi in 1933 and continued as a principal of the company for another two years. After that her appearances in opera became fewer though she still gave concerts till 1945. Moreover, she lived through harrowing times. The Revolution did not close the theatres but did bring a change of audience and direction. It seems that she adapted willingly. She had always resisted invitations to

136

sing in the United States and Britain (she did take part, with Caruso and Ruffo, in a brief season in Paris), and certainly she was not going to join the émigrés now. She entered into the communist era with apparent enthusiasm and was thrilled when Lenin came to her dressing-room. In 1922 it was felt that selected Russian artists should visit selected places abroad to convince the West that Russia had not descended into utter barbarism. Nezhdanova was ambassadress in this, appearing in Berlin, Prague, Warsaw, the Baltic capitals and other cities in Germany and Poland. In the USSR she was among the most honoured and hard-working of singers and teachers, continuing throughout the Second World War. Something of a national icon by this time, she received several of the country's highest awards, including an honorary doctorate in 1944 and a 'Defence of Moscow' medal.

We are talking now of a singer well advanced in years, and it is as well to remember this when listening to her later records. One of them is a rather pretty idyll called 'Collective Farm Song', and she sings it with charming purity and no weakening of the breath-control. The record was made, we note, in 1938, but perhaps other thoughts (this was after all the recently-purged Russia of jolly Uncle Jo) distract our attention so that we forget to do the sum: born in 1873, she was then 65. Something tells us that this delicate, girlish tone is not really a girl's, but it would be hard to say exactly what. In duets with the tenor Kozlovsky, made the following year, her voice sounds thin and worn, though a needly quality about the recordings themselves does not help.

For the true Nezhdanova of her prime it is best to go back to the early records, to delightful things from the Glinka operas or *The Snow Maiden*, or to her Queen of Night, Rosina, Marguerite in *Les Huguenots* and Elsa in *Lohengrin*. Or to songs by Tchaikowsky and Rachmaninov – but sadly not the one we most want to hear. In 1915 Rachmaninov at last finished a *Vocalise* he had worked at over a period of some three years; he wrote it (originally a tone higher than the published version) for Nezhdanova, who was also the dedicatee. Levik heard her sing it, and remarked that only when it was over did he become aware it was a song without words. 'Whole images of experience,' he said, had been created by the 'emotional richness of sound'. Occasionally lost treasures are retrieved from the record companies' archives. If only this could be one!

---

[1] The Levik Memoirs: *An Opera Singer's Notes*, trans. Edward Morgan, *Symposium*, 1995.

CHAPTER 28

Lily Pons and Lotte Schoene

They were born within the same decade, Schoene towards the end of 1891, Pons (as we now know) in April 1898. Both girls became singers, with light soprano voices, pure and sweet-toned by nature, trained to pass over a wide range with fluency and evenness. The careers of both began in their native countries, Schoene in Austria, Pons in France. In common they had typical roles in the *leggiero* repertoire: Rosina, Gilda, Philine, Olympia, Mimì. Schoene reached the top of her profession in Vienna and Berlin, Pons in New York. But Pons became a star, and Schoene a refugee. In 1933 when the star was singing Gilda, Lakmé and Lucia at the Met, Schoene made her last appearance as a member of the company in Berlin (of which she was also something of a star). By the outbreak of war, Pons was known the world over through films, while Schoene's closed inconspicuously as she went into hiding throughout the occupation. The Great Leveller came for them within months rather than years, finding both in their adopted homeland: Lily Pons died in 1976 at Dallas, Lotte Schoene in 1977, aged 86, in Paris.

When we listen now to their records and judge, qualitatively, on the basis of them and of contemporary assessments, it is hard to see justice in Fame's relative allocations. Still, that is an age-old story: what presses more immediately is the question of what it was that made the difference. Time-and-place, as usual, is one answer. Pons was 'discovered' in Montpellier by the retired tenor Giovanni Zenatello (Vol. 1, Ch. 38) and his wife Maria Gay, who brought her to the attention of Giulio Gatti-Casazza, hence securing an audition for the Met. This was in 1931, when the New York opera house had urgent need of a star coloratura, Galli-Curci having left the previous season. Personality and appearance also played their part. Pons was very French, *petite, jolie, charmante* and so forth. She took the public's imagination. She was 'the pocket prima donna', and she interviewed well. 'I like art, nice frocks, motor cars. I have a special love for animals and they like me ... I like life because it has been kind to me, and I can tell you that at this hour of the night, I like to sleep!' ('A lady who can scrimshaw a melody' by P.K. Thomajan quoted in Drake and Ludecke's *Lily Pons: A Centennial Portrait*, Amadeus, 1999).

None of this, it must be emphasised, would have brought her the great

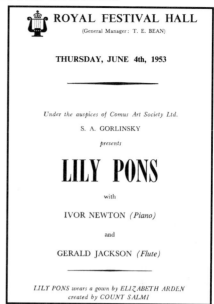

ROYAL FESTIVAL HALL
(General Manager: T. E. BEAN)

THURSDAY, JUNE 4th, 1953

Under the auspices of Comus Art Society Ltd.

S. A. GORLINSKY

presents

LILY PONS

with

IVOR NEWTON *(Piano)*

and

GERALD JACKSON *(Flute)*

LILY PONS wears a gown by ELIZABETH ARDEN created by COUNT SALMI

Lily Pons

success she made of her American career had her gifts and accomplishments not been real and special. Her voice, in those early years at least, preserved something of the characteristic French tang, but had also a gentleness, somewhat like Galli-Curci's in that respect but not common among coloratura sopranos who could also be described, in the more literal sense, as brilliant. She clearly was that too. Her singing had the power to excite, though the voice itself in the main part of its range was not at all powerful. She was also a neat technician: the scales, staccatos and trills had the fluency and ease that established her credentials with the public even if not with an old hand like W.J. Henderson. Really, what made the difference and turned a success into a triumph were the high notes. That is to say: the very highest, the Ds and E flats, the E natural that would stop the show at the end of 'Caro nome', the Fs which because of the keys used would elevate the final utterance of Lucia.

Schoene had her high notes too, very beautiful ones, if not quite as high as all that. They may not have been so joyously at command, and in the mysterious chemistry of stardom some other element may have been missing. It is harder to make an informed guess in the absence of live recordings, whereas with Pons the quality is recognisable instantly in at least one of the transmissions that survive from the stage of the Metropolitan. This is of a matinée at the end of 1940 when *La Fille du Régiment* was given in the triple glow of Christmas, a new production, and feelings running high about the war in Europe. Pons' arrival brings cheers; she

139

flourishes her cadenza, crowns it with something in *alt*, and, though the sound is small, it must be getting through, for the cheering is renewed. She was also said to be not in entirely best voice, and the tone on lower notes is shallow. As to the characterisation, she seems to accept readily enough the role's treacherous invitation to be pert and pretty, facetious and cute, yet without quite going over the top. But that is what the whole performance does – and with inspired success – at the very end, when in the 'Vive la France' finale Pons leads the whole company in the *Marseillaise*. Thoughts turn to her stricken country and to the momentous uncertainties of the year ahead. The tiny figure bearing the regimental flag is the emblem, the focal point of some strong emotions; but it could not have been so had she not sung creditably throughout the performance.

Whether – supposing circumstances were different – Lotte Schoene could conceivably have taken the place of Lily Pons and rallied the audience's enthusiasm to a comparable degree is doubtful. She was by all accounts a spirited performer and popular with the public, but her art impresses as having been of a more delicate kind. The *altissimi* would have been of the type favoured by the German school, taken with the head-voice and produced as a floating tone rather than with the triumphalism which coloraturas as different in other ways as Tetrazzini, Pons and Sutherland could summon to achieve a culminative *tour de force*. Marie, pride and joy of the Twenty-First, seems not to have been among Schoene's roles anyway; but if it had been, she would probably have been at her best in the reflective aria 'Il faut partir': her singing was much more of the lyric kind, its appeal intimate and refined.

Recordings testify to that and more. In the doomsday scenario they would be among the last to go. They date from the early years of her career which were also the last of the pre-electrical period of recording, and they extended to some made privately and probably in retirement. There are lovely things among the early ones – a heavenly (if bogus) gypsy song from *Cagliostro in Wien* comes enticingly to mind. Best as a group are those she made by the new electrical process starting in 1927. This was the year or her long-remembered appearances at Covent Garden as Liù in the first performances there of *Turandot*. 'The best singing', said *Musical Opinion*'s 'Figaro', 'came from Lotte Schoene who made a wistfully pathetic figure of Liù and acted with much power in the torture scene.' 'Once again the best singing of the evening came from a German artist,' reported the *Daily News*, and the *Sketch* headlined 'Lotte Schoene achieved a triumph.' Khaikosru Sorabji, a critic rarely pleased by anything he heard in Italian opera at Covent Garden, still singled her out, even when the name-part was taken over from the unwanted Bianca Scacciati by the ever-efficient Florence Easton: 'very beautifully sung … the best singing by anyone in the opera'. Back in Berlin, she recorded the solos with adorable chastity of timbre and style. The tenderness of *portamenti* gives warmth in the first, the firmness of her low notes endows the pathos of the second with

Lotte Schoene as Mimì in *La Bohème*

determination and a capacity for heroism. They remain touchstones: beauty, imagination and restraint combine to most cherishable effect.

She must also have been a delightful Mozart singer, to judge from the coupling which had on one side Despina's song in *Così fan tutte* about the lady of fifteen years and Pamina's lament from *Die Zauberflöte* on the

141

other. The first is sung with the lilting light-heartedness of a true Wienerin, the second with comparable lightness of voice but now infinitely saddened. The sure unostentatious skill of her florid singing contributes to the pleasures of Frau Fluth's feminist diatribe in *Die lustigen Weiber von Windsor*; less strong in character than Lotte Lehmann's record but utterly winning nonetheless, with the ideal rubato (the Viennese instinct again) for the 'Frohsinn' tune. In Verdi there are exquisite duets from *Rigoletto* with Joseph Hislop and Herbert Janssen (what partners!), and the Page's first song in *Un ballo in maschera* is charmingly sung, with the German language so musically handled that one hardly notices it is not Italian. Even more remarkable in that respect are the excerpts from Massenet's *Manon*, the Gavotte graceful and brilliant by turns, the farewell so full-hearted that when she tells of the tears ('Tränen') that are flowing we almost see them.

Another farewell is among these recordings, which, poignantly sung as it is, recalls Schoene's own. The story is told by André Tubeuf in an article for the *Record Collector* (Vol. 20, no. 1). No announcement had been made, but everybody in the Staatsoper that night seems to have known. The Nazis had come and Schoene had to go. After the performance of *La Bohème* on 12 June 1933, she 'was called again and again, and the door in the iron curtain had to be opened for her, against every rule'. They cheered her, he says, 'with compassionate silence' and she went into exile in France.

Pons also left France but under very different circumstances; and the lives of the two singers took opposite directions, one upward, the other down. I like to think of them united in one connection. The aria of Pamina in *Die Zauberflöte*, recorded perhaps ideally by Schoene, was also most beautifully sung by Pons, in French as 'Ah! je le sais'. It finds out the best in her; which is perhaps surprising for it allows no exhibition of 'star-quality'. And it contains none of those notes way up in the stratosphere which so excited her audiences in New York and which, as we have seen, 'made all the difference'.

CHAPTER 29

Maggie Teyte

Le style est l'homme: and if 'le style', why not 'la voix'? And, of course, if 'l'homme', why not 'la femme'?

'Voice is character, and character is fate: discuss.' Maggie Teyte might have found it a congenial line of thought (though no doubt she would have disposed of it in a manner too brief and pungent to satisfy the examiners). Her biographer, Gary O'Connor, pointed to an obstacle in the way of its application to his great-aunt when he wrote of the anomaly between 'the tough, in many ways imperious and utterly selfish woman' and the 'pure vulnerability, the extraordinary youthfulness and tenderness of feeling' evident in her recordings (*The Pursuit of Perfection*, Gollancz, 1979). One remembers, too, that the singer she most admired was Melba, in whom the anomaly was still more marked (the sweetness of tone and the sourness of disposition, the refinement of sound and the indelicacy of manner). Or perhaps the voice, like the heart, has its reasons which the character knows not of. Perhaps it tells the deeper personal truth after all.

Maggie, hard-boned, bright-eyed, bantamweight struggler as she was, could induce weeping, tender and affectionate weeping, in herself and others. Perhaps, as with a record of Melba that takes the listener offguard, the truth is that perfection in art generates its own rush of feeling. I suspect that with both of these remarkable singers the emotion aroused does have to do with character after all. To anyone who knows it well from records, Melba's singing is very far from impersonal, yet that is a description often given to it. Teyte's singing, never simply impersonal, nevertheless has something of the hard definition of her character. The emotion arises when so *un*emotional a sound reveals its heart. Voice is character, perhaps, though it bypasses those upper layers of identity through which a human-being becomes known, seen, marked and docketed as 'a character'.

Maggie Teyte was 'a character' sure enough. She would speak her mind, swear like a trooper and go her own way. It was a restless life and seemed even longer than it was. This was a woman who died in 1976 at the age of 88, who had taken New York by storm in her sixties, who had been rediscovered in her fifties, had gone into something like professional oblivion in her forties, become an international star in early thirties and at the age of twenty had been Paris's second Mélisande. As a teenager she had studied the role with Debussy, having trained with Jean de Reszke. And she started life on 17 April 1888, in Wolverhampton, England. She married a Frenchman and then the son of an American millionaire. Among her acknowledged lovers was Sir Thomas Beecham. Closest of all her friends was very probably the woman with whom she utterly and unforgivingly broke off relations when she (Grace Vernon) decided to marry. She never settled down as the member of an opera company; she would not take to the oratorio-and-concert routine that was the lot of most British singers in her time; and she was never satisfied, always wanting to try something new (taking herself in old age for instance to Vienna, to learn about Schoenberg, serial music and *Pierrot Lunaire*). She offended people all along the line and yet somehow retained their affection. As an old woman, and a Dame of the British Empire, she would scuttle unrecognised down the road in St John's Wood, rap on the door of a neighbour's house, announce that she had come visiting, and from the depths of a disreputable old raincoat produce a bottle of gin. 'A character.'

The career too had a character of its own, the kind that, with the folly of hindsight, causes people to believe in 'fate' as a purposive force. In pattern it was Churchillian. The adventurous, brilliant youth leads to a middle-age in the wilderness, with great things ahead. In the arts, this is as good a formula as any for becoming a cult-figure. Association with the legendary elders of a brilliant youth, then relative obscurity till all but the *cognoscenti* have forgotten the name, and finally re-emergence with powers undiminished, the living representative of bygone glory: cult status is the prize. And it would be easy enough to be cynical about it, but for that one phrase, 'with powers undiminished': a condition as easy to specify as it is hard to fulfil.

Maggie Teyte's return, or the start of the third period, was signalled by some unexpected, privately initiated, recordings made in 1936. Up to that time, the Teyte discography had been ... messy. She had had a spell with several companies (principally Columbia, Edison and Decca), recording mostly popular songs and a few numbers from operetta or musical comedy. Then, out of the blue, came Joe Brogan with what must have seemed a harebrained proposition for an album of songs by Debussy to be performed by Maggie Teyte and Alfred Cortot. It was an enthusiast's pipe-dream, except that Brogan had some clout in the record industry as the founder of the famous Gramophone Shop in New York. They still turned him down at RCA, and he had no better luck with Walter Legge in London (he, after all, as the man behind the comparably uncommercial Hugo Wolf Society records, might have been counted on as supportive). In the end the go-ahead came from HMV's Fred Gaisberg, and after that it was only necessary to obtain the agreement of Cortot himself – luckily and readily forthcoming. The records sold well in America and scored at least a *succès d'estime* in Britain. Without them it is unlikely that Teyte would have been

144

Teyte as Manon

asked to make her series of French song recordings in wartime, and without those she would not now be the Maggie Teyte we know and love.

And 'love': 'love' is the word, is it? I do believe it is, though I hadn't used to. I loved, it is true, the very first word I heard her sing. That was 'Asie!', the invocation at the start of Ravel's *Shéhérazade*. She brought to it such

145

promise: all the enchantments of the story-teller's art coalesced with the exotic romance of our illustrated Omar Khayyám at home. The year was 1943, and though still quite young I had heard some good singers – but never one who so commanded attention and caught the imagination. She did not keep it, however. Voice was the thing I cared for then, and it was disappointing to find another famous singer with what I called 'wear on the top'. The middle and lower notes seemed fine, though not rich or vibrant and if the upper notes at a *forte* seemed hard or thin I cannot now say, but they were of a kind which (in the way of youth) made me mentally transfer her from one list ('my' singers) to another.

The records adjusted this impression in that they never revealed anything corresponding to 'wear on the top', and they did show, beyond question, a grand, old-fashioned soundness of method: not the faintest suspicion arose of the wobble that seemed (even then) endemic among

146

modern singers. But the fine attributes that were commonly supposed to distinguish her singing of French song – variety of shading, delicacy of suggestion, subtlety in the comprehension of music and text – were not features that I could discern to any marked degree. Her Debussy, and particularly the recordings with Cortot, compared unfavourably in such respects with, for example, those of Gérard Souzay or Janet Baker. Close comparisons of the *Bilitis* songs with Baker, Crespin and Merriman brought plentiful revelations from the others, but Teyte seemed plain, unresponsive to detail. Even in simpler *mélodies* by other composers it was possible to imagine performances that might dispense more successfully with formalities, achieving a more Gallic effect of charm and intimacy.

But then came Duparc's 'Extase'. I think it was this, this setting of a six-line poem so slow that motion seems almost to be suspended, that moved things on. A haunting song which crept into the mind with insidious intent, it brought always Maggie's voice with it: 'Un sommeil doux comme la mort.' A late piece of writing by the critic Philip Hope-Wallace nudged further. Talking about singers who were inimitably, unmistakably and irreplaceably themselves, he instanced Maggie Teyte. The fact that I would have been unlikely at that stage to have thought of her in this way myself made me think about it now, and the feeling was implanted. Very soon I found the mind was full of her, the special timbre, the personal style.

In particular, one Maggie-ism, the downward *portamento*, became a companion-spirit, always at hand when French song was sung without its aid. Hear Barbara Hendricks, for instance, sing Fauré. She brings the clarity and grace befitting the French salon; also something impersonal, disengaged. Turn back to Teyte, and we hear 'Après un rêve' as a love-song, affectionate and yearning in mood. Or in 'Le secret', again, we find a different, and new, warmth of feeling; and in both songs, the *means* is the downward *portamento*.

And it is not a mere mannerism, an indulgence, but in fact sparingly and pointedly used. In 'Le secret' it occurs just twice: at 'la nuit' and 'il s'évapore'. In the first – 'Je veux que le matin l'ignore / le nom que j'ai dit à la nuit' – it points a distinction. The morning is the time for public fact, the night for private feeling. Morning suggests the 'clean' factual progression of the keyboard from note to note; night is the time for the slow curve of the gradual violin. The singer then wishes that at the first breath of dawn, noiselessly, the secret emotions of the night would evaporate like a tear. This, the evaporation, brings the second *portamento* – on account of the tell-tale 'comme une larme'. The name, secretly and lovingly confided to the night, is told with a sigh and a tear: the *portamento* is the sigh. And that is the secret of the art of Maggie Teyte.

CHAPTER 30

Richard Lewis and Heddle Nash

Everyone – everyone, that is, who sometimes listens with the kind of concentration that occasionally turns into love – has known the experience of the painting showing through, or the photograph striving up and out to get free of an image superimposed. It happens quite often with voices. They can be clear, single and unopposed one moment, and then the music will change, bringing in a ghost-voice, ever so faintly at first but with ever growing insistence. Normally it is the voice you heard originally in this particular piece of music, and through which you came to know it. But on the occasion I have in mind it was the other way round, for 'my' Gerontius on records had always been Heddle Nash, and he it was whose voice was being spooked. 'Jesu Maria, I am near to death', sang the well-known, well-loved tones; and somewhere beneath them the ghost-voice stirred. ''Tis this new feeling, never felt before': but of course it *had* been felt before, and it was the word 'new' that made me know it. The ghost was Richard Lewis.

A strange encounter, this; and there was something ghostly about it too, for I never in my conscious mind did this man justice. There were reasons, no doubt, some of them not utterly shameful. One was the old human weakness of taking home-cooking for granted and preferring some tasty little mess because it is foreign, or marvelling at the landscape abroad and ignoring the woodland not five minutes from your own door. Another reason, and a much worse one, I'm afraid, is the insidious bullying of authority. The record-collecting connoisseurs of my youth did not rate him, and that was that. Youth, knowing its inexperience, hesitates to trust its own ears. But mine had told me, when I first heard Lewis 'in the flesh', that this was a voice I liked. He was singing Peter Grimes with Covent Garden on tour, and it came to me, in the first place, as a voice of exceptionally pure quality. The year would have been 1947 or 1948, and it was my first 'live' *Grimes*. The voice of Pears was very much in my mind then, as Lewis's own was all these years later as the ghostly, inward-singing Gerontius; but Lewis's voice (I remember the experience very clearly) came as a relief. It had a sweetness in its tone, with no wear or hardness, and yet it was also very adequate in strength. I know I thought (till taught

148

Richard Lewis   Heddle Nash

to think differently) that here was a tenor who belonged with the good if
not the great.

Lewis at that time would have been 33 or 34, and it would have been
just a little *after* that that I at last caught up with the older tenor, Heddle
Nash, 'live' as opposed to the voice I seemed to have known for ever on
records. Born in 1894, he would then have been in his mid-fifties and, loath
as I am to admit it (but this is the time for truth), I was not greatly, but
slightly, disappointed. He sang Gerontius in the Chapel of King's College,
Cambridge, then later appeared in a concert or two, and in 1952 sang in a
performance of *Messiah* where he was wilful throughout, and in the aria
'But Thou didst not leave his soul in hell' so wayward that no two
consecutive bars seemed to be in the same tempo. Five years after that the
still potent name turned up in a cast-list at Sadlers Wells, where in the
premiere of Arthur Benjamin's *A Tale of two Cities* (1957) he sang the role
of old Dr Manette. The reiterations of 'One hundred and five North Tower'
were memorable, and just once or twice there came as it were the ghost of
the voice which was Heddle Nash. But that was all, and in 1961 he died.

Of both tenors, what principally remains now is their records, but also
the written record of their respective careers. These are instructive to
compare, for, overlapping as they were, they reflect the changes that befell
the singers' world in the middle half of the twentieth century.

Significantly in that respect, and exceptionally too, Nash ended his
career in the premiere of a modern opera; Lewis spent a large part of his
in such events, but playing major roles of immense difficulty so that

149

sometimes no one could take over the part if he fell ill. He was the first Troilus in Walton's opera, Mark in Tippett's *The Midsummer Marriage*, the first Achilles in *King Priam*. He was also involved in the explorations back into opera's early days, beyond Handel to Monteverdi. Nothing comparable with this came Nash's way, for they were not part of his time. The nearest he came was probably the pioneering Glyndebourne production of *Così fan tutte* in 1934, when most of the audience were hearing the opera for the first time. In concerts he would sometimes include songs by Delius, Moeran and Warlock. Vaughan Williams's *On Wenlock Edge* was in his repertoire and he was one of the soloists for whom the *Serenade to Music* was written; but essentially he managed to get through his career as a busy contributor to musical life while making hardly any contact with modern music.

His was the last generation that could do this, and to some extent he was exceptional even then (his contemporary Widdop sang, for instance, in broadcasts of *Wozzeck* and *Oedipus Rex*, which also had in its cast the then-famous Welsh tenor Tudor Davies). Nash's career developed along traditional lines: local choir, prizes, study, small parts, training in Italy. His teachers, it is true, had some clout as international names: Marie Brema at Blackheath and Giuseppe Borgatti in Milan. There was also the 1914 war in which he suffered badly. But once started, promotion came fast. A successful debut in *Rigoletto* at the Old Vic led to a recording contract with Columbia and engagements with the British National Opera Company and Covent Garden. He was even permitted – an Englishman! – to take part in the 'grand' international seasons, and his Ottavio in the *Don Giovanni* of 1929 brought a personal triumph with headlines in the national newspapers. What was more wonderful still, he was asked back and over the next few years appeared as Rodolfo, Almaviva, Rinuccio in *Gianni Schicchi*, the Italian Singer in *Der Rosenkavalier*, Pedrillo in *Die Entführung* and (greatly admired) David in *Die Meistersinger*. Perhaps international recognition would have followed (for many thought he sang the Italian lyric roles as well as Schipa and better than Dino Borgioli), but the Second World War intervened, and cut across his career just at that crucial point.

So it did with Lewis, but at a much earlier stage. He had trained with Norman Allin, the leading British bass of his generation, and began promisingly with the Carl Rosa Company, but was over thirty before making a real start. In his favour was the change in attitude to British singers on the part of the national opera house, and indeed of the world in general. Lewis became indispensable to Covent Garden, especially in their plans for British opera; to Glyndebourne also, where he had one of the longest associations of all. He made his American debut in 1955, singing Don José in San Francisco where he returned regularly over the next thirteen years. He sang there in a wide range of roles not heard in the UK,

THE CAMBRIDGE PHILHARMONIC
SOCIETY

IN ASSOCIATION WITH THE ARTS COUNCIL OF GREAT BRITAIN

DREAM OF GERONTIUS
(ELGAR)

THURSDAY, MAY 18th, 1950

At 8.30 p.m.

KING'S COLLEGE CHAPEL
(By kind permission of the Provost and Fellows)

NANCY EVANS Mezzo Soprano

HEDDLE NASH Tenor

NORMAN LUMSDEN Bass

GARTH BENSON Organ

ERIKA BACH Leader of the Orchestra

Conductor - - FREDERICK RIMMER

This programme, price 4/-, admits one person to the Ante-Chapel

and remained in demand throughout the States though never singing at the Met.

Like Nash, Lewis was essentially a lyric tenor but with a stronger, more robust instrument. When he undertook as heavy and dramatic a role as Herman in *The Queen of Spades* at Covent Garden he gave some impression of being overparted, yet Troilus also needs power and stamina, and for that he seemed ideal. Nash would never have contemplated such roles: he was a delicate singer, highly distinctive and appealing in timbre, elegant in style, agile and adept in *fioritura*. The operatic composers for him were Rossini and Donizetti, but there was little of them to be heard in those days. He could have made an internationally first-rate Nemorino in *L'elisir d'amore* or Ernesto in *Don Pasquale* – a part he did indeed sing

151

with great beauty and refinement in a broadcast performance of the opera in English. In his own time, English singers, even of his eminence, still drew a large part of their income from oratorio and other choral society engagements up and down the country. Lewis had his share of that in earlier years, but once he attained a seniority comparable in his day to Nash's, it had ceased to be a bread-and-butter routine.

Not that Handel was ever a routine matter for either of them, though both in their time found themselves criticised by one side or another. For some years Nash was admonished by the critics not to bring his Italianate operatic ways into oratorio, and Lewis fell foul of the connoisseurs on account of his technique. Today, their recordings make an interesting comparison. Lewis is never as anti-vocal as he was made out to be, though Nash shows himself the better singer. In Jephtha's 'Waft her, angels, through the skies' he supports his soft notes so that the head-voice does not take on a separate identity, and his runs are smooth where Lewis uses more of a *marcato* style suggesting that the ascent 'above yon azure plain' will be an altogether bumpier process. In 'How vain is man' from *Judas Maccabæus* Lewis has more justification for this style, but Nash preserves *legato* when he wants to and then makes a far bolder effect of vigour, reading Handel's arrogant shakes and strutting intervals as satire on the blusters of 'gigantic might'. A comparison of two operatic arias again favours Nash. In the Dream Song from *Manon* he preserves the tenor tone, soft but firm, where Lewis relaxes into a near-falsetto; and in the aria from *Les Pêcheurs de perles*, while Lewis can claim credit for singing in the original key (Nash a tone down), all the magic is with Nash, where Lewis, again bumpy on the quavers, forfeits the lulling motion and unbroken serenity of the dream.

But both were artists. Both could work a spell with simple things, Nash (for instance) in the song 'Macushla', Lewis in 'There's none to soothe my soul to rest'. And both could rise to greatness, which is how the voice of one could haunt the other's Gerontius. They were also, like the other great singers in these studies, distinctive and memorable. Lewis's voice comes across the years in phrases from *Grimes*, in Mark's 'summer morning dances in my heart' and Troilus's 'You are frightened by dreams like a child'. And as for Heddle – with a few well-chosen words for invocation ('All hail, thou dwelling' will do), his voice will come on the instant, clear, unmistakable and ever-welcome.

CHAPTER 31

Alfred Deller and Andreas Scholl

The sub-title of Michael and Mollie Hardwick's excellent biography of Alfred Deller is *A Singularity of Voice*. The phrase originates in an account by Thomas Coryate, of *Coryates Crudities*,[1] 1611, of a singer he heard at a solemn feast in Venice. This was a man of middle age and not 'an Eunuch': a 'rare fellow for his singing' especially as 'nature doth more commonly bestow such a singularitie of voice upon boyes and striplings'. The sound was such that 'had a nightingale beene in the same roome' the bird might possibly have excelled beyond the man, 'but I think he could not much'. The authors remark that the traveller might almost have been writing about Deller. Their book was published in 1980, and at the point where the quotation is introduced they were thinking back to the late 1940s, when Deller was 'discovered', aged 36. The rare fellow with the singular voice, then an alto in Canterbury Cathedral Choir, was to restore the word 'countertenor' to current usage. In *The Record of Singing*, a compilation which includes and represents some 500 singers who made gramophone recordings in the first half of the twentieth century, there is only one countertenor; and that is himself. Singular indeed.

Half a century later, the picture is different. Countertenors abound. The record catalogues in the year 2000 do not carry handy lists of artists in categories of voice or instrument, as they used to when Deller came on the scene, but a rough check nets some eighty countertenors or altos, according to editorial decision about what they are to be called – which is still a matter for tiresome debate. Of this number, perhaps no more than five or six might justly claim a place in any future *Record of Singing* to cover the second half of the century. Still, the singularity has certainly been diluted. Middle-aged gentlemen who sing like nightingales are now, if not exactly two-a-penny, at least numerous enough for the supply to match an ever-increasing demand.

In 1950 Deller stood in solitary eminence. Fifty years later the serried ranks have no universally acknowledged chief, but prominent and perhaps best among the present generation is Andreas Scholl. He also, like Deller, stands physically tall, well over six foot, and the strength of his voice is commensurate. There is also a similarity of timbre. Words such as 'disembodied', 'unearthly' and 'ethereal' are commonly used to describe the

Alfred Deller

countertenor voice; and Deller certainly had, as it were, a department of his voice which answered the description. Yet the instrument itself was sturdy, even vibrant; and Scholl sings with a forthright manner, ample power and full-bodied tone. Some countertenors sound womanish; Deller and Scholl do not.

Do they sound male? Or is that other commonplace word, 'sexless', right? It is more appropriate, I would say, to Deller's singing than to Scholl's, but if so that may be more on account of style and repertoire than of the voices themselves. Deller was essentially a spiritual singer. It was not that he lacked the capacity for light-heartedness, gaiety or normal

154

Andreas Scholl

human passion: when he sang Dowland's 'Fine knacks for ladies' it was with zest, and the sensuality of Purcell's 'Sweeter than roses' was never more potent than in his flecked colouring and sinuous movement. But the fine knacks were a prelude to 'Sorrows, stay' or 'In darkness let me dwell', and his Purcell had the sensuousness of illuminated darkness in a Byzantine church. Deller's way of retreating into the head-voice became more marked as he grew older and less able, or inclined, to risk the high notes at a forte. This may have become a technical necessity, but it was also at the expressive heart of his singing, a setting free of soul from body. It is hard to think of him without some such spiritual dimension, a way in which the voice achieved singularity of a different and richer kind.

Scholl's art belongs, by comparison, to daylight. But then, he has still, at this point of achieved fame and well-tested accomplishment, to arrive at the age by which Deller was 'found'. And Scholl is the child of a very

155

different time. He, it is true, grew up with a background of church music, a chorister like Deller. But Deller, born in 1912, spent his early years in a world under the shadow of one war and then moving towards the gathering storm of another. The household itself lived in the strangely mixed sunshine-and-shadow of the father's military ways. Known as 'the Sergeant', he is a character to whom one warms when reading the biography, even while being thankful for not living under the same roof. Scholl's was a musical family, with a fully supportive father. Time and place were propitious. The war-shadows had lifted. The 1960s had swung, the 1970s rocked, though perhaps in the provinces near Wiesbaden not too deafeningly. As a teenager, Scholl knew all about pop, and now, at an age when miserable old codgers (like myself) might say that he ought to know better, makes rock music for himself electronically at home. Deller hated the stuff.

The countertenor voice has, of course, to quite a remarkable extent been newly liberated, the principal agent being opera. Scholl made his operatic debut in 1998, when it was described as 'long-delayed'. He was then 30, and enjoyed a huge success in his role of Bertarido in Handel's *Rodelinda* at Glyndebourne. Deller was 48 when he sang in *A Midsummer Night's Dream* the role of Oberon which Britten had written with his voice in mind. Scholl appeared to take to the boards as if by nature; Deller did not. Conscious of his physical size on the small stage at Aldeburgh and not very happy with the production as far as he himself was concerned, he met with discouraging reviews; and when the opera was introduced to Covent Garden his replacement by the American, Russell Oberlin, came as a bitter disappointment. He appeared later as Death in a one-act opera of *The Pardoner's Tale* by Alan Ridout, but it was obvious that no stage-career would open up for him. Since that time, the revival of baroque opera has involved the countertenors to such an extent that the whole professional outlook has changed. Then, with the example of Jochen Kowalski, who made such a powerful, intensely male and dramatic, impression as Gluck's Orfeo, the 'image' changed again. When Andreas Scholl reached his 30s, the kingdom had been thoroughly prepared; it was an extensive realm too, and he entered it amid a general sense of historical inevitability.

It is also a kingdom with a court, wide enough to harbour rivals, civilised enough for the rivals to be known as colleagues. A change in its recent constituency is the displacement of the British hegemony. A sizeable representation remains, James Bowman now its honoured elder statesman; but a swelling party of Americans has David Daniels prominently in their midst, and even the Far East has its members, with the remarkable Yoshikazu Mera as one who has captured fascinated attention. The court even has its jesters, and Scholl, when not yet heir-apparent, made one of them. 'The Three Countertenors' appeared on record in 1995, and it was probably through this unlikely event that many listeners came first to know his voice. He sang the Habanera from *Carmen*. His fellows were Pascal Bertin and Dominique Visse, a wicked elf deliciously tipsy on the champagne of Offenbach's *La Périchole*. Scholl himself stood out as having the best voice, and also as a musician who could contribute a lute-song of his own composition. The record did not outstay its welcome or try too hard for its laughs. But it says a certain amount for the maturity of the countertenor voice in its relationship with the rest of the world that it can afford to laugh at itself and let the public laugh too.

Laughs of the wrong kind still arise occasionally. Scholl himself has known them in one of his native German towns. Deller had to take many a jibe, much of it merely coarse, some ill-natured. The 'bearded lady' story cannot have been untypical in kind. Paul Beard, leader of the BBC Symphony Orchestra, standing in the wings with Sir Malcolm Sargent, remarked 'I see we have the bearded lady with us tonight'. Sargent, to his credit, seemed not to have heard. Only a few years earlier, our own Cathedral alto had said to me in response to my aspirations to altodom, 'Oh no, be a tenor. You can't do anything with a voice like mine. I couldn't get up and sing a song. Everybody would be expecting me to wear a skirt.'

That man, our alto, could, I am convinced, have been a valued professional countertenor had he lived now. Like Deller and Scholl, he had what he had been told (somewhere around 1910) was a 'natural alto'. He had simply continued to sing treble till it became more convenient to move into the men's choirstalls and sing alto.[2] But the musical time was not right. There was no BBC Third Programme, devoted to good music on radio and ready to champion Purcell as Britain's greatest composer. There was no Michael Tippett, hoping ardently to find just such a voice as Deller's for the Elizabethan repertoire. Scholl can now sing fearlessly in solo recital, his magnificent voice and thorough musicianship commanding a full house as it does whenever he sings in London. But the ground was prepared in earlier days, when suddenly the conditions came right and the man with a bit of genius in him (for Deller had that) could flourish. I can hear him now, from fifty years back, singing in a Cambridge chapel Byrd's Lullaby, which I've never heard him sing on records. Perhaps it was a unique sound then and therefore doubly memorable. But it was more than a sound. The voice may no longer be 'singular' as it once was; but the soul is.

[1] The full title is *Coryates Crudities, Hastily gobled up in five moneths travells in France, Savoy, Italy, Rhetia, commonly called the Grisons country, Helvetia alias Switzerland, some parts of high Germany and the Netherlands; newly digested in the hungrie aire of Odcombe in the County of Somerset, 1611*. Odcombe was Coryate's birthplace and on his return from Venice he hung up his shoes there in the parish church.

[2] For more about 'Alto Smith' see *Voices, Singers and Critics*, Duckworth 1992, p. 56.

CHAPTER 32

Ian Bostridge

The singers' world has seen no more remarkable advent in recent times than that of Ian Bostridge. When he first came to notice in London in the early 1990s, his voice was slender as his figure, which was that of a lanky first-year sixth-former. The voice had been trained but sounded like a gifted amateur's. It had a pleasant drawing-room quality but of a very English type, without much in the way of ring or body. The manner of his singing was modest, and a good mind lay behind it. But hearing and watching this youngster (as he appeared to be), it was hard to see more than a limited, specialised future for him as a professional singer; and an operatic career seemed out of the question.

Evidently there were people observing more closely and perceptively, for his name continued to circulate and was usually mentioned with admiration. I went with curiosity but no great expectations to hear his attempt upon one the summits, *Winterreise* no less, at a midday concert in the Southbank Purcell Room. The suitably intimate hall was not full but the audience was well-informed, and in it were several, perfectly sympathetic to the singer, who at the conclusion judged the venture premature. For myself, it brought a totally unexpected revelation. In all the many performances heard in concert halls and on records, I had never really believed in the 'ich', the protagonist: his emotions rang true and were moving, deeply so, but that day's experience made me realise that I had never truly thought that there was any such person: or *such* a person maybe, but no individual, with a childhood, a nickname, a particular way of tilting his head. Now he stood in full view. Even Fischer-Dieskau – even in most masterly form as in a performance some years previously with Brendel – had dramatised the character, representing him with all the feeling, understanding and power of communication a great artist might command; yet the person, the 'ich', achieved only a kind of theoretical, literary existence, a mouthpiece for poet, composer and singer rather than an individual, with a name, a way of parting his hair, a suit of clothes.

It may have been the suit that did it. This being lunchtime, dress was relatively informal. More likely, it was the singer's age, his obvious youth. Almost certainly, it had to do with the individuality of his appearance, the look of somebody to whom the world could be an inhospitable place, his

refuge a library maybe, or in harsher circumstances a cardboard box and a doorway. The voice told of its troubled heart without any literary touch and without a suggestion of the music schools or of singing learnt from gramophone records. A fine intelligence was clearly operative, and yet its expression had remarkable directness and essential simplicity. It did not make the 'I' particularly likeable: in fact that was part of its truthfulness. This was a lad you could see wouldn't fit in, just the kind to be turned down by a girl and her parents; resentful too, egocentric, a loner, even a little bit mad. I fancy now that that exaggerates the features of the character Bostridge created, to the point of embodying it, in that remarkable performance of 1993. Certainly there was nothing melodramatic or starry-eyed about it, and it was sung with refinement and vocal skill. But there for the first time stood the 'ich' of *Winterreise*; you saw him at once with the insight of his own heart and as the person he presented to the world.

159

The danger of such an early experience of a singer is that it may never be repeated. That is not quite as it turned out here, but certainly a year or two elapsed before anything quite of that kind recurred. In the meanwhile young Ian Bostridge sang on and very soon found himself famous. His art developed; the repertoire grew; the understanding deepened; most notably the voice strengthened. It did so both in volume and in stamina. In early recitals he was plainly sung-out by the end, and in the friendly atmosphere of the Wigmore Hall would not mind saying so come encore-time. Very soon he was undertaking heavy programmes with no sign of tiring or of strain. What was more, he showed that he did have a future in opera. His roles included Tamino in *The Magic Flute*, for which he was praised though not so emphatically as for his Peter Quint in *The Turn of the Screw*. He revealed a delightful flair for comedy as the stuttering Vashek in *The Bartered Bride*: that was one of Peter Pears's roles too, and Bostridge's development may be akin to Pears's, with a distinguished Aschenbach in *Death in Venice* to crown it. It is hard to imagine him having the physical toughness to make a convincing Grimes, but then that might at one time have been said of Pears himself.

One thing about his future career and repertoire: it does not look like involving much in the way of nineteenth-century Italian opera. He was asked about this, or, rather, the matter was raised but in the form of those Latin questions which have the answer written into them, during a public interview at the Edinburgh Festival of 1999. A further assumption was made that he would probably not find Italian opera to his taste anyway. The directness of Bostridge's reply went straight to the heart, in both senses. It wasn't, he said; that he didn't like it, in fact he enjoyed Italian opera and liked listening to it. The point was: 'I don't have the voice.' Italian operas need Italianate voices, and: 'I don't have an Italianate voice.'

These are the words of a sensible man, which may seem a patronising thing to say about a man of such evidently high intelligence. Bostridge is regularly referred to as an intelligent singer, even as an intellectual among singers. He was, after all, a Post-doctoral Fellow at an Oxford college, an historian, and is the author of the book *Witchcraft and its Transformations 1650-1750*. He has acquired, according to an article about him in *The Times* (23 November 1999), an 'extraordinary aura of aestheticism'. In the circumstances it is not quite such a platitude to say that he is also 'a sensible man'.

This 'aestheticism' and intellectualism, in fact, may not be the most accurate of pointers to the distinguishing feature of his art. They are even a little suspect: he looks 'aesthetic', has an intellectual background. The intelligence is beyond question, but perhaps a little detour may be allowed at this point in order to pursue the immediate matter of a *singer*'s intelligence. For instance, virtuoso-displays are often thought of as completely brainless but may involve *singer*'s intelligence to an exceptional degree. When Tetrazzini sang a 'brilliant' cadenza, with staccatos going off in all

160

Bostridge with Julius Drake in *Diary of One Who Vanished*

directions amid scales and arpeggios of dazzling rapidity, it was described as 'vocal fireworks' and indulgently dismissed as such. But it really (amongst other things) involved the busy exercise of a *singer*'s intelligence: nothing would function without the mind, and the mind taps out at lightning speed on a vast complexity of little keys. Any mental imprecision or sluggishness, and these 'mere fireworks' will be a damp squib. Another exercise of the particular kind of intelligence that is appropriately a singer's may involve the disciplining or cancellation of messages sent by other kinds of intelligence. In a song such as Schubert's 'Litanei', linguistic intelligence will urge the accentuation of certain words or syllables at the expense of others, where singer-intelligence is pre-occupied (and it is a highly demanding occupation too) with preserving an unblemished sing-ing-line. That also is a mental exercise, though it may not sound like it. When we talk about an intelligent singer it should not mean, as it usually does, one who can speak or think intelligently about text.

The question remains; why has Bostridge captured the public interest as he has done? It is not because of vocal quality (to take some English tenors in a comparable field, Ian Partridge produced a more beautiful tone with a finer line, and Robert Tear and Antony Rolfe Johnson were stronger in volume). Nor is it quite a matter of emotional intensity (there is more of that in Philip Langridge). In such respects Bostridge is fine but not

161

exceptional. In what I would call singer-intelligence he does well too (difficult scores are assimilated by the voice as well as by the mind, and he cares for tone and evenness), but not to a degree that places him in the special category where he now finds himself. Textual intelligence (or what people generally have in mind when they say 'He's such an *intelligent* singer') is certainly a notable feature; yet as much, or more, of that is demonstrably present in the recordings of Bryn Terfel, about whom it is *not* generally said (no 'aura of aestheticism' there).

Bostridge possesses these many qualities, but the really distinctive strength lies in something else. Physical appearance undoubtedly has something to do with it. The power of that first *Winterreise* still haunts, and it was visual as well as aural. Its impression, slightly blurred by a later performance in more formal circumstances and dress, was defined afresh in the film version, semi-dramatised and made some years later. In this the producer's hand intervenes and obtrudes throughout, but Bostridge's face, figure and voice will long identify that 'I', the 'ich' of the songs. Recently, within a fortnight, we heard him giving (with his marvellous partner in many concerts, Julius Drake) the first performance of the 'Arabian' cycle (*Sechs Gesänge aus dem Arabischen*) written for him by Hans Werner Henze, and in Janáček's *Diary of One Who Vanished*. The first is a strongly personalised composition; the second was given in a staged production, where, as in *Winterreise*, we saw Bostridge making a real, and unforgettable, individual out of the commonly more generalised character. His special gift – among many other talents – lies in character. At this stage in his career he is good in a wide repertoire, good-to-great in the musical dramatic monologue.

CHAPTER 33

Matthias Goerne and
Peter Schreier

When Fischer-Dieskau retired in 1993, the position of senior figure among Lieder singers, male, became Peter Schreier's. Among the younger generation, the likely successors at one time appeared to be numerous, with several fine German baritones such as Olaf Bär, Wolfgang Holzmair, Thomas Quasthoff, Andreas Schmidt and Stephen Genz, the young Englishman Simon Keenlyside and the Canadian Gerald Finley to be ranked as full equals. At the time of writing, the baritone who has excited most interest and held it with the most distinctive individuality is Matthias Goerne. Like Fischer-Dieskau and Schreier he brings insight, an intensity of concentration that offers the perpetual prospect of a special experience. With the others (and I particularly find it in Finley and Keenlyside) there will be real enjoyment and satisfaction, and in all honesty I am not sure that Goerne gives more in the same currency, but with him we can always be aware of possibilities, as with 'the famous stone that turneth all to gold'. Delete the 'all', be realistic and bring it down to earth a bit, and this is still the touch of the *great* Lieder singer, as opposed to the good.

Goerne has also a most distinctive voice. The beauty of its timbre is instantly striking, but almost as immediately it raises doubts about the production. The tone is so round and warm that it seems impossible for it to be thrustful and penetrative too. This concern has so far been largely theoretical in my own experience, which is mostly (but not entirely) confined to hearing him in the relatively small Wigmore Hall in London, ideal as it is for Lieder recitals. Even here songs such as Wolf's 'Prometheus' (with its accompaniment like a Wagnerian orchestra and its call for a Wotan-voice to match) carries to the back rows with the effect of power increased but at a distance; by contrast, in that same hall and in a comparable seat, the voice of Thomas Quasthoff has seemed, at a fortissimo, to be right in front or all around, while Goerne's at fortissimo comes from the platform. As an allied feature of his production, certain vowels have tended to sound as though going back towards the throat: the 'ei' of 'heiss' or (in Schubert's 'Das Fischermädchen') the German 'Land' are examples. These represent perhaps the more problematic side of a method which has the very great virtue of preserving the voice from that over-brightness, metallic impurity or raw openness which so frequently coarsens a singer's tone. Whether this has indeed to do with use of the soft palate I do not know (and singers, I find, tend to hedge their answers to questions about such matters), but to a layman's ear that is how it sounds.

It is, however, an extraordinarily beautiful voice as heard in the flesh, and so is, or has been, Schreier's. This may need to be stated somewhat emphatically because it might not accord with the impression received by those who have heard Schreier only on records. By one of a series of coincidences and accidents such as can dog one's path from time to time, I was very late myself in hearing him 'live', though had long been familiar with his recordings. It came as a surprise to find that features which limited enjoyment on record were relegated, while the purity of tone emerged as a primary constituent in a way for which records had left me unprepared. In this respect he was like Pears, Lewis and to some extent Gedda. In kind, the timbre was as expected, chicken (let's say) rather than roast beef, eglantine rather than red rose. But in effect the sheer purity, the beauty of tone, ensured a heightened pleasure and, in the case of Schreier, the characteristic that I had been hearing as a kind of yowl, flattened in tone by the elimination of vibrancy and hence of resonance, disappeared from the foreground.

It is still present and has its place in his art, which in turn belongs to a well-established German tradition. As a boy he sang with the famous Dresden Kreuzchor. Some recordings made at that time show a strong alto voice (he was by then presumably a 'mature' chorister), of forthright but unvaried tone. The choral background is one we have to thank for much, but it also has its drawbacks, one of them being the insistence on a 'straight' tone, natural to a boy perhaps but then continuing as the desirable sound-image when the boy becomes a man. It is potent in the English tradition also, so that, in addition to the tenors already named, others from earlier times such as Edward Lloyd, John Coates, Gervase Elwes, then Eric Greene and Steuart Wilson, produced tone which, however powerful, sounds bloodless to Mediterranean ears, and quite often, it must be said, to our own. The sound at best is spiritual rather than romantic, and it does not suit Italian opera. Schreier's operatic career, accordingly, has centred on Mozart. In early recordings especially he could come very close to the elusive ideal: 'Un' aura amorosa' (*Così fan tutte*) from 1968, for instance, is honeyed in tone, beautifully phrased, with an excellent legato and an elegantly-turned shake at the end. Yet over a larger operatic canvas the palette has a limited range of colours, and the lack of vibrancy, together with the openness of certain vowel sounds, tends to nag. Even so, and allowing for the difference in background, it is a little startling to read in a footnote in Rodolfo Celletti's *A History of Bel Canto* (English ed. Oxford, 1991) that 'if this [a record by Schreier of an aria by

164

Matthias Goerne

Agostino Steffani] is anything to go by, Schreier also sings his Lieder badly and is not fit to sing Mozart'!

Goerne has also been associated with Mozart in his operatic career, making his Salzburg debut as Papageno in 1997. He, however, has other interests in opera – as indeed Schreier had – and more recently has appeared with success as Wozzeck. Dramatically, that must be a part ideally suited, and, to judge from recitals heard since then, it seems not to have harmed his voice. Yet, like Schreier in the general view, he remains at present above all an exponent of the Lied.

In a recent recital at the Wigmore he was accompanied by Graham Johnson, who has worked with him on many occasions and never without some wonder. Rehearsing, he realised that his mind was going back to his own early days as an accompanist. There was only one man in his

Peter Schreier

experience whose working habits were so driven by a passion for discovery and improvement. This was Walter Legge, who above everything else was a teacher (all the rest, the talent-spotting, record-producing, concert-management, were essentially means to that end). Goerne, for instance, will take the opening of a song in six or seven different ways, each time coming up with something new, always intelligently experimental, much as Legge would do in those sessions with accompanists which were called 'crucifying the pianist' but which gave invaluable lessons in digging deep. If those two had worked together, Graham Johnson says, they would have stormed at each other, for Goerne also has passionate convictions and at the present stage of his life is very much for or against: the integrity is fearless and there is no fudging the issue, but essentially he and Legge would have been looking for the same end – to make the performance revelatory.

And this he does, in his early middle age as Schreier has done for many years now in his maturity. Schreier has broken ground perhaps most revealingly of all in his characterisation of the romantic poet's 'I' or alter-ego. 'Poor Peter', the unhappy misfit of Schumann's mini-cycle op. 53

166

no. 3, becomes painfully vivid in the tones Schreier finds for him, sensitive like Thomas Mann's Tonio Kröger or almost like T.S. Eliot's magic-lantern throwing 'the nerves in patterns on a screen'. Over a time his various recordings of *Dichterliebe* coalesce and collectively enact the protagonist's cherishing, the resentments, ambivalences and violent swings of mood, with a power and clarity which very probably nobody had achieved before him. In some wonderful Schubert evenings with Andras Schiff he gave a *Schöne Müllerin* and *Winterreise* that also went to the very heart. At the end of *Winterreise* they prepared for an encore, and one wondered what on earth could come after that, but it was the one thing possible: the 'Wanderers Nachtlied', 'Über allen Gipfeln ist Ruh', and it came as a benediction.

Goerne has also wandered by the brook, up to the mill and come sadly back. He also has trodden the icy road, dreamed of Spring, rested at the graveside inn and heard the organ-grinder play. If a similar benediction were to be asked of him as an encore on a similar occasion he could well consider 'Die Sterne', Schubert's setting of Schlegel's poem which tells how benignly the stars could cause earthly suffering to vanish within the sacred radiance of heaven's love. For this, the young singer fashions a tone that is gently enveloping, and he exercises a breath-control that is of the soul itself, for it seems to be quite free of the body. One would hope that even his own restless pursuit of excellence may have been satisfied with this, as he sings it to Johnson's accompaniment in the complete *Schubert Song Edition* on records. In it we can find something like the sublimity of spirit such as Schreier gave us in that 'Nachtlied'. Mixed with it is another element, precious to the lover of singing, and this is the gently vibrant tone, rich in humanity, which recalls a master of earlier years before Fischer-Dieskau's re-energising arrival on the scene, Herbert Janssen. When such forces combine within a young, devoted and independent artist they surely provide the conditions for greatness among the Lieder-singers of our time.

CHAPTER 34

Anne Sofie von Otter

It was in 1985 that we started getting signals from Switzerland. They came via *Opera* magazine, where news of a wonderful Cherubino had the ring of conviction: she gave 'unqualified pleasure' and was 'as mischievous in character as she was polished in style'. The name reappeared ('marked out for greater things') as Hansel, and then, rather more urgently, as Clairon in *Capriccio*. Anne Sofie von Otter, said the report, was an artist 'who could have dominated the stage with her statuesque appearance, easy manner, and slinky, sexy good looks, but she tailored her perform- ance intelligently to the activity around her, building the character on music and words, and with just the right hint of overacting'. There was definitely something intriguing about this: a figure statuesque yet slinky, a capacity to dominate but also a self-restraint that kept it in check, and a delicacy of style (she dealt in hints) that was combined with a capacity for fun.

Prior to this, one day late in 1984, a parcel arrived, containing a record, and the postmark was Swiss but the record Swedish. Its programme was of music by Monteverdi, Handel and Telemann, and an accompanying hand-written letter warmly commended the singer in terms that were echoed in the sleeve-note. She had come from her native Sweden to Basle and was doing at least well enough to convince my correspondent that 'a great career might lie ahead'. 'Listen to this young singer,' advised the writer of the sleeve-notes, 'a warm and rich mezzo-soprano just about to embark on her grand international career.' The notes also drew attention to her awards and scholarships, to the thoroughness of her musical studies in Stockholm and her successes in concerts abroad. 'At present,' they added, 'she is studying with Vera Rozsa in London, and has thus joined the ever-abundant flow of Swedish vocal exports.' If this was hype, at least it was hype's more acceptable face, for a Swedish mezzo-soprano who sings Monteverdi probably deserves all the help she can get.

The record itself certainly lived up to its promises. The voice, as they said, was warm and rich. It also could boast a range of over two octaves, with easy movement between registers and between all levels of volume; it was also pure in quality and firmly produced. Yet the sense of an exciting discovery arose not so much out of the voice itself as from the skill and

168

intelligence of its usage. Individuality lay in character rather than timbre, and the character was essentially that of a lively mind responsive to both music and words. Two songs from Monteverdi's *Scherzi musicali* were included, the performances delightful in every respect but particularly in their feeling for rhythm. These are charming pieces, the instrumental parts dancing with a lightness that has also to be caught by the voice. The young singer seemed absolutely at one with the players and had the ability to make her voice smile. Then in the following number, the great lament of Arianna, she brought a fine concentration of tragic tone, duly darkened to reflect the sombre harmonies and search the deep places of the soul in its wish for death. Still more impressive was the scene from Handel's *Hercules* in which the conscience-stricken Dejanira wills herself into mad-

169

ness and finds 'the furies of the mind' eager to come into their inheritance. This is a supreme test of even the most experienced singer's dramatic power and technical mastery, and perhaps von Otter, straight from college, could hardly summon the uninhibited intensity of a Janet Baker. Yet, taking it at a feverish speed as though goaded by desperation, she articulates every note of the runs with clarity and without aspirates, and is vivid as a video in her enactment of the wretched woman's torment. It was an outstanding achievement.

This debut-recital made it clear that von Otter was a natural for the recording studios. Yet, as audiences in Basle's opera house were well aware, and as the rest of the world would soon discover, the impact of her performances was much strengthened by her remarkable stage-presence. When *Opera*'s reviewer observed that even in the secondary role of Clairon she could have dominated the stage, he was no doubt calling to mind, along with the voice, that strikingly tall figure and the long expressive face. It is also true that both of these could appear to enjoy a fuller, freer life when the role she played took her out of skirts and put her in trousers. Cherubino and Octavian beckoned to her from the start; Hansel and Nicklaus in *Les Contes d'Hoffmann* were also among her early roles on stage; and with the Composer in *Ariadne auf Naxos* and the Orfeo of either Monteverdi or Gluck, here was a ready company of *Six Characters in Search of a Singer*, all with an interest in the young mezzo from Sweden.

The long legs and boyish face did of course bring with them the danger of type-casting. There may also have been a temptation to exploit the reaction which an artist so strongly individualised by appearance as well as by her singing can readily draw from an audience. If so, she appears to have resisted, and in this respect too that first LP of 1983 was reassuring. Telemann's 'Canary' cantata ('Funeral music for an artistic canary, following its demise this year to the immense grief of its owner') affords ample opportunities for self-conscious exhibitions of winsome sentiment and gawky innocence – and to her great credit she almost entirely declined the invitation. Listening again now to the recording (conveniently reissued on compact disc), one catches just occasionally what might be the tone of incipient Hoydenism, but essentially the charming piece is left to speak for itself, without intrusions of facetiousness or even of overt personality, at least till the time comes for cursing the murderous cat.

It has to be admitted, even so, that the return to this particular recording came about partly by way of a check-up. In later years the heavily humorous touch so happily avoided in the Canary cantata has sometimes arisen and could be mildly irritating. Some of Mahler's quasi-folk, quasi-naive songs may indeed invite such treatment but are none the better for it. The children of 'Verlorne Müh' become not so much childlike as childish; in 'Aus! Aus!' the weepy voice of the girl whose boy has marched away with his regiment is too broadly characterised, and even

170

AMI
Artist Management International Ltd
in association with
The South Bank Centre presents

ANNE SOFIE VON OTTER
mezzo soprano

BENGT FORSBERG piano

Villanelle	Hector Berlioz
La belle Isabeau	
La mort d'Ophélie	
Gestillte Sehnsucht, Op 91 No 1	Johannes Brahms
Geistliches Wiegenlied, Op 91 No 2	
with MATS LIDSTRÖM cello	
Nuits d'étoiles	Claude Debussy
Fantoches	
Chansons de Bilitis	

INTERVAL

from *Die tote Stadt*	Erich Korngold
Sonett für Wien, Op 41	
Sterbelied, Op 14 No 1	
Liebesbriefchen, Op 9 No 4	
Du reine Frau, Op 18 No 3	
Lieder eines fahrenden Gesellen	Gustav Mahler

*Members of the audience are requested to stifle any unavoidable coughing
and to check that digital watch alarms are switched off for the duration of the recital*

Queen Elizabeth Hall

Thursday 12 December 1991 at 7.45 pm

Programme Price £1.50

(Anne Sofie von Otter appears by arrangement with Lies Askonas Ltd)

Concert Management: Jane Gray

the charms of 'Rheinlegendchen' are compromised when an assumed 'character' voice is imposed.

Her recorded Mozart songs also suffer intermittently from some less than elegant pointing of the humour. These, however, also draw to notice a tendency that might become more pervasive: the habit of treating individual notes to a swelling, rather as period stringed instruments will sometimes do *ad nauseam* – and indeed, taken to extremes, the habit can beget a kind of nausea, just as a perpetual wave-motion makes for sea-sickness. In a relatively mild form it drew attention as a feature of von Otter's singing in a concert to which she contributed songs by Purcell and it may well be that contemporary English practice has encouraged a notion

171

that this is an essential feature of authentic performance. In the Mozart songs on record, the pushing or swelling of notes became one of several traits which collectively disrupted the legato singing-line. It is true that singers face an eternal dilemma in balancing the claims of 'pure' singing against those of expression. But by the late 1990s it seemed to me that von Otter was tilting the balance in favour of 'expression' dangerously far.

The dilemma is one which critics face too, and perhaps no less dangerously. My own belief is that modern critical opinion, concerning itself above all with expressiveness, undervalues the two qualities most fundamental to the art: beauty of tone and mastery of legato. But, for the critic as for the singer, it is a matter of balance. The verb 'wallow', flabby and flaccid as are its connotations, sticks sharply in my mind. Used incidentally by a respected colleague, it occurred in a context the meaning of which was, roughly: 'Here is an expressive performance, alive with emphasis, contrast, notes that are detached or semi-detached, which I personally find most satisfying; and those with different tastes may go away and wallow in legato to their hearts' content.' Such a view might be mine exactly if keyboard performances of Bach and Handel were concerned. But do we who insist so on the mastery of legato in singing – do we 'wallow'? And in the final balance may it not be that our insistence on the value of a true legato and of beautiful tone risks reducing the singer to a kind of aural masseur/masseuse? In which case, if a singer so gifted as Anne Sofie von Otter gives increasing right-of-way to 'expression', should we not adjust our critical balances accordingly, for assuredly the gain outweighs the loss?

In general, I would resist any such conclusion (which is based on the premise that legato is anti-expressive, whereas a legato line may be *infused* with feeling, which does not inevitably have to resort to emphasis to gain expression). Yet with this singer's most recent recital-disk at hand it is sorely tempting to concede the point. In this, entitled *Lamenti*, the beauties of singing, in tone and evenness of production, are often great as ever, yet at times she will sacrifice these qualities and so tilt the balance uncomfortably. The critical concession has to be made nevertheless: with the great, almost as a condition of their greatness, the balance is of their own choosing. Whether this singer, still a relative newcomer, has achieved that status must remain a question. Comparing her recent record, made in 1997, with the debut-recital of 1983, we can hardly fail to recognise the comprehensiveness of her artistic development. Then, thinking of all that has gone between, even on records alone (the Bach and Handel, Gluck and Mozart, the glorious Grieg and Sibelius), the achievement of these years is colossal. Both programmes include versions of Monteverdi's 'Lasciatemi morire', and both are fine. The balance between 'pure' and 'expressive' singing has certainly shifted, but something very like greatness has emerged.

CHAPTER 35

Elisabeth Söderström

Turning to Söderström brings some pleasant prospects into view. One is that of taking down from the shelves those wonderful LPs she made with Ashkenazy of Rachmaninov's songs. Another is the re-reading of her delightful book. If every young singer should study Janet Baker's *Full Circle* as serious preparation for life in the singing profession, Söderström's *In My Own Key* should follow, and without too much delay. Like the Baker diary-book, it gives a realistic picture of what to expect, but it can also make you laugh. A cheerful irony pervades the horrors and the glories. It is a toughener of the spirits, and the student who is a survivor by nature will think, first, 'What *is* this that I have set my mind upon going into?', and, secondly, 'Well, if she can take it, so can I.'

Let's listen first to one of those Rachmaninov records. Here is one with all the winners, several of them at least, starting with 'Oh, never sing to me again' and ending with the Vocalise, which perhaps should be put aside for a delicious encore at the end. And that opening song – how it brings back the radiance of her voice. I used to think that if anything could reconcile me to the thought of never again hearing Schwarzkopf in recital it might be the prospect of Söderström in songs such as this. She has the authority for Rachmaninov as well as the voice. These songs, however tender and private in their sadness (as this one becomes), need some grandeur of style, some drama in the utterance. Söderström's voice was not large, but, like others in these chapters (Julia Varady for instance), there is concentration in the tone, vibrancy in the timbre. 'The Harvest of Sorrow', which follows, develops passionately out of its simple folk-song beginning, and Söderström's voice rejoices in the high tessitura, as soon it will do with the grand sweep of lament and the long sigh of its last sung note. 'How fair this spot' is fairest of them all, better perhaps when a tenor can float his head-notes, but lovely in Söderström's gentle handling, so that one could wish the sequential phrases to succeed each other *ad infinitum*. 'In my garden at night', 'To her' and 'Daisies' lead in the programme to one I'd entirely forgotten – 'The Pied Piper', subtly playful, almost in the mode of Wolf's 'Die Spröde'. Then 'Dreams' with its Ravelian accompaniment, and 'The Quest', delicate, fascinating, and growing towards the climax of a great passionate cry. It's all too much.

Which of course is only a manner of speaking, or if meant seriously then it must be in reference to the music itself, which one should perhaps take in moderate doses. It is *not* too much in any stylistic sense in reference to the performances. Go back a generation and play records by Nina Koshetz, and then Söderström sounds restrained, almost under-characterised. Koshetz (45 and short of breath) tells of a deeper nostalgia for the songs of Georgia in 'Oh, never sing to me again': her pianissimo fades slowly into silence, and her more generous allowance of *portamento* finds a readier way to the heart. 'How fair this spot' with Koshetz is rather more a personal, many-shaded utterance. Did she therefore feel it more acutely? Or is it like (what shall we say?) a film-star of the old days, Nazimova or Theda Bara, whose style, however valid then, could not be brought into the performances of later times? Rather to the contrary, the comparison does in fact make me conscious of a limitation in Söderström's art, or the art of her period; and yet I read the music and then listen to Söderström and Ashkenazy on records and they bring it to life with such fullness that one has little wish to ask for more.

Her book is a delight – and absolutely non-Rachmaninovlike in tone. A singer's life, we gather, is a hazardous business, poised between sublimity and bathos. As Katya Kabanova on stage she concludes that amid all the beauty of this world she must die, and, having hurled herself into the river, hears a voice calling 'Vite, madame, levez-vous' as arrangements are made for her to be dowsed in water and lifted back on stage 'so that Tichor Kabanoff has a corpse to throw himself over as he sobs out: "Katya! Katya!"'. Well, perhaps we know all that, but Söderström's account, among all the biographies and autobiographies of singers, is the only one which finds space for realities such as that central part of a singer's life which is spent in learning and trying to remember. Not (that is) learning to sing, but memorising the music and words themselves. Perhaps singers and their biographers think that to reveal such conditions of their workaday life would be like taking their readers into the kitchen, the bathroom or even the toilet; but such delicacy might encourage a supposition that singers simply open a score, breathe in, and there it is, in the system and obedient to call. Söderström opens up this dark cave of the mind which somehow can learn and retain (she dived into Octavian's clothes for Act 2 of *Der Rosenkavalier*, not having sung the part nine years), and yet may at any moment go into spasm or paralysis and refuse to function at all. She tells most vividly of an experience at the Festival Hall in London where she was due to sing Britten's *Les Illuminations*. The rehearsals had gone well, but *en route* to the performance a notion lodged in her mind that the French words (at home she had sung it in Swedish) would not come. The horror of standing there with the knowledge that the concert was being broadcast, seeing members of the audience following every word of the text printed in their programmes, of her confusing French and Swedish, perhaps remembering neither, appeared overwhelming. Right up to the moment of

Söderström as Cio-cio-san in *Madama Butterfly*

taking her place on the platform she felt that she simply must cancel; and then on the way out from the wings she fell over a chair and the horrible spell was broken. The audience sympathetically laughed at the accident and applauded her recovery: the music started and she sang. She says that it may not have been the best performance of her life and next day one of the critics did observe that she had sung a sharp instead of a flat somewhere or other; but 'there was no scandal' and the nightmare passed without notice. Nevertheless the incident was related to memory and the learning-process, and nowhere else can I recall a singer going into this essential part of the singer's life with, at any rate, Söderström's fullness and frankness.

There are many other accomplishments she has mastered more fully than most other singers. The mastery of languages, for instance: Scandinavians are widely known to be among the best linguists of the operatic world, and Söderström, like Nicolai Gedda, had an advantage in the nationality of her parents – the mother was a Russian. For her part in the Janáček operas, however, she learned Czech, and that was something of an achievement even for a Scandinavian. As to repertoire, she has proved an invaluably adaptable musician among singers. As the Governess in Britten's *The Turn of the Screw* or Ellen Orford in *Peter Grimes*, or as the wife in Henze's *Elegy for Young Lovers*, or the pop-singer Daisi Doody in Blomdahl's *Aniara*, she has played her part in the development of modern opera. She has also been among the best Mozart singers of her generation, and one of the most versatile, charming New Yorkers (for instance) with her Susanna in *Le nozze di Figaro*, and then delighting such as were lucky enough to be present with a one-off Musetta in *La Bohème*. Butterfly, Mélisande, the Countess of *Capriccio*, Emilia Marty and Jenufa are all roles in which her performances have been distinguished by the fine interplay of intelligence, voice and stagecraft. Her acting had the controlled naturalness of high professionalism, and yet (as her book illustrates) there were times when her emotional involvement became almost dangerously complete.

She has also been the proud Director of opera at Drottningholm – a Stradivarius among opera houses, she called it, and the one in which some 45 years earlier, in 1947, she made her own debut. As a concert-artist of apparently infinite resource, she has appeared widely in orchestral programmes, oratorios and solo recitals. Her vocal gift was essentially lyrical, yet in recital her 'Erlkönig' could be as powerfully dramatic as any. In earlier years especially, when she rounded off her programmes with the 'Echo Song' beloved of Jenny Lind, she could produce an enchantment of sophistication and simplicity combined in rare union.

But we must go back to the Rachmaninov records, and, before succumbing to the call of the 'Vocalise', take in the first side of Volume 2, affectionately opening with 'In the silence of night' (shades of McCormack and Kreisler), then on with the fine frenzy of 'So many hours', calming as the

voice rises with its early-morning clarity and freshness high above the piano's quiet chords in 'The Little Island', then a gloriously impulsive start to 'Believe it not', and ending with the excited outpouring of 'Spring Waters'. Listening afresh, one can understand that there will be some listeners for whom such vibrancy will be excessive, and more for whom the music itself over-indulges. The spirit of delight which Shelley says comes so rarely is nevertheless a fairly constant companion in these records, and the long-promised, richly-anticipated 'Vocalise' is a delight. My copy, however, has its full share of the clicks and other ills that LPs are heir to, so the hearing, lovely as the performance is, proves not quite the Elysian delight that was expected. It is, in fact, an experience in keeping with the spirit of her book. This is the real world: after the ecstasies on stage, a voice from the wings cries 'Vite, madame, levez-vous'; and as the voice in the 'Vocalise' soars and swoons in the bliss of its dying fall, the stylus encounters a minute impediment and Elysium is startled by a click and a bump.

CHAPTER 36

Yevgeny Nesterenko

Most of us associate singers with particular works, and for myself, Nesterenko's is the voice of Shostakovich's Michelangelo. It was his recording that introduced this late masterpiece, the *Suite on Verses* by Michelangelo op. 145a, to us in the West: a searing expression of sublime fretfulness, voiced by a singer schooled in the finest traditions. The profound impression made on record was confirmed in many countries by recitals in which this work had a dominant position. On some occasions the composer himself would be present, and, rightly or wrongly, one assumed there to be a closeness of understanding and sympathy that stamped the performance as definitive.

As an artist, Nesterenko has become the voice of much more in addition to this; but he has also been a *figure*, and as such becomes a focal point in a wider range of thoughts concerning his country and the bewildering developments of its history in his time. He was probably the supreme operatic star among singers in the last years of the Soviet Union and the first of the new Russia. Perhaps the mezzo-soprano Irene Arkhipova (Vol. 2 Ch. 9) shared the position; others such as Galina Vishnevskaya (a thorn in the flesh of the old authorities, and one they were pleased to be rid of), Yelena Obraztsova, Vladimir Atlantov and Yuri Mazurok also ranked highly. But in a country where hierarchy counted for so much, this stardom brought an institutionalised status that had no exact counterpart in the West. In the West you might hitch your wagon to a star; in the Soviet Union the star in turn was hitched to the State. Nesterenko's stardom began in the old order, ended in the new, and had reached its zenith at just about the time when the State inaugurated the most momentous programme of unhitching known to modern times.

Born in Moscow in the January of 1938, Nesterenko was very much a child of Stalin's USSR. He was brought up to hardship in the war years when the family travelled as evacuees to Tashkent, returning in 1943, then moving on to Chelyabinsk beyond the Urals. He was fifteen when Stalin died, which meant that his adolescence coincided with the beginnings of a new age. He would have felt it in the air at Leningrad, where he went in 1955 to study at the Institute of Engineering Construction. Even then his secret ambition was to become a singer, for his head was full of

Nesterenko as Ruslan in *Ruslan and Ludmilla*

the sound of Chaliapin's records and to his ears the voice he was developing sounded not altogether dissimilar. At least he learned, via the gramophone, a basic repertoire, including the 'Song of the Viking Guest' from
Sadko, which he sang, a tone down, at a concert of amateurs. People were
impressed; he went to a teacher, and for some years combined vocal
studies with training as an engineer. This is a young man, growing up in
a country without political freedom and governed through a rigid bureau-
cracy which takes the arts within its orbit. But he makes progress in both
directions, the sun shines (it did on the day he started singing-lessons),
and the world is not such a bad place.

It witnesses, for instance, the thawing of the Cold War, the beginnings of official de-Stalinisation, and Yuri Gagarin is up there in his spaceship. For this engineering student and fledgling bass it is the start of a decade that will take him to the very top of his profession. He found an ideal teacher of technique in Vassily Lukanin – also a link with his boyhood hero, for Lukanin had sung Pimen to the Boris Godunov of Chaliapin. At the Opera Studio in 1962 he sang some small roles, then Gremin in *Eugene Onegin*. The following year he joined the Maly Theatre, singing the King of Clubs in the company's first production of *The Love for Three Oranges*, and gaining experience in a wide range of opera, Russian, French and Italian. He won the Silver Medal at Sofia in 1967, bringing promotion in Leningrad to the Kirov, and in 1970 the Tchaikowsky Festival Gold, with a contract for the Bolshoi.

As a species, the Russian bass is as proverbial as the Italian tenor. Russia is a land of basses, deep as wells and sonorous as cathedrals. To be principal bass at the Bolshoi is to be chief of basses in a population of (then) roughly 250 million. Nesterenko came into his kingdom at an auspicious time. The singers of the previous generation were no doubt celebrated in Russia, but for the most part not even their names were known at all widely abroad. Nesterenko had just time to establish himself at the Bolshoi when the prospects began to open up. 1973 was the year when the company brought Russian opera, with its language and traditions, to La Scala, Milan, and Nesterenko starred in *Ruslan and Ludmilla* and *Prince Igor*. Two years later they visited New York and in the capitalist heartland played to warmly appreciative audiences, for whom the centrepiece of the season was *Boris Godunov*. Nesterenko won emphatic acclaim in the title-role, which many at the Metropolitan still associated with Ezio Pinza and Alexander Kipnis, while some veterans must have been able to recall Chaliapin himself. Again Nesterenko was treading in his hero's footsteps and again he stood as the worthy representative of a noble tradition. A decade earlier, opportunity would not have been open to him; the more outgoing policy of the regime, however guarded, came just at the right time for him.

The successes abroad confirmed his pre-eminence at home. For the next ten years he remained in his prime, roughly up to the age of fifty, which he reached in 1990. At the Met, *Opera* magazine (September 1975) reported 'a bass of rich, even vocal production and awesome tone, a major artist in every way'. In *Eugene Onegin* he gave 'a suavely sculptured account of Gremin's tuneful aria'. In *War and Peace* he was a Kutuzin 'of magnificent voice and warm, commanding presence'. His Covent Garden debut followed in 1978, with a Don Basilio in *Il barbiere di Siviglia* which William Mann said 'brought the house down not only with the cavernous glory of his bass voice and its quality and generous artistry, but with the joviality of a young, well-nurtured face, highly mobile, a robust, athletic figure, slit eyes, a torn-pocket mouth, an athlete's stride'. His other roles

180

in the house were Méphistophélès in Gounod's Faust and Khovansky in *Khovanshchina*. We never saw his internationally admired Philip in *Don Carlos* or the role in which he was said to be most ideally suited, the King in Tchaikowsky's *Iolanta*.

The parabola of his career started its downward curve in the late 1980s. It was a fairly gentle process, but reports began to come in of a voice losing the deeper resonances, and even before this he had been victim of some miscasting, as when he sang Rossini's Mosè and the Inquisitor at *Don Carlos* at La Scala. An interesting extension of his repertoire, and a bold one, came when in 1986 he sang Bartok's Bluebeard in Hungarian at Budapest; and yet limitations, both artistic and vocal, were increasingly noted as he went into the 1990s. It was almost as though his fortunes were bound to those of the old Soviet Union. The Berlin Wall fell in 1989. The disintegration of the Union and the Communist order had a profound effect on every aspect of life, including the cultural. I do not know what Nesterenko or other artists of his generation have thought of it, but it would be very natural if they associated the old regime with their own heyday. And no doubt, for better or worse, others will do so too.

I saw his Covent Garden operas, thinking his Khovansky a fine fellow, the Méphistophélès somehow unsatisfying (probably having hoped to match memories of Ghiaurov in the role, missing the full sonority and not finding quite adequate compensations). He sang also in a Verdi *Requiem*

181

at the Albert Hall: fine but not special. The great Nesterenko experience was a concert at the Wigmore Hall. In the second half he sang Mussorgsky's *Songs and Dances of Death* and then a group of songs that filled the concert platform with an astonishing gallery of characters: the village idiot, the Spirit pleading with the Creator to be allowed to comfort Mankind, and, most vivid of all, the seminarian. He was generous with encores, including favourites by Tchaikowsky and Rachmaninov, and even the 'Song of the Volga Boatmen'. During one of these, a political protester advanced to the front and spoke passionately in Russian while the singer looked stonily ahead, only turning to face the man with an annihilating glare at some telling point of denunciation in his next song. In all of this the voice itself was magnificent and its production possibly the most even and finely textured that I had (or have) heard in a bass. But the greatest impression was made by song and singer together in the first half of the programme, consisting of Shostakovich's *Suite on Verses by Michelangelo*. Like others present, I had come to know the songs through his recording and, at the same time, the voice through the songs. Hearing them then 'in the flesh' could have been a let-down (as sometimes happens when turning from records to the 'live' occasion); but it was in fact still more powerful, both in expressiveness and in the quality of the singing.

Today, Nesterenko's star has waned somewhat. At no very great age (60 in 1998) he still sings, teaches and enjoys a prestigious reputation in Russian musical life. But considering that he was pre-eminent among those who came to the West and brought with them the intimation of untold riches (riches that became much more familiar to us over the last decade of the century), he is not remembered so much as one might have expected. Perhaps the currency of a video and a sound-recording of excerpts from *Boris Godunov* has modified the initial conviction that here was the true successor to Chaliapin and Christoff. Up to a point, that is what he was: the fine resonance and evenness of voice go with the dignity, humanity and authority of his stage-presence to create such an impression. But the agonised soul of Boris seems not to be caught, as it was by those great predecessors.

Better for capturing the great singer that Nesterenko undoubtedly was, is the more lyrical repertoire. King René's prayer in Act 1 of *Iolanta* places him immediately among the century's best. His singing of Glinka's *Ruslan*, possibly wanting a touch more bass and weight to it, still sets the standard *as* singing. In some ways most exciting of all are the solos from the Tchaikowsky Competition of 1970, typified by the note-by-note exposure of vocal gold in Khan Konchak's solo from *Prince Igor*. But essential – and amazingly no longer available in our record catalogues – is the Shostakovich. And how rich that the singer who so prospered in the post-war USSR should be the voice of the composer who so chafed under its yoke.

CHAPTER 37

Irmgard Seefried

What songs shall we call upon to evoke the shade of a great singer? Answer: hundreds, or as many songs as there are singers or listeners with memories to revive. But usually there is one song for each singer, and with Irmgard Seefried we have only to hum, softly to ourselves, a few lines of a folk-song:

> Da unten im Tale lauft's Wasser so trüb
> und i kann dir's nit sagen, i hab' di so lieb.

Then the second verse, and it is that which really that does the trick:

> und a bissele Falschheit is au wohl dabei.

The song is tender, rueful, realistic, and it goes to the heart with the note of truth common in folk music, it having been tried in the fire of time over generations. 'Down in the valley the water runs dark, and I can't actually tell you how much I love you. You're always talking about Love and Truth, but there's always a little bit of falsehood around.' The song goes on to reach a sadly sensible conclusion – that 'if I tell you ten times and you still won't understand, then I'll just have to go away and move on'. It's really, I suppose, a man's song, but that doesn't greatly matter. Tune and sentiments ring true, and Brahms (it is one of the *Deutsche Volkslieder*) graces them with his respectful non-intervention. Seefried included the song regularly as an encore in her recitals. It took her back to her Swabian childhood, and up to a point she sings it (as we hear on records) with a wistful childlike simplicity. For all that, it is wise in the ways of the world: 'a bissele Falschheit is au wohl dabei'. And that is where the song works as an evocation: a kind of sly sincerity, innocent realism, serious playfulness, comes over the expression, and there she is. As we listen (even in our minds) she comes into focus: Irmgard Seefried as to the life.

She was one of the most vivid singers of our time. One would almost say that she was clearer to the eye than to the ear, but that would not be true, for the visual memory (I find) needs the ear to summon it, and even then the essential value is that it leads us back to the hearing. I was once well rebuked on that score by Seefried's close colleague of many years, Elisabeth Schwarzkopf, with whom I had been recalling Seefried's performance of the 'fish-sermon' (Mahler's 'Des Antonius von Paduas Fischpredigt'). I described how at one point she would make what I thought of as a fish-face while she sang. 'You remember that?' Schwarzkopf asked. Yes, I replied with bashful pride, feeling that I had remembered it rather well over all those years. 'Well, you shouldn't,' said Schwarzkopf, and added, 'You should be ashamed of yourself. You should.' Ah well, I said ('a bissele Falschheit' coming in handy), perhaps I was. She meant, of course, that what should impress is the singing, the expression-through-music, and not any incidental entertainments on the way. But then, that's the way of the world too: memory is well aware of its status as an indispensable servant with licence to misbehave.

Seefried, remembered so vividly, is also remembered affectionately and not least by Elisabeth Schwarzkopf herself. They were not close personally (professional etiquette and mutual respect required a 'Sie', not a 'Du', in greetings and conversation), but as fellow-artists in the unforgettable years in post-war Vienna and Salzburg they worked so often together that they grew almost by symbiosis. They would regularly listen in the wings to each other's solos, and though no words would be exchanged about voice, style or technique, she felt they had enough common ground in the nature of their training to share a tacit feeling for standards. One of the qualities at which Schwarzkopf marvelled was Seefried's boldness. Maybe the results did not always justify it, and maybe a company cannot afford to include many artists of such strong impulse, but this vitality and independence were essential conditions of what Seefried so valuably was. They permeated her Lieder singing as much as her stage-work. In that most exact of composers, Hugo Wolf, she had a natural affinity with the girl of the *Italian Songbook* as well as a profound religious belief that prepared her spiritually for the *Spanish Songbook* too. But it all seemed to be done so easily: in these things, Schwarzkopf felt that she herself had to work while Seefried seemed to make them hers by instinct.

Then there was the voice, with that strong middle register which so shaped its character. In duets with Schwarzkopf it would seem natural for Seefried to sing the lower voice-part, and this she did as Octavian to the other's Marschallin and Sophie, or, on records, Hansel to her Gretel. But it was not always so: in *Le nozze di Figaro* Seefried was the Susanna, Schwarzkopf the Countess, and in the harmonised phrases of the letter duet Susanna has the upper part. Then, when they gave their duet-recital, which was such a lovely Maytime event in 1955, the disposal of the voices alternated. The remarkable thing, as the recording shows, is that the voices matched so well. They were quite distinct but both of a distinctively German school (Seefried's first teacher was Albert Mayer of the Augsburg Conservatory, after whom she worked with Theodor Rehmann of Aachen Cathedral, and Schwarzkopf felt that they must have taught many of the

principles she learnt from Maria Ivogün). Neither of them had an Italianate vibrato, and though Schwarzkopf could produce something of the kind at will, Seefried's tone was always 'straight'. When they sang their Monteverdi duets, there was no anachronistic lushness or looseness of timbre. On the other hand, their 'straightness' was not the deliberately ironed-out tone of the modern early-music school – though, listening to Seefried now, I sometimes wonder whether, in other circumstances, that strong boylike sound might not have been recruited by a Schola Cantorum Guillaume de Machaut or something of that kind.

Certainly, in combination, the voice and impetuosity made her, in those respects at least, prime-choice for the trouser-roles in opera. She might have made a wonderful Cherubino in *Figaro* had not Susanna been her

Elisabeth Schwarzkopf and Seefried at Abbey Road Studios, London, 1947

part. Her Octavian in *Der Rosenkavalier* was so charismatic that when she was on stage it could be difficult to look elsewhere even for a moment – unless (as when I saw her in the role) the Baron Ochs was Kurt Boehme. They played together in the opera quite frequently and with a matching *joie de vivre*. They were neither coarse nor refined, but, unlike so many middle-ways between polarities, their partnership was utterly positive, potent and great fun. Her supreme creation, however, was the Composer in *Ariadne auf Naxos*. In this she found exactly the character for her

186

temperament and the music for her voice. I never saw her perform the role on stage, but feel that I do see her through the records. A pirated recording has her 'live', and this is the version sometimes preferred, but the studio recording is inspired and all the better for its discipline: there was never any danger of Seefried's Composer being unduly inhibited. This character, the young genius caught in the very descent of the divine spark, finds in her an exponent who is already alight. The sublime egotism of mankind's unacknowledged legislator is brilliantly caught, so too the Cherubino-adolescent who learns the lessons of life (the 'bissele Falschheit' of compromise being one of them) from the enchanting lips of Zerbinetta. The sense of almost unbearable beauty in his own writing, the intake of breath as it grips him by the throat, the conviction of holiness in art and its profound power of metamorphosis through the gods of life and death, and then the outrage of purity profaned – 'ich durfte es nicht erlauben!', how she loathes that word 'erlauben' – all is brought to the furnace of Seefried's art; and at the same time, the notes are well and truly sung.

Her singing, as such, was not always so well-judged in what it attempted and in its technical security. She could, for instance, make a success of Fiordiligi on stage, but records show places where in live performance it would be easy to mistake the will for the deed. With the further strengthening of that tough middle register, the high notes needed more and more to be prayed for. The famous accompanist Gerald Moore noted in his memoirs what many observed, that she regrettably 'changed her method': 'In the effort to increase the volume of her voice, the tone has lost some of its quality.' That was written in the early 1960s. When I myself heard her in some of the last recitals she gave in London, she generated, as did the audience, much warmth; but more was done by character and vividness of communication than by pure singing.

And yet, almost hot from the press at the very time of writing, there arrives a Salzburg recital of 1969, newly released on compact disc, containing so much of the true and best Seefried that it instantly admonishes these critical misgivings. This is quite late in her career, and in Mozart her legato is not flawless, but a real legato is still available, and that is by no means so common as many suppose. Her Bartók *Village Scenes* are still subtle in colouring as they are bold in spirit. Schumann's Mary Stuart is still noble in the pathos of her farewells. Strauss's 'Gefunden' is lovely in the purity of tone and sensitivity of response. And then at the end, as a final encore, 'Da unten im Tale', simple and heartfelt. And ne'er a 'bissele Falschheit' in the whole recital.

CHAPTER 38

Alexander Kipnis

Out of the blue and over the telephone, unprovoked and unsolicited, in the year 2000 came a voice which said 'He was a god'. It was an old friend who rang, an old friend in more ways than one since he had first heard the god in question in 1927. It was on a dreadful evening at Covent Garden when hisses were reported from every part of the house including the well-bred stalls. *Les Huguenots* was billed, or rather *Gli Ugonotti*, for the first time in fifteen years and expectations were high. As early as January Ernest Newman told his readers in the *Sunday Times* that it was the occasion he was looking forward to more eagerly than anything else in the scheduled summer season. In the event, as Newman said, it turned out to be 'one damn sing after another'. At the end the cast faced a thoroughly jaded audience – which did not include the King and Queen, who had left long ago. As to the cast, 'none rose to the rank of the good second-rate while several of them were well on in the D4s'. To this there was a single exception. Among what in days of old were known as the seven stars, only the Marcel was worthy: the Ukrainian bass, Alexander Kipnis.

My old friend seemed to think I might have been there as well, but as I explained I had not then quite been born. 'But of course,' I hastily added, 'I know his records.' 'Oh but you can't believe records,' said my friend. 'I've never believed records since ...', and he went on to tell, as though it were yesterday, of a certain Alessandro Valente who had made a best-selling record of 'Nessun dorma' and was so unwise as to appear in public shortly afterwards. That would have been sometime around 1930.

It is of course to be hoped that we *can* believe the records where Kipnis is concerned, for they are practically all we have of him now; at least until son Igor produces that biography which seems to have been in the offing for a good many years. We have to say 'practically all', because there also remain the written records. These, or such as I have of them, make an interesting collection. Most are glowing, but after that initial success in *Les Huguenots*, his reappearance in the season of 1929 brought mixed reviews. Sorabji, who had been immensely impressed by his Gurnemanz in *Parsifal*, found his voice in *Das Rheingold* 'sounding veiled and even a trifle muffled' (a fine distinction, surely, between those two). Herman Klein in *The Gramophone* thought his Pogner in *Die Meistersinger* ('so far

Kipnis as Rocco in *Fidelio*

as voice was concerned') 'an even greater disappointment than his efforts in *The Ring'*. And the *Musical Times*'s critic compared him unfavourably with the Norwegian Ivar Andresen: 'no one who heard those two singers as Hagen could have the least doubt of their respective merits.' Kipnis, he said, had undoubtedly a great bass voice but was 'inclined to bottle it up'. In 1933 his Baron Ochs was admired by *The Times* for the richness of voice and the artist's refusal to allow 'the coarse humour of Ochs to degenerate into nothing but roaring'. In 1934, on the famous opening night when Beecham, disgusted by the philistinism of the chattering classes during the Overture to *Fidelio*, shouted 'Shut up you', Richard Capell wrote that in Kipnis's Rocco he missed 'a true fruity *basso profondo*', while as Hunding he was 'a bit hampered by the beauty of his voice'. That, happily, did not prove a disadvantage the next season (which was his last in the house) for his King Mark in *Tristan und Isolde* was 'magnificent' (Cardus) and 'a thing of pure beauty' (Newman).

This was not his last operatic appearance in Britain, however, as in 1936 he sang at Glyndebourne in *Die Zauberflöte*. Walter Legge was there and reported for the *Manchester Guardian*: 'The great artist scaled down the volume of his noble voice to the requirements of the theatre without robbing the music or character of any of its dignity'. He thought it probable that only those who had heard how the superb voice would fill a large house could appreciate the technical skill which this adaptation involved. In Legge's other role as assistant to Beecham at Covent Garden in the last two seasons before the war, he had wished that Kipnis could be Covent Garden's Sarastro when they revived the opera, and, still more important in the long run, that he could have taken the part in the first complete recording, which he produced in 1937. But in those days there was no place for Kipnis in Berlin, where they decided to record, and as a result they had to make do with Wilhelm Strienz.

But of course we do have something of Kipnis's Sarastro in a complete recording after all. In that same year he sang the role in some famous performances at Salzburg under Toscanini. One of these was recorded, though privately, presumably from a broadcast. 'You can't believe records' said my old friend; but you can't entirely disbelieve them either, especially when the performance is recorded 'live'. So the majestic sonority is preserved, and the god achieves immortality. The trouble is that two gods are at work here, and that mere mortals, and gremlins, get in the way too. Toscanini is all energy and drive; just occasionally he will seem happy to relax a little, but mostly he wants to move it on, and Sarastro's music, especially, calls for breadth. The gremlins compound the mischief by seeing to it that Sarastro's music from his aria onwards is the most inadequately recorded of all. In effect we have, in full sonority, Sarastro's part in the finale of Act 1 and 'O Isis and Osiris' from Act 2. The prayer is fine, with a genuine legato and a sense of the voice going out towards the audience. So in this instance, though we cannot entirely believe the record

ALEXANDER KIPNIS

(for that would mean that Kipnis was frequently inaudible), we can at least trust part of it, and be thankful.

Still more – indeed infinitely more – must we be thankful for the Kipnis discography as a whole. Other live recordings exist, and in better condition than the Salzburg *Zauberflöte*: his Leporello to Ezio Pinza's Don Giovanni, for instance, or his King Mark beautifully sung in 1943, his Boris Godunov, vividly characterised, each of them presenting a different side of his art. But we still know him best through those studio recordings from 1916 to 1946 in which his repertoire is generally so well represented. As for their reliability, it is true that he is regularly placed very close to the micro-phone; nevertheless, such sonority as this is not of a kind that can be faked. Moreover, the faults are exposed very clearly too. He aspirates quite badly and quite often; occasionally (the great *Simon Boccanegra* record has examples of this) a soft note will fall slightly flat in intonation; more disconcertingly, and increasingly so after 1939, the vibrancy will some-

191

times loosen so that the tone spreads. But this is a magnificent legacy. Parading them mentally, one 'hears' with a thrill the Good Friday music in *Parsifal*, Wotan's Farewell, Schubert's 'Aufenthalt' and 'Der Wanderer', Brahms's 'O Tod, wie bitter bist du' and Grechaninov's 'Over the steppe'. And merely to list these few is to evoke as many again, which in turn will summon others.

Again, turning the records over in mind and then playing a few of them, one realises afresh the extent to which more than voice accounts for the special place they hold in the affections. There is a group of Schubert songs on American Columbia, made in 1927 and 1928. Extraordinarily moving to hear again, these have him at his finest and most characteristic. Part of the vocal character, it must be admitted, derives from the Russian background which, to our ears, heightens the dramatic element in 'Der Wegweiser' and makes 'Der Doppelgänger' a thing of genuine horror. But essentially the joy of these performances lies in the combination of strength and gentleness. In 'Der Lindenbaum', the consolation of 'Hier fändst du deine Ruh' is almost palpable, and the hushed 'Du fandest Ruhe dort' promises rest with the most inner-sounding of *pianissimi*. 'Der Wanderer', too, is a marvellous study in detail. Something, perhaps, of the grand gesture of an old-school actor attends its changes of mood, but how vivid they are, and how heartfelt.

In that song it is easy to believe that he was indeed singing from the heart; and perhaps, when he was recording it, in an American studio and about to go to Chicago for another season at the opera there, his mind went back to the start of his own traveller's life. A childhood spent very largely on the move with a small theatrical company took him from the Ukraine to Poland. From Warsaw to Berlin, Hamburg, Wiesbaden and back to Berlin again, but now as first bass in the State Opera; across the Atlantic with the Wagner Festival Company in 1923; Buenos Aires in 1926, London in 1927: he was a world-singer already, and so it remained until his retirement from opera in 1946. He settled then, teaching at the Juilliard in New York and at his studio in Westport, Connecticut, where he was active until suffering a stroke a month before his death in 1978.

'A god,' said the old friend: perhaps not a proposition for public debate. But 'Best bass of the century': a case could certainly be made for that.

CHAPTER 39

Margaret Price

On 1st October we received a letter from Dame Margaret Price to say that from that day she had decided to give up her work as a singer. Her recital on 26th January, listed in the Master Series brochure, will therefore no longer take place.

In her letter she paid tribute to Wigmore Hall and 'in particular the great audiences'.

So it is farewell to a great artist, one of the best musicians of the century.

The printed notice came on a slip inserted into the Wigmore Hall's *Master Series* leaflet. And thus passed from sound and sight one of the great singers of our time. The beauty of her voice was unsurpassed in its day, and she became an artist of the front rank, singing with ever deeper feeling and steadily maturing powers of expression. She has given incalculable pleasure over a career of more than thirty years and fully deserves her freedom from the duties of public life; but she will be sorely missed.

The voice was rich and pure, strong and firm. There was an element of the mezzo about it, and indeed it was as a mezzo that she started. At times it had a tubular quality which on records and even in the flesh could evoke the ignoble word 'hooty' – instantly to be dismissed, not so much on account of its inelegance as because it did a grave injustice. The sounds in question were well-rounded and without vibrato, but the tone was still healthy and the production free from breathiness. The highest notes were latterly not her crowning glory, but those around the G or A flat were among the most lovely within memory. There was royalty in the timbre, but nothing stiffly monumental: she maintained a well-practised fluency and sang with a very human warmth. Mozart provided her testing-ground, in which she gained immediate distinction, Verdi and Strauss opening up their treasures to her as did Brahms, Schumann and, over the years and by degrees, Schubert. Wagner also had a place in her career but she was much too sensible not to know what that rightful place was. And no doubt this same good sense told her when the time had come for retirement.

Few singers can say they have no regrets, and Margaret Price will have had her share of them. So will we as members of the British public, for it is a sad fact that for many of her best years she was not to be heard in our leading opera house. She worked her apprenticeship with the Welsh National Opera, the Scottish and the English Opera Group. She made highly successful appearances on television, in *Eugene Onegin* and *La vida breve*. In 1963 her opportunity arrived with Covent Garden's *Zauberflöte* in which her Pamina was outstanding. The same year brought a Glyndebourne debut as Constanze in *Die Entführung*. Klemperer himself asked for her as his Marzelline in *Fidelio*, and in 1970 she made her American debut as Pamina at San Francisco. One success followed another, with reviews that reflected the glow of her voice and paid tribute to the charm and steadily increasing confidence of her stage-presence. On her return for a second season at San Francisco, the critic Arthur Bloomfield wrote in *Opera* magazine that she 'floated legato phrases and sustained tones with unsurpassed security and loveliness', while, singing her first Fiordiligi, 'she stopped the show'. This clearly pointed to a singer of international stature. But in those precious years, the 1970s, when it would have been a joy to have watched the growth of her art, Covent Garden engaged her but rarely.

Wherever the fault lay, it reflected adversely on the house, for it looked as though the old snobbery which preferred a foreign name to a more homely one was in action again. The years in question saw the rise of Kiri Te Kanawa, who made a triumphant success in one of Price's most cherished roles, Countess Almaviva in *Le nozze di Figaro*. There was no good reason why both careers should not have flourished side by side, and indeed the two sopranos did appear together in some performances of *Don Giovanni* – one of those combinations that become legendary, like Lehmann and Leider, Rethberg and Ponselle, Schwarzkopf and Welitsch. That was in 1974. In the next few years, Te Kanawa sang regularly and gloriously at Covent Garden, while Price sang gloriously elsewhere.

In the States, Chicago followed San Francisco, with the Met in 1985, welcoming her in Mozart. Paris, Vienna and Milan acclaimed her also in Verdian roles such as Elizabeth of Valois in *Don Carlos*, Desdemona in *Otello* and Alice Ford in *Falstaff*. Cologne and Munich took her to their hearts most enthusiastically of all. She appeared, completely unknown, and, as Alan Blyth reported in *Opera*, 'swept an elegant Cologne audience off its feet': 'for a first Donna Anna anywhere it was in its way as amazing an achievement as Sutherland's Lucia'. After another *Don Giovanni* in Munich, another of *Opera*'s critics, Greville Rothon, found himself wondering 'if she is not perhaps the most musical of all the sopranos before the public today'. It is not surprising that for many years she made Germany her home.

At Covent Garden the great nights lay ahead. If a single date has to be chosen it might be 5 February 1980. Such events are rare in any opera house, but, as Harold Rosenthal wrote, 'this was one of them'. Domingo was singing Otello in Britain for the first time; Carlos Kleiber conducted with memorable intensity; the production ranked among Covent Garden's

best; and like a gold necklace caught by a beam of light in a painting by Rembrandt, Price's Desdemona cast a glow over the whole performance. We had heard several sopranos, including Te Kanawa, give most lovely accounts of the role, and this was the noblest of them all. She moved well and acted convincingly, but essentially she worked through the voice. Moreover, she phrased well, sang scrupulously and articulated her words with feeling: but essentially it was a matter of timbre, of voice-quality. We

had heard other powerful voices before but not of this purity, or other voices of comparable purity but without such depth and roundness. With her, Desdemona lost some of her girlishness, so that she was perhaps less pathetic as an object; but she gained in mature humanity, in authority (still an innocent but more active than passive) and hence in tragic status.

Norma was surely a mistake. She sang the role first in 1979 at Zürich. Accounts of this and subsequent performances suggest that from the first she was a plausible misfit. This at any rate was so at Covent Garden in 1987, by which time the upper notes at a *forte* were no joy at all. Lovely things were done ('Teneri figli' was sublime), but on balance one came away with a sense of having witnessed the beginnings of decline.

Even so, it was several years after this, in the 1990s, that one of my own reviews ventured the claim (or admission) that 'if she is not the greatest soprano presently before the public, I do not know who is'. By that time her concert work had developed remarkably in what one has to call its soul. She had built up a substantial repertoire of Lieder since early days, but for long the singing, particularly of Schubert, impressed as careful and correct rather than expressive: there was not much sense of inner 'possession' of the songs, or of ability to communicate in this more personal and intimate medium. Sometime around 1990 this changed. In that year she gave two wonderful recitals at the Wigmore Hall, the first of them culminating in an unforgettable performance of Wagner's *Wesendonck Lieder*.

The heroic voice, under perfect control, was thrilling to hear in the climaxes of the second and fourth songs ('stehe still' and 'Schmerzen'), and its softer quality was idyllic in the third, 'Im Treibhaus'; but she held us also with a concentration upon the songs as intense personal experience. Of course these are not typical Lieder, but in the second concert we encountered the same spiritual conviction in Brahms's 'Der Tod, das ist die kühle Nacht'. From then onwards, a Margaret Price recital was increasingly an event to be looked forward to for what Lotte Lehmann called 'more than singing'.

And now we shall hear her no more, except in memory and on records. Can I 'hear' the voice in my head? The alto element, which memory so insists on, probably has to be mentally adjusted and reduced. Rather as with Victoria de los Angeles and Jessye Norman, the very real presence of true soprano tone would often take one by surprise. This mental association with Norman reminds us that when they sang together in the *St Matthew Passion* it was Norman who sang the alto part, Price the soprano. Searching back in the mind for the high notes of earlier days, one recalls Mozart's 'Vorrei spiegarvi': something of a miracle that so rich a voice should rise so blissfully to the high Bs, the C sharp, the D. And how beautifully she would sing Liszt's Petrarch sonnets with their demand that the high notes should come to the voice as naturally as they would to a violin. It was those, as I remember, that first aroused the suspicion (how cautiously we prowl around such an idea when it first materialises) that here was not merely an uncommonly good singer but possibly rather a great one.

Even now, inveterate sniffers and prowlers, our critical selves return to the scent. That frightful word 'hoot' will not entirely go away, and it coalesces with those moments of flattened intonation which became troublesome in late years. But, marvellously and as though to dispel any such doubts, the morning's post brings, from a kind friend, a cassette; and I listen to a *Così fan tutte* from Munich and an *Otello* from Paris, both 1978. This is not *'rather* a great singer': it *is* one. The triumph of that 'Come scoglio' ... and the very first phrase of Desdemona, 'Mio superbo guerrier': that is the voice of a woman who herself, when put to the test, will be dauntless of spirit. From this phrase to the sustained rise of the octave at the end of her prayer, all has not just the beauty of great singing, but a greatness of affirmation.

Singers take their retirement in different ways, and we are told of some who do not want to hear a note of singing, their own or anybody else's, ever again. Let us hope that in Margaret Price's Pembrokeshire retreat the tape of that *Otello* will sometimes be given a hearing. If any reassurance is needed, it will confirm, for its Desdemona's satisfaction, that she was indeed a truly great singer, her art warmly appreciated, and she herself deeply loved.

197

CHAPTER 40

Eleanor Steber

On the whole, Europe, including Britain, missed out on the Steber generation.

In wartime the *names* of these new American singers crossed the Atlantic, but not their records. After the war we were preoccupied with what was coming from Vienna and to a lesser extent Milan. Snobbism and nostalgia entered into it too. This was Metroland, meaning in this instance the Metropolitan Opera House, its history and traditions. The home of the great names was losing them: one by one they slipped out of view and were replaced by the native unknowns. It was not a pretty picture – our prejudice and conservatism, that is. Irving Kolodin, in his History of the Met, might assure us that the *Simon Boccanegra* of 1949, with Warren, Varnay, Tucker and Székely was vocally no second-best after Tibbett, Rethberg, Martinelli and Pinza, but we didn't believe him and didn't want to believe him. The Victor record catalogues and other memorabilia from America contained photographs of these new principals; and they looked like film-stars.

Steber was part of this, and early acquaintance with her singing on records confirmed rather than counteracted the predisposition to reject or at any rate to relegate. She was undeniably efficient (in fact she often showed herself to be exceptionally able, but that was as far as we were prepared to go). Her voice was firm, but firmness was also part of its character, and here it registered more as a charmless intransigence. The timbre was bright rather than warm; behind it one sensed a strong personal will but not a personality that induced either a smile or a tear. And there, for an indecently long time, it rested.

The first nudge to sit up and take an interest came with the recording of Berlioz's *Les Nuits d'été*. Made in 1954 with Mitropoulos and the Columbia Symphony Orchestra, this introduced the lovely work not only to the record catalogues but to most listeners the world over. It seems to me that I did not hear it myself for some years, having become familiar with perhaps two or three other versions first; when I did, the quality that most impressed was freshness. Perhaps it was after having reached saturation-point with Régine Crespin's tragically inflected singing that Steber's way with it brought less of the nights, maybe, but more of the

198

summer, and some slightly sticky residue in the Crespin (the momentary downward pulls of intonation being part of it) was wiped clean. The performance was less introverted but not cold or prosaic. The softness that warmed this strong, outgoing voice in the later phrases of 'Le spectre de la rose' was particularly touching, and, as one plays it again now, the opening of 'Sur les lagunes' – 'Ma belle amie est morte' – is almost shocking in the new coloration evoked by the suddenness of death. 'Comme elle était belle' is so generous a giving of the self, and the last reiterations of 'Que mon sort

199

est amer' are fine in their darkness, which is deeper by virtue of the bright soprano tone that greeted us in the opening 'Villanelle'.

The other recordings in which Steber made an impression at this still very interim stage were of works by Samuel Barber, *Knoxville: Summer of 1915* and *Vanessa*. The opera, recorded in 1958 with the splendid original cast, gained for Steber constant admiration, but it was *Knoxville* that went to the heart. That perhaps is in the nature of the piece itself. Its evocative text (all the more potent for its factual porches and buggy, streetcar and quilts) is unashamedly nostalgic, and Barber's opening music plays wistfully on the 'soft' third note of the scale. And Steber's way with it is an antidote: her tone is as clean as her intervals, and she doesn't mess about. But her voice comes back to the mind with the strange emotional force that the 'cold' voice of Melba can have. To think of those phrases, 'Now is the night one blue dew', in Steber's voice is to catch a vocal perfection which so matches the music that it surprises the emotional system and holds it captive.

I suppose the next stage in the recognition of Steber was a putting together of bits-and-pieces. A lot of unpublished or previously unfamiliar recordings began to appear. Some showed her at the very beginning of her career: one, Lia's aria in Debussy's *L'Enfant prodigue*, was a private record made in 1938 and showed not only the youthful freshness of voice but also a mature authority. Her *Auditions of the Air* of 1940 included the *Ernani* aria, and even then she had the technical assurance to sing those rarely observed staccati on the arpeggio down from the high A. Everything here is in place, the triplets, the chromatic scale, the trill. Also one senses the strength of personality: this is a live performance, and she concludes it with a dazzler of a trill and a triumphantly launched high B flat, winning not just applause but cheers.

Steber was of course a personality, as all (all?) the great singers have been, yet this was not quite something that could be appreciated at a distance. Londoners were given the first direct experience when she appeared at the Wigmore Hall for three concerts in 1964. Though unable to attend, I had a vivid first-hand description from Edward Greenfield, whose review in the *Guardian* is quoted in Steber's autobiography: 'if in the last few decades America has produced a grand lady of singing, it is Eleanor Steber who came sailing in, be-sequinned in crimson, a commanding and imperious figure, but tremendously engaging.' The Wigmore is an intimate hall, and generally artists do not come 'sailing in'. Audiences there have high standards, and if the singing had not justified the grand arrival their reaction would have been politely cool. In fact the concerts were said to have been among the year's best, and the infusions of colour and grandeur were welcomed. Mr Greenfield noted that the voice was much bigger than records had led him to expect; 'a marvellous voice: and it projects beautifully on the half-voice, with an individual, sweet tone'. Furthermore, 'in the interpretations there is great command'. It also came

200

Preparing for *La fanciulla del West*

as a surprise to many that her first programme included a Handel cantata, the second songs by Alban Berg, and the third Britten's *Winter Words*.

Yet still the personality was one that had to be lived with, as only Americans could do, for it to be really known; and by that time it was not so much personality as character. There is plenty of that in the autobiography (*Eleanor Steber*: with Marcia Sloat, Ridgewood NJ, 1992). It tells of her private life with its two failed marriages and its problems with drink, food and impulse; also much (and more than most singers' autobiographies do) about the music in her life. But the character that comes across, even here, and at this remove, is moving and infectious as an exponent of human energy. The exceptional feats – singing *Così* in the afternoon and *Otello* the same evening, or agreeing on the Saturday to sing a first Metropolitan *Fanciulla* the following Monday – with her are not so much exceptional as typical. Or when she went on tour – in the States or the then unknown Yugoslavia or the Middle or Far East (for all of these have their

201

chapters) – it is not to sing and rest in between shows, but to meet people, see life, enter into the company-spirit. She learns new music all the time – Marie in *Wozzeck* at a late stage when most would be retreating to their core-repertoire, and at the very end of her career taking on Mrs Grose in *The Turn of the Screw*, Miss Wingrave in *Owen Wingrave* and that half-hour of concentrated nightmare, the woman in *Erwartung*. All is done with a tremendous attitude of 'roll up the sleeves and get in there', which perhaps after all *is* very American and a reason why she struck a chord among her countryfolk not only as a singer but as a person.

That reception they gave her on her unforseen return to the Met for a one-off *Fanciulla del West* – the stage gold-miners greeting her not with 'Hello, Minnie!' but 'Hello, Steber!' and the audience rising to their feet as one on her entry – that speaks volumes.

On that occasion they hailed character and musicianship no doubt, but, more, the singer: those other qualities would not have brought her to that place and that reception otherwise. Steber was, and is, essentially a voice; and the voice probably owed as much to its training as to its natural endowment. At the centre of her story, albeit in the background, stands 'Mr Whitney': William L. Whitney, teacher of singing at the Boston Conservatory, aged 72 when Steber became his pupil: 'a gentleman of the old school' and firm founder of technique. Others helped – Paul Althouse as coach, Dmitri Mitropoulos as musician – but the assurance of production, the no-wobble, no-gear-change, clean-as-a-whistle athleticism of her singing, owes itself to Mr Whitney. And so we are back where we started, with these qualities correctly observed in the first records heard but not properly appreciated.

This has been the story of a progress; and, like the pilgrim's, it ends with an arrival. An American friend sends the *Don Giovanni* of 14 December 1957, on LPs: the Metropolitan, Böhm conducting, Steber as Anna. Mr Whitney, we remember, schooled her in Mozart, and here is the reward. But along with the secure technical mastery the performance has a warmth, to which, not before time, the pilgrim can instantly respond.

And indeed, he can almost stand with the miners, look at the top of that staircase and shout 'Hello, Steber!' too.

CHAPTER 41

Frances Alda

Alda was a fighter, and, while the full menace of its title, *Men, Women and Tenors*, may not have been entirely borne out, her autobiography is still an energetically combative document. At this safe distance of time and place it may even be rather likeable. One warms to the girl from New Zealand (real name Frances Davies) who could cry out 'Damn it to hell' when playing golf with the King of England. Her stock rises further when Oscar Hammerstein's new company is faced with the telegraphic ultimatum 'Either Alda or me', signed 'Melba'. She had new loos installed backstage at the old Met, cleared up the whole area and even furnished the dressing-rooms with water on tap. That she could do this was a result of her marrying the Director, which might look like another smart move but in fact brought her a great deal of trouble, for she was the inevitable object of jealousy and subject of innuendo. Her stories may not reach us from the most impartial of sources, but if there is any truth in the tale of her first appearance in *Faust* at the Metropolitan, where she found that another of the company's Marguerites had caused the spinning-wheel to be immobilised for the occasion, one would willingly place at her disposal the retributive powers of a Medea.

She could no doubt be an infuriating woman. Rosa Ponselle recalled how, if given half a chance, she would take imperious charge of rehearsals; one result was that, when practically all retired members of the company (or as Alda herself put it, all 'who could limp or hobble in at the stage entrance and still sing a note') were recruited for a 'Save the Metropolitan' Gala, she was not asked. Her book, and indeed the many stories told of her outside it, suggest a woman who lived life to the full and upset a few apple-carts in the process. Hell hath no fury like a prima donna scorned, but there must always be vacancies in the heavenly choir for voices like hers. I once heard her name mentioned most unexpectedly at a dinner-party in Tuscany. A florid American had known her well and produced his *bon mot*: 'Her singing was divine, but she was a bitch.' I remember thinking that a great number of people who had encountered her in public and private life must have thought much the same.

But 'Her singing was divine'. Most of the critics seemed not to think so. Her debut at the Metropolitan was hardly auspicious. The role of Gilda in

Alda as Manon

Rigoletto may not have been tailor-made to suit, but she had sung the part successfully in Europe and it generally suits the audience: they like the music and the character. In the performance on 7 December 1908, Alda had the support of Caruso and Pasquale Amato, and though the conductor was not Toscanini, with whom she had worked previously and whom she felt to be sympathetic, it was the experienced composer-conductor, Francesco Spetrino, who was entrusted with no less than 80 of the season's performances. The new soprano was acknowledged as one capable of doing 'useful work' with the company, but that hardly constituted a triumph. Credit-marks in agility and power were offset by minuses in vibrato and intonation. Especially dismissive was W.J. Henderson of the *New York Sun*, not that his words, influential though they were, meant that Alda was likely to be dismissed. As Mrs Gatti-Casazza she was there to stay. After a *Manon* with Caruso, Henderson derided her vocal registers (he counted 'at least five'), and for many years gave her no peace. By 1913 he conceded that Desdemona was 'one of her best roles' and added in almost conciliatory mode that if 'her tones are unsteady' it was probably due to 'bad training in early studies'. So much for the achievements of Madame Marchesi, who having auditioned Alda in her Paris studio reputedly announced that she had discovered another Melba.

Quite possibly the New York critics were objective and accurate, but the keen edge of their hostility suggests the presence of a personal factor. The community of feeling that unites present-day critics in the face of a perceived 'hype' may well have been at work here. Their severities diminished over the years, and even Henderson became sufficiently well-disposed to grant that in Walter Damrosch's *Cyrano de Bergerac*, sung in English, Alda's words were the clearest; but then, Henderson had himself written them. To that extent he had a personal involvement in the production, and a softening of the usual asperities is noticeable when, at the second performance, he wrote that Alda had 'one of her clearest successes'. He also found a little niche for her where congratulations were in order. After the premiere of Victor Herbert's opera in 1914, he wrote that Alda 'who seems to be the high priestess of opera in English at the Met represented Madeleine with genuine art'.

Records tell more than this. She seems to have been a 'natural' for the studios, recording often and usually with good results on the first 'take', rarely producing anything, even in undistinguished music, which does not have a touch of distinction about it. Her first record was made after Caruso had visited her in search, as he explained, of a soprano with whom to record the Miserere scene in *Il trovatore* (he had tried it with Johanna Gadski and been dissatisfied). This was not an opera in Alda's repertory, but that is a fact one would never guess any more than that this was her first experience of making records. Listening with the specific complaints of the New York critics in mind, one finds very little that corresponds. Intonation is reliable, the vocal registers are well integrated (and not too

Alda as hostess with guests (left to right): De Luca, Martinelli, Jeritza, Toscanini

numerous), and the only vibrato is of the even, close-knit variety that does so much to enrich a voice's character and colour. The training which Henderson thought deficient vindicates itself in another impressive feature of her singing, the cleanness of its upward intervals and particularly of the optional top C. Remarkably, she appeals to the mind's eye as a true Leonora, tense with foreboding in this night-and-fear-ridden opera, responsive to the taut rhythms and plaintive accentuations. Two recordings were made (the second one, with chorus, a week later) their consistency indicating a reliable artist rather than a lucky rush of adrenalin.

Her first solo recording was of the Willow Song and 'Ave Maria' from *Otello*. Here, the vibrantly dramatic voice of the 'Miserere' changes character: nothing of the prima donna now remains, but, instead, the warmth of an anxious and affectionate heart finds expression in pure, maidenly tones with a finely judged interplay of clean, precise movement from note to note, as on a keyboard, and a violinist's curve or *portamento*. If it is hard to reconcile a singer who showed such command of her art in the recording studio with one who deserved the kind of review meted out after her performances in the house, then it is doubly difficult to do so when a single day's recording in 1912 produced no less than nine published solos, varied in scope but constant in the excellent quality of their performance. Among them was what probably remains her masterpiece, the aria from Catalani's *Loreley*, an opera she was eventually to sing at its Metropolitan premiere ten years later.

Alda's career at the Met did indeed prove durable, as Henderson rather cynically predicted it would. In fact there is little to suggest that her marriage brought managerial favours: more often than not, she waited for an opportunity while rivals (notably Geraldine Farrar) continued to prosper in coveted roles which she could well have sung. She retired in 1929, having appeared in every season since 1908/09. Though the Metropolitan formed the centre of her career, it was reached only after some busy years in Europe, moving from Paris (with a debut at the Opéra-Comique) to Brussels, Covent Garden, La Scala (she was their first Louise), the Opera at Warsaw and elsewhere. In the 1920s she sang in Buenos Aires with colleagues such as Gigli, Ruffo and Chaliapin. She also travelled extensively in the States, in both opera and concert work. In her memoirs she expresses disapproval of recital programmes which include operatic excerpts – an opinion she must have formed after 1907, when at concerts in London's Wigmore Hall she sang 'Divinités du Styx' from Gluck's *Alceste*, the *Loreley* aria and Violetta's solo (both sections) from Act 1 of *La traviata*.

'Her singing was divine': I can hear that sentence now, the last syllable prolonged like a limp handshake. Also the 'bitch', wryly realistic in its emphasis rather than deliberately venomous. This man had known Frances Alda well and later took me to see, there on the wall of his living-room, the original testimonial presented on her retirement and signed by all those eminent colleagues, many of whom heartily detested her. He also told of a wonderful party at her house and of photographs he had taken of Toscanini playing accompaniments while Martinelli and De Luca sang, with Jeritza and the hostess herself looking on, all with smiles of blissful content in the pleasure of what we used to call 'a musical evening round the piano'. That is how I now like to think of the woman. As for the singer: perhaps greatness did elude her, on records as on stage, and yet her voice still haunts the mind. It does so, for instance, in the music of Mimì – and how curious that this large, extravert character, as Alda appears to have been in life, should on stage have found such affinity with the shy, tender girl whom she sang more often than any other role. Or we perhaps hear it in that inspired trio from *I lombardi* with Caruso and Marcel Journet, singing like souls possessed, with Alda so sensitively, and almost physically, feeling out to trace with her voice the growth and retraction of her phrases. Rather as with Maggie Teyte (Ch. 29) and perhaps Melba too, the art and the personality seem so disparate and yet must have been interdependent. Strange harmony of contrasts.

CHAPTER 42

Frieda Hempel

The whole critical process is a sifting, where by due discrimination excellence can be appreciated: it rewards the great and the truly distinguished artist, and its motivation is love of the art. Yet I sometimes wonder whether the artist concerned could possibly guess this to be so, singers especially:

> *You give us song, and we bring you prose: you cast forth notes as a garment for the naked of the earth, and we fashion a report.*
> *You sing true, and we say 'Tush, and so she should': you err, and though it be ever so little we say 'Aha, aha, she singeth not according to the law and the prophets.'*
> *You live by that which is within you, and we say 'Lo, she stumbleth': you utter words unto the scribes of the gutter, and 'Behold,' we say, 'she hath the voice of a nightingale and the brain of a sparrow.'*

The publication of Frieda Hempel's *My Golden Age of Singing* (Amadeus, 1998), is a genuine manifesto of love, or of devotion at least; yet in the reader it inevitably induces thoughts that cannot quite simply accept the gift of song and the fact of a life. Over the years, a deadly word has gained substance in my mind in association with this singer, and this latest publication does not banish it but merely shifts it somewhat to the side of the central figure.

Let us recall who she was. Born in 1885, she had become a star in Berlin by the age of 20. She sang the coveted coloratura roles, Lucia, Gilda, Violetta, Daughter of the Regiment and Queen of the Night. The Kaiser made a fuss of her, greeting her from his carriage ('Guten Morgen, Fräulein Hempel, wie geht's?') as she drove to rehearsal in hers. She sang at Bayreuth and in London, where everybody adored her except Melba and Sir Thomas Beecham who considered that she asked too much for a night's performance pointing out that she was merely engaged to sing. The years of fresh-voiced youth and beauty continued, and in 1912 came the call to New York. A terrible sea-crossing took some of the bloom from her cheeks, and the voice was not in best condition when she made her Metropolitan debut; but gradually the house, public and critics, began to see what they had in her and to realise that it was a richer compound than the airy

Hempel as Violetta in *La traviata*

coloratura of reputation. Before 9 December 1919, she had appeared at the Met as the Queen in *Les Huguenots*, Rosina, Queen of the Night, Olympia in *Les Contes d'Hoffmann*, Violetta, Gilda and Lucia, but on that date she presented New Yorkers with their first Marschallin in *Der Rosenkavalier*. She had sung the role in the Berlin premiere also, having first been

209

Strauss's choice for Octavian, then for Sophie and finally, when he found himself short of a singer to impersonate that great lady, the Marschallin – or Princess – herself. This revealed a new Hempel, or, rather, it confirmed a notion that some had formed about her already – that she was at least as good a lyric soprano as she was a coloratura, and that it was in this repertoire that her future might more profitably lie. She found other congenial lyric roles, in Weber's Euryanthe, Wagner's Eva and Bizet's Leila, but with the outbreak of war, and then more especially when America entered the fray, German artists had to keep their heads down. Hempel married an American and kissed the French flag at the end of *La Fille du Régiment*, but that only alienated her own compatriots when they heard of it, and altogether life was not easy. She gave her last performances with the Metropolitan late in 1919 and after a few appearances with the Chicago Company, renounced opera altogether. An energetic career in the concert hall followed, lasting over two decades, and it may well be that in the earlier years of this period she was to be heard at her most accomplished and fulfilled.

Yet it is also about this time that the dreaded and as yet undeclared word begins to hover. In 1920 she was approached by the President of the Swedish Society with a request that she would sing in an important forthcoming concert to honour the centenary of Jenny Lind. Imagination took flight: the concert (to be followed by a tour) would be given in period costume, with flautists and pianist dressed up too, and an actor would represent the legendary manager P.T. Barnum. The concert at Carnegie Hall on 6 October reproduced a programme of 1850 and met with a huge success. It was a show that ran, in the States and in Britain when she brought it to London. There the critics were duly appreciative but with that kind of politely indulgent smile that should be a word to the wise. They welcomed her as Jenny Lind but hoped she would return as Frieda Hempel.

Gerald Moore, who was the accompanist for one of the later Jenny Lind concerts, adds a note which is out of key with the melodious prettifications but may chime in with some of our own feelings. He declined to wear the pianist's togs. The prospect of climbing into garments that had been passed from one player to another did not appeal ('Besides,' he added, 'I look bad enough already'). In fact, the whole business must have seemed to him rather ... now, what would the word be? And then there was the matter of 'Ich hab in Penna', Wolf's song about the girl who has boyfriends in a number of Italian towns, including ten in Castiglione. Hempel would feature it as an end-of-programme item but shorn of its postlude, which, she said, made a better ending for her. That postlude is the devil of a challenge to the pianist, and Moore put it to her that even accompanists have their professional pride, so on this occasion the postlude (which also happens to be part of the song) was restored.

The last of the Jenny Lind concerts was scheduled for 1932 and though

normal recitals continued, they became ever more intermittent. By 1940, reviews were largely exercises in euphemism, and gradually Hempel faded from public view. Her name returned to the headlines in an unexpected connection in 1942, when the *New York Times* of 7 February announced: 'Singer and Police in Row over Dog. Frieda Hempel seized in Park as she leaves Meat for a Mongrel she Fed Five Years'. Then, more ambiguously 'Eats it to Prove Story'. The dog was called Brownie and is possibly the most vivid character in her autobiography. Or autobiographies. Just before she died, in 1955, the singer was able to see and hold the dust jacket of *Mein Leben dem Gesang*, the story of her life dictated in English to her friend Elizabeth Johnston and translated for publication in Germany. The strange – indeed, rather weird – thing is that there already existed an autobiography, in English, which Hempel had completed with a previous secretary and of which Johnston was told nothing: she found it by accident when clearing up the New York apartment for a tenant during Hempel's illness. It was then put aside for safe-keeping and retrieved in 1990 when news of its existence aroused interest, leading to its present publication. The German version is obviously related to it by more than subject-matter, but the English is fuller, more detailed and with relatively more in it on matters which, if not exactly musical, do relate to music. Elizabeth Johnston adds a prologue and an epilogue, and William Moran supplies annotations, a valuable independent 'chronology' and a discography.

Such a book inevitably brings one closer, in personal terms, to its subject. In particular, Johnston's devotion to Hempel during her last years and in memory since her death, is a moving testimonial to a lovable woman. The brutal, unchivalrous word, which even now I hesitate to write, is as it were deflected. Yet if 'silly' is not a word for Hempel herself, it surely is for much of the world around her: a vacuous world, where platitude passes for intelligent commentary and interest quickens only with society-chat, dresses and pets. What also sticks, in Hempel's narrative, as in that of so many celebrated singers, is the absence of any real evidence of an interest in music. Perhaps she did not want to 'talk shop'; on the other hand, there is plenty of gossip concerning the musical world but not really about music itself. What a difference it would make if one were to come upon sentences (I'm now making them up) such as these: 'That morning I discovered Mozart's "Vorrei spiegarvi", a heavenly piece, perfectly suited to my voice, and I decided to explore further' or 'For many years I had sung the same few songs of Schumann and now I began work on the great cycles, particularly *Frauenliebe und Leben*' or 'My accompanist brought along a book of Elizabethan song-writers, including John Dowland, and I realised what a wealth of beautiful music is to be found here'. There is of course no sentence of this kind to be found from start to finish. Hempel was commonly thought of, especially in America, as a particularly musical singer. In her books she pauses twice to discuss points concerning an opera – but even then her subject is the character and not the music. In a thoughtful, musically-centred person's life-story, sentences such as those invented ones would introduce a paragraph; as it is, even a single sentence of that kind would be as welcome as water in the desert.

So, grateful for the contact, the information and the photographs, yet with a hollow where we would have wished for substance, we go back from the book to the records: there to find one of the loveliest of voices, employed with dazzling technical skill, mastery of production, and a genuinely fine and imaginative musical sensibility. She recorded the song from Handel's *Joshua*, 'O had I Jubal's lyre' with the runs beautifully fluent yet clearly articulated. Her 'Voi che sapete' is a thing of light-and-shade, alive with the fresh impulse of the adolescent song-maker. In the Queen of Night's first aria her voice and style testify to her kinship with the daughter who will also soon be expressing her sorrow in G minor; to the second she adds, in staccato, a couple more sparklers to the display. As Rosina in *Il barbiere di Siviglia* she sings the famous aria with touches of dreamy magic.

You bring us prose, and we hear your song: you fashion a report, and we hearken to your voice.
   Not when it tells of praises and of pets: but when it sings of Jubal's lyre and Cherubino's love, of vengeance shot in alt by Night's high Queen, and Seville's rose transformed into a nightingale.

212

CHAPTER 43

Pol Plançon

Even Plançon ... had some faults
W.J. Henderson

Even Plançon. W.J. Henderson, no stranger to these pages, was writing on 3 August 1921 to mark the death of Enrico Caruso. He was music critic for the *New York Sun*, and his writings date back to the early 1880s. When Caruso made his debut at the Metropolitan, Henderson had already the experience of two decades of opera-going, having lived through what to so many of his generation was the golden age of singing, when the principal tenor was Jean de Reszke. Of that 'golden age', the bass Pol Plançon was the most steadfast of leading lights. He remained with the company till 1908, and his continuing memory shed its glow over the rest of the Caruso era. At any rate, when Henderson, even on this solemn occasion, could not refrain from striking a proper critical balance, reminding his readers that 'Mr Caruso's art was far from faultless', it was Plançon whose name came to mind as having been the nearest to perfection in his long experience. 'There never has been a faultless singer,' he wrote. 'Even Plançon, one of the greatest masters of vocal technique that ever trod the stage, had some faults.'

What those faults were he does not say, and, as far as his singing is concerned, it is very unusual to find any hint of criticism from contemporary writers whether in New York or London. So (the present age may ask) who was this paragon, and wherein lay his mastery?

He was Paul Henri Plançon, 'Pol' being presumably a familiar version of 'Paul' rather than (as sometimes suggested) a contraction of Polydor. The year of his birth is now accepted as 1851, though earlier reference books give 1854. From his birthplace, Fumay in the Ardennes, he went to Paris for training with Gilbert Duprez, 'creator' of numerous tenor roles in Donizetti and famous exponent of the high C from the chest, which apparently changed the whole direction of tenor-singing in the mid-nineteenth century. According to Henry Chorley, Duprez's voice was 'half gone' before the age of 40, though he could still turn in a magnificent performance through sheer passion and musicianship. He ran his own school in Paris, wrote a treatise on the art of singing and lived to a grand old age. Perhaps as a teacher he profited from his own excesses, in the midst of which he was still noted for smoothness as well as declamatory force. Still, his is not quite the line or vocal tradition in which one would expect a singer of Plançon's elegance to have been reared. His later teacher was Giovanni Sbriglia, also a former tenor, whose pupils included the De Reszke brothers. Whoever was responsible for what, Plançon was a credit to his teachers: there has probably never been a singer more unanimously praised as being 'well-schooled'.

As was usual practice, the young bass went out first into the provinces to gain experience, making his debut at Lyons in 1877. This was as St Bris in *Les Huguenots*, an opera that remained closely associated with him throughout his career. His Paris debut followed in 1880 at the Gaieté, graduating to the Opéra, after a season at Monte Carlo, in 1883. Here he sang as principal bass for the next ten years, during which he took part in several premieres including those of *Le Cid* and Saint-Saëns's *Ascanio*. His international career dates from 1891 with the first of his fourteen consecutive seasons at Covent Garden. The Metropolitan followed in 1893, bringing him eventually a total of over six hundred performances with the company and a position among the seven most highly paid singers.

In London all aspects of his art commanded admiration. 'A magnificent performance' was the *Musical Times*'s phrase for his Mephistopheles in 1892. As Jupiter in Gounod's *Philémon et Baucis* he 'sang superbly and his fine presence was most imposing'. The previous year his Rocco in *Fidelio* displayed 'rare excellence of method, fidelity to the text and beauty of voice'. In 1896, 'M. Plançon's splendid voice and dignified bearing' distinguished his Pogner in *Die Meistersinger*, and they could conceive of no way in which his Ramfis in *Aida* could be improved upon. His single failure appears to have been in Boito's *Mefistofele* (1895) when *The Times* reported that Plançon was 'scarcely as well suited ... as to the more suave demon of Gounod's opera, and he was hardly convincing in the part, though the superb richness of his voice told as well as ever'. Although he was said to have had at no time more than a few words of spoken English at his command, he nevertheless sang in that language for the premieres of Stanford's *Much Ado about Nothing* and Isidore de Lara's *The Light of Asia*.

In that opera, according to George Bernard Shaw, he saved the first scene. Shaw is always a joy to read on opera in the Golden Age (this particular venture, he said, was stifled in production 'with goodwill and hundreds of pounds worth of silks and precious-looking metals, when it was perishing for want of two penn'orth of skill and fancy'). Legend passes down the phrase 'Nights of the Seven Stars' apropos *Les Huguenots* in those years, but Shaw took his score with him (or had it in his head) and was less enchanted. 'Nobody who does not know the score,' he wrote in 1894, 'can have any idea of the mutilated state of the work as performed at Covent Garden, or how completely obsolete is the phase of public taste

214

Plançon as St Bris in *Les Huguenots*

215

which influenced the mutilators in their choice of cuts.' Of the conductor, Enrico Bevignani, he writes: 'I admire the obligingness and adroitness with which he accompanies the principal singers through all their extremely *ad libitum* readings, and the determination and briskness with which he thwacks the choruses along so as to get the opera over early and leave plenty of time for very long waits between the acts.' Of the singers, 'Plançon carried off the honours'. This was in the role of Marcel, which Shaw found a relief, since 'he happens to have that first important requisite for the part, a true bass voice'. This was in contrast to 'the attempts of Edouard de Reszke to squeeze it into the compass of a somewhat limited *basso cantante*'.

A few sharply focused observations of this kind tell us more about the 'Golden Age' than do all those incantatory lists of great names supposed of their own accord to inspire faith. But of course with a singer such as Plançon the essential documents are the recordings. However primitive, they are of sufficiently good quality to have drawn the comment 'Oh, but he might be in the room!' from one of his most eminent former colleagues. Emma Eames, a soprano who shared many performances with the great bass, was then a severe old lady and no lover of the gramophone; but in the 1930s she paid a visit to the critic Desmond Shawe-Taylor who played for her some good original copies on good equipment. Her spontaneous reaction is one of the best testimonials those old records have.

Let us listen with a few comparisons at hand: nothing too exhaustive but enough to get the measure. The first record he made for the American Victor company in 1903 was the Count's aria from *La sonnambula*, 'Vi ravviso, o luoghi ameni'. It is sung to piano accompaniment and without chorus, but has the phrases of introduction, 'Il mulino ... il fonte ... il bosco!' The nobleman has returned for the first time to the village of his childhood, and he looks around at the once-familiar scene. Rather marvellously, Plançon lives it: the tempo of the exclamations, the affectionate recognition seeping deeper into the voice with each, shows immediately that for him at least this *bel canto* business is essentially an expressive, dramatic art. Then, with the opening of the aria, what takes us is the sense of a great instrumentalist. Each of these phrases is not merely so evenly 'bowed' but is also shaped by judicious growth and retraction (not fussing, but always within the overall concept of the phrase), *portamento* and *rubato*. With the minor modulation the pace is slightly quickened, a *rallentando* compensating as the first melody returns. At several points we are aware of the virtuoso, but only in passing, and his cadenza is taken as by a master-cellist, first *legato* and lithe, then with accentuations, settling to the final note with a beautifully sustained and gracious *diminuendo*.

Going then to the admirable Nicola Zaccaria in the Callas recording of the opera in 1957, we welcome the warm Italianate voice (Plançon's less vibrant timbre might not quite satisfy Italians), but then note that nothing really happens. He sings smoothly, and the materials are there for a performance as finely developed as Plançon's, but nothing *is* developed. Those light shadings and delicate fluctuations of tempo have gone, and so has the reality of the Count's nostalgic encounter. With the sonorously named Francisco Ellero d'Artegna in a concert performance of 1990 the treatment is similar, but the effect duller still, as the voice has less colour and its management less assurance. But to come then to the richly endowed Samuel Ramey (1986 recital) is to experience still more of a non-event. Here the tone is surprisingly loose in texture, and the handling of the melody if anything still more unimaginative, for if there is any definable expression it is of an ill-judged severity. The sense of a precious, affectionately lyrical encounter is lost entirely. Back to Plançon, and the imagination glows: he is not only much the best singer in all these comparisons but infinitely the most expressive artist.

217

CHAPTER 44

Samuel Ramey

Do what you will, this world's a fiction,
And is made up of contradiction.
                                    William Blake

So the reader may think on finding that the man about to be hailed as nearest successor to the legendary Plançon is the very one who at the end of the previous chapter was compared to him in the least favourable terms. The limitations shown up by his recording of the aria from *La sonnambula* are real enough; nevertheless it is Samuel Ramey who has shown most impressively the technical capabilities of the bass voice in the later years of this century as Plançon did in the earliest. He even recorded Plançon's old favourite, the song of the Drum Major in Thomas's comic opera *Le Caïd*, with the bravura scales all in place and a cadenza to match the master's. He also did what the Master did not – sang lots of Handel and Rossini, the kind of virtuoso music that was neglected for generations, partly on the plea that modern singers could not be expected to cope.

In the year of writing, Ramey (born in 1942) will be approaching his sixtieth year. Records have begun to show signs of age in the fabric of the voice, in quieter passages if not at a *forte*, though he is reported to be still giving full value in performances at the Met and elsewhere. His prime was probably in the middle and late 1980s, when at Covent Garden he sang and acted so well as to imprint those years with his name and memory. Old opera-goers, looking back, will identify them as 'the Ramey years'. He sang first at the Royal Opera House in 1982 as Mozart's Figaro: 'an ideal voice for it, dark and incisive but still lightweight enough to keep fast music flowing easily' wrote William Mann in *Opera* magazine. The following year Harold Rosenthal found his Don Giovanni likely 'in a year or two' to become one of the great interpretations, and 'his beautifully schooled *basso cantante* is always a joy to hear'. The Gounod Méphistophélès, Don Basilio, and the various Evil Influences in *Les Contes d'Hoffmann* made a still stronger impression, and a concert performance of *Semiramide* revealed more clearly than anything else had done the exceptional quality of his technique. Here among operatic basses was at last the true virtuoso. In this *Semiramide* the runs were articulated clearly and without cheat-

Ramey as Don Giovanni

ing. He used no aspirates or any of those less blatant 'separating' devices whereby the even flow of sound is broken by *martellato* emphasis or semi-staccato or a light easing by the breath. These were genuine and comparable to the passage-work in the old records of Pol Plançon; they were sung with the straightforward honesty of Peter Dawson practising the method taught him by his master, Charles Santley.

Most fundamental to the art of singing, however, is what may (erroneously) seem to be the simpler skill of *legato*, the binding of notes to sound with the evenness of a stringed instrument. The *Sonnambula* aria, used

219

for comparison with Plançon, might suggest that Ramey would be deficient in this, but that would be a wrong conclusion, as Plançon's superiority here lies in the shading and shaping of his *legato* phrases. In fact most comparisons with other basses will favour Ramey in this respect. In the prayer from *Nabucco*, for instance, you don't catch Ramey breaking the line as the imposing Nazzareno de Angelis did in his famous recording of 1928, and in Attila's dream he preserves an Italianate flow better than does Ruggero Raimondi, his nearest Italian counterpart. Assur's 'Deh, ti ferma' in *Semiramide* was also memorable for what certainly appeared to be a faultless *legato*, the wide range (low G to high F) manipulated flexibly with unobstructed evenness. Here too was singing in the noble traditions of the art.

Yet the tradition does require more. At Covent Garden, for example, Ramey's singing of the Mirror song in *Les Contes d'Hoffmann* was among the chief pleasures of the evening, and the fine tone and well-sustained *legato* were by no means its only assets; for instance, he led back into the 'Scintille, diamant' melody with a gracefully-spun link and in a later phrase moved, note by note, to the high octave with ably supported *piano* tone. Yet he did not quite woo the melody (or, through it, the mirror which is to capture Hoffmann's soul for him). There was nothing of the light caressing touch of imagination; and this is what he lacks. It was so in the *Sonnambula* aria: an apparent inability to get through to the *poetry* of song.

In song itself, and in recital especially, the lack of intimacy and charm was felt more acutely. At best in 'character' songs such as Charles Ives' 'Circus Band' and 'Charlie Rutlage' (where his *parlando* effects recalled Lawrence Tibbett), he could also sometimes catch the warmer, softer emotions of songs such as 'In the Alley'. Perhaps language was a liberating force here, for at the same concert in which these were highlights, his singing of Schubert's 'Der Doppelgänger' conveyed no pain or thrill of horror, and the prayer, or 'Chanson épique', in Ravel's Don Quichotte songs carried little sense of its being addressed, let alone any hint of an affectionate smile in the voice. Even in his recording of Copland's *Old American Songs*, which are thoroughly homeground, the sound remains fixedly unsmiling in 'The Boatman's Dance', and in 'Simple Gifts' something formal, almost severe, replaces the easy charm one would have hoped for.

In opera, the wide variety of his repertoire contrasts with the narrow range of vocal expression. Records show this inescapably, where in stage performances effective acting would at least partly compensate. In 1989, for example, a recital disc appeared with arias from ten different operas, Italian and French. In the opening number, 'Infelice' from *Ernani*, you look for a softening of the emotions, for a heart. In the tutor's solo from *Le Conte Ory*, which follows, you hope for a tang of ironic humour. Fiesco's 'Il lacerato spirito' in *Simon Boccanegra* wants sadness, Nabucco's vision of

skulls, hyenas and snakes wants some imaginative relish, Procida's greeting to his native Palermo wants affection, and with the 'sérénade moqueuse' of Berlioz's Méphistophélès we want ... mockery. Yet a single expression predominates in all of these: that of stern authority. The immobility of vocal characterisation is striking.

On stage, his tall, athletic figure, his strong features, with those dark eyebrows and the teeth that can glint with satanic glee or seductive charm, all effectively supplement the voice; and indeed no written criticism comes to mind or hand that complains of sameness or ineffectiveness in his acting. It is sometimes said that he is not so good in comedy, yet his Don Basilio in *Il barbiere di Siviglia* still raises a smile in the recollection of that hat and umbrella and some funny half-remembered play of spidery fingers. There was a way too in which voice and figure matched. His Nick Shadow in *The Rake's Progress* at Glyndebourne seemed 'all one', compact and saturnine, voice and figure together. A video of Boito's *Mefistofele* from the San Francisco Opera House in 1989 shows him unequivocally and firmly the charismatic centre of the production.

His achievements have been remarkably comprehensive. In an interview with Martin Meyer published in *Opera* (April 1986) he says of himself – and Meyer adds that it was 'not a boast, just a fact' – that 'there's not another bass capable of the wide variety of repertoire I sing'. By that time he had added Bartok's Bluebeard (in Hungarian) but not yet Boris Godunov, which he was to sing (in Russian, it almost goes without saying nowadays) at the Met in 1997. For the alleged 'fact', I fancy it might not go entirely unchallenged by the basses' union (Robert Lloyd, for instance, could make a pretty fair bid). But ultimately that is not what is going to matter. The great thing is the specific contribution, and that brings us back to Handel and Rossini.

For specimens of his Handel, take the first aria in *Ariodante* or Argante's 'Sibilar gli angui d'Aletto' from *Rinaldo*. Both are kingly – sung by a king and sounding like one. This is the voice of authority, but what validates it in operatic terms is the mastery of technique. These runs are marvellously precise and even. The first has a two-octave range (F to F), the second needs to be thrown off in a vaunting manner (he's King of Jerusalem and arrives in his chariot). All is accomplished with the assured skill of one who has learnt the hard way, taking no short cuts. Similarly with Rossini. The entrance aria in *Maometto Secondo* will serve for an example here – fine *legato*, fluent cadenza, brilliantly smooth and rapid runs in the cabaletta – but his whole performance in the recording of this opera can stand as a crowning achievement. The old French master himself never had the opportunity of singing in this repertoire. He would no doubt have brought to it his own imagination and individuality (in which there was a spicy element of high camp). But in sonorous authority and well-schooled technique, even Pol Plançon might have found that Sam Ramey would give him a run for his money.

CHAPTER 45

Thomas Hampson

The role of the 'classical' singer in modern times (and it is a sign of modern times that we should have to specify 'classical') is perhaps debatable, but most will agree that Thomas Hampson is the man to fill it. Gifted with strikingly good looks that do not conform to the model of an old-fashioned film-star, he has a stage-presence that makes him a popular favourite. He could so easily have been a pop 'singer' (the inverted commas now transferred). As an American he would have found the style come naturally to him, and then, when he died, the professional description as singer could have gone unqualified.

That such a man should choose to become a 'classical' singer – or since we are among friends let us say a real singer – is a matter for rejoicing in itself. But Hampson is a trophy. He is also an artist, like any other, and his place in this gallery is secured by the merit of his art; in a peculiarly modern context, however, he carries particular weight. He is one who demonstrates the value of the 'classical' tradition by his allegiance. Almost by inference, the forces that so potently and persistently degrade the vocal art – designating as 'singers' people who produce sounds as though from a throat full of gravel, or otherwise abuse an immature voice, or rap out words without musical pitch – can recognise something in Hampson's gift which would be wasted in their line of business. His kind of manly baritone did have a place in popular culture as represented, say, in films of the 1930s or the musicals of a decade later; but these are now dated in a way that the nineteenth century repertoire no longer is. People of whatever age can in fact see that a voice like Hampson's deserves music like Verdi's. In other words, popular culture still has somewhere in reserve – a disused room that is spared from incorporation in the universal disco – a notion that perhaps better does exist. Such a voice is still, if not in so many words, acknowledged as 'better': and perhaps it would not be forcing inference too far to hope that such a notion (however unformulated and unadmitted) that 'better' exists in respect of voice might be extended to the music that is perceived to suit it, and even to the culture of which that music is part.

Hampson, moreover, is a man of the modern age. However thoroughly schooled in traditional methods, and however deeply imbued with the culture of past centuries, he sings as one whose stimulus and responses belong to his own time. For instance: switching on a radio broadcast from the Met and coming in in mid-*Traviata* where the as-yet unidentified baritone sings 'No, generosa, vivere, e lieta voi dovrete', one feels immediately the modern touch. It is partly that the focus of attention is not upon the opulent tone which these phrases so warmly invite and which this noble voice is so richly providing, but that a *protest*, a spirited contradiction, is being voiced. Violetta, with implacable realism, has foreseen her future: 'Morrò' ('I shall die'). Germont sings 'No you won't', and with Hampson he means it. The sequence has its musical logic, Germont's phrases following the pattern of Violetta's, so that, musically, they seem to go along with her though in fact they are opposing, or more accurately are intended to fortify her through their opposition to her pessimism. Hampson opposes: his 'No' is strong, his 'vivere' carries conviction. Later comes the 'Di Provenza', and again his style has the conviction of someone *not* with a song to sing but with a message urgently to be communicated. Such an approach to the famous aria brings inevitable loss: this is not the way Giuseppe De Luca sang it. De Luca's voice was so even and well-rounded that one felt the appeal of father to son lay essentially in that tone – the ideal beauty of singing establishing, or embodying, the stability of home, family life and the natural blessings of Provence. But Hampson's intensity of emphasis corresponds more closely to Verdi's markings, and it answers to the needs of the dramatic situation. Enough in his singing testifies to the capacity for a beautifully-voiced, smoothly-produced performance in the *bel canto* tradition; the modernity – a fusion of intelligence and independence – lies not in any rejection of this, but in its extension to accommodate dramatic truth.

He has not always seemed so strongly and individually expressive a singer. In Lieder, and especially the great song-cycles, he has not, in my experience, been among those who bring a new light or who intensify existing feelings. His recording of *Winterreise* with Wolfgang Sawallisch, for example, has remained in my memory for not being memorable. Listening to it again, I find indeed much to enjoy, but principally because of the great pleasure of hearing *Winterreise* sung by a voice of such beauty and with this evenness of production. His performance is not inexpressive, and sometimes will come a song ('Auf dem Flusse' is an example) where real pain is caught. But it's intermittent: the man with bitter yearnings at heart and a terrible progressive weariness of spirit and body slips in and out of view, his place taken by the singer *telling* of him but not *being* him.

Winterreise is of course the summit, and so perhaps cannot be accepted as fairly representative; and yet I think it is, for take (for instance) *An die ferne Geliebte* or *Dichterliebe* and one finds the feelings generated by Hampson's recordings to be very similar. In the Beethoven cycle, the opening song brings little sense of the implicit pain of absence, and thereafter there is little of the tension that should eventually become overt in the Florestan-like feverishness of excitement in the last song. In the

Hampson as Rodrigo in *Don Carlos*

Schumann, a tenderly flowing melody such as that of 'Am leuchtenden Sommermorgen' will be caressed and most beautifully sung, but we don't hear in those healthy tones the 'trauriger, blasser Mann' (sad, pale-faced) observed by the whispering flowers.

Perhaps the exceptional beauty of the voice is itself a liability in these songs: with Fischer-Dieskau, Peter Schreier or Ian Bostridge the tone sours or bites or drains more readily. Hampson's kind of beauty is also less amenable to the characterisation implied in these sad, pale-faced men with their loneliness and hurt resentment. I find too that, while I can call the voices of those other three to mind and hear them internally, I cannot quite do that with Hampson. A generalised beauty of sound appears, but

225

there is no idiosyncrasy to lay hold of and so bring the rest into focus. In this, too, Hampson may be increasingly representative of the 'classical' singer in the modern age: his voice-character is so very much that of a norm.

But we seem to be caught in a chain of anomalies, for Hampson is a very *exceptional* singer; at least, if he were the norm we would be living in a very fortunate age. He is also exceptional in the nature of his interest in the art. 'Interest', moreover, is a feeble word for what seems to be a consuming passion. All accounts tell of a man who, within the time-limits permitted by a singer's busy life, is a devoted musicologist. Whatever a listener such as myself may find missing in his *Dichterliebe* (for example) it cannot be through a want of care and thought on his part, for this is also the man who has made a comparative study of manuscripts and given the first performance of an important critical edition. His editorial work on Mahler has involved a growing belief in the merits of the original versions of songs for voice and piano as opposed to orchestra. The history of American song has long been central to his programme-making, resting (as he writes in his notes) on a 'musical balance of Classic form and Romantic freedom; in the poetic juxtaposition of vernacular and elevated speech; and in the essential contraries of naive and sophisticated sentiments'. He is not only a singer for modern times, but a thinker too.

From first to what in the normal course of events must be now the ripe

226

centre of his career, he has distinguished himself as among the most talented of his generation. A sign of it is his position as the last of that long and illustrious line of singers spotted and advanced in their career by Walter Legge, and it was under the auspices of his wife Elisabeth Schwarzkopf that the young Hampson made his debut at the Wigmore Hall, where he was hailed as 'a great discovery'. This was by David Murray of the *Financial Times* who observed that 'the modest house was enraptured; it must be bigger next time'.

Hampson has been one of those fortunate singers who achieve public celebrity and yet retain the respect of the music critics and the profession in general. In opera he is an instant favourite with the audience whatever rival attractions may be on stage with him; and he never compromises standards of taste and musicianship. I myself heard him in opera last in Szymanowski's *King Roger*, where he sang supremely well, and in Polish. In concert it was in a programme that included his beloved Mahler (with piano) and settings of poetry by Walt Whitman. He ended with 'Long time ago', and the reception of this gentle, fireside musing, beautiful in tone, heartfelt in expression, showed that nostalgia can be very modern too.

Chapter 46

Barbara Bonney

The light soprano voice is a charming gift, and plenty of charming music has been written for it. And, like a charm, that very word will hang around its owner's neck, with its equally inevitable appendage: 'youthful'. To her, also, will go the songs of Spring, happy, pretty and charming, but hardly expressive of more than a seasonal segment of human experience and emotion. The light soprano is limited on several fronts. Youthful charm may have its reserves of energy and stamina, but not strength to withstand the big orchestral battalions. It does not thrive in large opera houses or on a declamatory style of writing for the voice. The voice of youth and springtime must also face the passing of these seasons, and the question of what to do when they are gone. The voice may change its nature, put on weight, darken the timbre and thicken the tone, fitting it for a different repertoire. Or of course the light soprano may remain true to herself and be condemned to a life of perpetual prettiness.

Barbara Bonney has squared the circle, or at least brought off a quite considerable feat, for she has remained true to her voice-type and yet developed it to outlast Spring and to outgrow mere prettiness. Now in her mid-forties (born in 1956), she has not taken the usual step from light soprano to lyric, or from Susanna to Countess, Sophie to Marschallin. So far from risking heavier roles, she has increased her vigilance and, having tried (for instance) Micaëla in *Carmen*, has found even this a step too far from the light soprano's rightful repertoire. Yet at the same time, voice and style have matured. The prettiness remains, but now with nothing 'mere' about it; Spring is still in the air, but not every day is cloudless and temperate.

Her presence on the concert platform – which rather than the operatic stage seems to be increasingly the place where we shall look to find her – is refreshing, cool, classical in the clarity of its definition. But in fact there is more. Increasingly, her singing tells of deeper emotions and of a less simple state of being. We sense a strength of conviction, and indeed it does seem from all that she says in masterclasses and interviews that a kind of proselytising zeal works within her. The classical coolness and Scandinavian cleanness of her singing almost belie the urgency of feeling. She herself stresses the desire to communicate as a prime artistic motivation.

Bonney as Sophie in *Der Rosenkavalier*

She is also aware of the hold which the modern world has upon its young, year by year weakening their ties with those three or four precarious centuries of European culture which for the so-called classical musician are central. The urgency of conviction and the passionately felt need for this communication relate directly, for with this awareness comes the wider understanding that the centrality of this culture is not the specialised concern of 'the so-called classical musician' but of civilisation itself. Our light soprano is involved in weighty matters.

Her career has been very largely based on Europe, physically as well as artistically. Born in New Jersey, she came to Europe on an exchange course when barely twenty. At home she had studied cello, and planned to go to Salzburg as she had seen the film of *The Sound of Music*, loved it and wanted to go where the hills were reputedly alive with it. At the Mozarteum she took lessons in singing, did a lot of work with choirs in the City, and in 1979 sang as an extra in the Festival chorus of Karajan's *Aida*. There she was spotted by an agent and recommended to the opera at Darmstadt where she stayed as a hard-working principal member of the company for four years. She sang in a wide repertoire, German, Italian and French, with roles coming her way such as Manon and Gilda, which would have been a trophy for any traveller who happened to be passing through at that time. Four performances a week and extras at the weekend might well have left their mark, but her voice remained pure and firm, so that when we heard her first at Covent Garden it was as a Sophie who, in quality of voice, took her place in the cast worthily alongside Te Kanawa and Baltsa. This was in 1984 and the following year was to bring her further notable successes, with *Semele* at Ludwigsberg and a debut in *Die Zauberflöte* at La Scala. This ended with Pamina marrying Papageno, Håkan Hagegård, and going off to set up house in Sweden; so the European base was further consolidated.

A deeper affiliation with Europe, however, lay in song rather than opera. Opera brought her plenty of good reviews ('her limpid soprano bathed in sunshine with pearly shimmering coloratura', Horst Koegler on her Semele, while Nannetta in Geneva 'looked and sounded a golden teenage beauty' and Sophie at Monte Carlo was 'radiantly innocent'), but it was through her recitals that we came to know her. In London (where, with her second husband, she now lives) they have been for the past ten years or so highlights of the musical year, looked forward to with the confident expectation of fine vocal quality and steadily growing artistry.

One of these, a concert given at the Wigmore Hall in December 1996, was the subject of a review by Max Loppart which deserves to be quoted in full. He reported that the concert 'offered some of the most beautiful, most captivating and, beyond that, most completely *achieved* Lieder singing it has ever been my privilege to hear'. The particular thought behind that italicised word probably lay in his later remark that 'she manages to create a small dramatic *scena* out of each song'. The programme was of Mozart and Strauss, and at the end the critic found himself moved to tears by her final encore, Strauss's 'Ständchen'. Let that be a lesson, for I was there too but must have left by then. Consulting the programme, I find the first encore 'Der Rosenband' ('exquisite') but nothing after that. My own memory of the concert is dominated by the sense, at the start of the second Mozart group, that we were hearing, if not exactly 'a new Bonney', then a

Bonney with Geoffrey Parsons

significant extension or intensification of the Bonney we knew. The feeling came first with 'Das Lied der Trennung', and then the song about Luise burning the love-letters – and what impressed so much there was not the anger of the opening (almost anybody can make an effect with that) as the reflective sadness and seriousness of the end. It was perhaps this kind of thing Max Loppart had in mind when he wrote that the voice had become 'a vehicle for artistry of strikingly deep seriousness'.

A further written note in that programme, I see, shows warm approval of Strauss's 'Die Nacht' but with the additional comment, *'almost* as before'. Investigation reveals that the 'before' in question was 5 June 1991, so the comparison was not remarkable for immediacy. Even so, it suggests that the impression made by that song in the earlier concert must have been very strong indeed. And I remember the performance, as an event, very clearly, for I turned to my neighbour, a rather uncommunicative colleague, and said 'That was *lovely'*. The song perfectly matched the voice, and I think that it was this concert, and that song in particular, which brought the first realisation that, among the many light sopranos of the time and the numerous Americans prominent among them, this was a singer of richer gifts and higher promise. The programme also included three songs of Grieg, with 'A Dream' as the one which also induced a sense of wonder. And, seeing now that the group opened with Solveig's song, I am reminded of another occasion, this time in Edinburgh, and with orchestra, when she sang that song to dreamlike perfection. It brought one of those moments when the listener seems to hover in between the here-and-now and the sense of a beauty beyond it.

There have been other memorable recitals, not least those with an all-American programme (for Barbara Bonney has not become completely Europeanised). One of these included as an encore 'Over the Rainbow', aginst which I see written in my programme the startlingly legible comment 'Best song yet!' A view of the 'extended' Barbara Bonney was afforded by Edinburgh's Hugo Wolf Festival of 1998 in a programme when, announced as just having recovered from a seven-to-eight-week cold, she gave lovely performances of 'Das verlassene Mägdelein' and 'Sankt Nepomuks Vorabend' and ended with the Mignon songs invested with a vibrancy and depth far beyond the designated limits of 'the light soprano'. This remarkable artistic growth can be followed on records too, and at the time of writing by a recent collection of Scandinavian songs which takes its title from Sibelius's 'Diamonds on the March Snow'. Some of the titles are of songs that have long been in her repertoire, but several have a fullness of heart and voice that marks the mature artist. To pick out one which will serve as a not too portentous symbol – Grieg's 'Der Rosenzeit'. It is a hauntingly beautiful song no matter who sings it, but the springtime voice with the bright cool sunlight in its tone needs to have warmed into Summer and the resources of coloration to have deepened towards damask. And that is what it has done.

CHAPTER 47

Cecilia Bartoli

The morning's *Guardian* has its obituary of Henry Pleasants, born 12 May 1910, died 4 January 2000. He was for many years London music critic for the *New York Herald Tribune*, and his books include *The Great Singers* (Gollancz 1967). As a singer he took lessons from Giuseppe De Luca and Riccardo Stracciari, and the tenor of his first opera in the 1920s was Martinelli. He had heard them all, listened attentively, reacted strongly, and thought for himself. He had also kept his interest alive into old age, looking, as Alan Jefferson says in his obit, 'forward as well as back'. Among modern singers one he considered outstanding was Cecilia Bartoli, 'and he extolled her vocal brilliance and star quality up to his final week'.

The praise of such a man is worth earning. Experience which goes back so far in time and has been so extensive can often make the latest talent seem small; to be picked out and praised in terms which might have fitted the famous ones of old must bring reassurance even to a singer whose popularity is so great that she may not seem to need it. Bartoli is indeed one of those, a bearer of the sacred flame, who have the life of their art within them and with it can for a while transform the quality of life itself.

In spite of which, I wish she would change her ways in three respects. The first is incidental but not insignificant. Her concerts usually include a virtuoso aria to conclude the first half and another to bring the programme to a final climax. In a piece such as Vivaldi's 'Agitata da due venti' the fast runs are accompanied by a rhythmic movement of neck and head, rather in the manner of disco-dancers who emphasise the 'beat' by pushing the head forward in time. It is hard to see any technical justification, but the audience seem to find it fun. Perhaps that of itself is considered justification enough. As the ingenuous play of a pretty girl it may perhaps be endearing; as the habitual play of a mature celebrity it is less attractive.

Allied to this, in so far as what started as an incidental effect now seems to have become habitual, is something which appears to be the deliberate infusion of breathiness. Traditionally, a principal aim of the singing-schools has been to inculcate a way of conserving breath and controlling its emission so that the tone admits no admixture of breath. A breathy tone may occasionally be used, quite consciously, as a musical sigh or exclamation, perhaps, of longing. In the course of Bartoli's recitals it will quite

233

Bartoli as Angiolina in *La cenerentola*

often characterise a whole phrase, or sometimes, as in Caldara's 'Sebben, crudele' or Bellini's 'Vaga luna', almost a whole song. The tone inevitably suffers, and the purpose of expressiveness is itself defeated when the method is used with such frequency. It may be that the audience's reaction, or some other kind of 'feed-back', encourages this too, perhaps not unsurprisingly as it is in line with a more popular kind of vocalism, and so, maybe, makes the pretty young 'classical' singer more acceptably 'modern'.

That practice, affecting music at a slow tempo, must be connected in some way with the habit of aspirating runs. This, which in Bartoli's earliest Rossini recital on records was a feature the young singer might have disciplined and eliminated had she so wished, has also become habitual, and by now it has simply to be accepted as a fact of life: this is how the runs are going to be taken. Some people don't mind it; it is often said that the whole Italian nation doesn't mind. It facilitates clear, rapid articulation, and, in different degrees and taking a variety of forms, is common practice. Like many other listeners, I personally deplore it. But there we are. This is a listing of three ways in which I personally wish Bartoli would change her style of performance. In most other ways I am blissfully content.

The voice itself is a lovely instrument, enriched by its reserves of contralto depth. That was one of the most striking features on first encounter: Isabella's 'Cruda sorte' in *L'italiana in Algeri* and part of the *Giovanna d'Arco* cantata showed it up well in her early Rossini recordings, and in concert at the Wigmore Hall it gave flavour to the voice particularly in songs by Caccini, Scarlatti and Paisiello. Fears that the low notes might lose their sumptuous quality as the voice grew accustomed to a higher tessitura proved unfounded, and, in what at the time of writing is the most recent occasion of hearing her 'live', the genuine contralto quality made especially welcome appearance in Caccini's 'Dolcissimo sospiro'. Nor has the voice shown any sign of breaking up into registers: the registers are there in place, but the transitions remain smooth and unobtrusive. Happily, too, the richness at one end of the scale and brilliance at the other have not dulled the middle register, where most of the singing is done.

With this instrument she accomplishes wonders, and the sheer virtuosity of her singing seems (for the most part, at least) inseparable from its expressiveness. A recent example, where excitement was a real presence, the audience seeming to hold their breath as one, was in the singing of a Haydn aria in an out-of-season concert at Glyndebourne. 'Al tuo seno fortunato' is sung by the Genio in the Orfeo opera, *L'anima del filosofo*, with souls flying upwards and out of sight in scales of dazzling rapidity. The music does not so much serve the sense as enact it, and that is what the singing did also. It was one of those occasions when the audience became united by a thrilled conviction that if the phenomenon called

golden-age singing exists anywhere in the world today, they had just heard it.

The excitement in this instance was certainly aroused by singing as singing and not (in the manner favoured by our contemporary opera reviewers) as the work of a specialised department of the acting profession. The performance had meaning none the less, and Bartoli is essentially an expressive singer. Again, those early records showed from the start a live artist, sufficiently so for the name of Conchita Supervia to come to mind more than once. The *Italiana* solo, for example, ran through a lively range of moods, with vocal manners to match. There was one gentle mood with velvety tone and smooth legato; and then, if not quite the counterpart of Supervia's playfulness, there came a new mood of eager determination and impetuosity. Always you saw a face. It was so too with the songs: in Rossini's 'La pastorella' she finds an enchanting way of characterising the girl who has discovered a snake beneath the rosebush, and in the *Regata veneziana* songs her cries of encouragement and alarm are vivid as any running commentary.

As to deeper forms of expressiveness, the music she sings imposes its own limitations – it tends to avoid emotional extremes and yet hardly makes a prior requirement of subtlety either. But then, the ability of a song and its singer to communicate and move the listener cannot quite be

236

assessed in such terms (the apparently artless performance of an apparently simple folk-song has sometimes proved to be the most moving event in an evening's recital). Bartoli's mastery over her material and her audience can be judged in a comparison of two recordings she has made of Caccini's song 'Amarilli'. The version from 1990 (a studio recording) impresses as a lovely song well sung, but it is easy to pass on to the next one and forget it. In 1998 (admittedly with a live audience, so that may account for some of the difference), the experience is altogether richer, the song commanding concentrated attention. It is now addressed, the opening words calling out to the beloved, the mood taking on a new urgency with a *stringendo* at the words 'Credilo pur'. The word 'dolce' is caressed, the repetitions of the loved name are affectionately breathed. Returning to the earlier recording is like experiencing the difference between static and dynamic: the first has its beauty as a statue has, but the developing, impulsive breath of life is in the other.

Bartoli's career has come a long way in a short time, and a large proportion of that time has been spent at the top of her profession. Starting at 19 (though, with opera in the family, she made an off-stage debut as the shepherd boy in *Tosca* at the age of eight or nine), she spent little more than two years in secondary European opera houses before her Rosina at Lyon, followed by a recording, brought her into the front line. Her record company promoted her with genuine conviction, not just hype and hope. Her successes – Paris, London, Milan, New York, Vienna – have been spectacular, winning her a sincerely devoted popular following. Sometimes those who have heard her first on record have been disappointed to find the voice has not the power they expected; most find themselves reconciled quickly enough by the quality of her tone and the charm of her personality. She very sensibly restricts her appearances in opera to roles in which the voice is not covered by a large orchestra and in which a big volume of sound is not a prime requisite: I heard her not long ago, for instance, at the Met and found her voice, though delicate, perfectly clear. The outlook could hardly be brighter.

Perhaps a little prayer is in order. This one should be in every mezzo-soprano's handbook, and goes roughly as follows: 'Give me not the wings of desire that I may soar above the middle ground wherein I dwell. Let not the tempter win, but grant a quiet mind, content in the knowledge that unto a soprano much is given but everybody loves a mezzo. Amen.'

CHAPTER 48

Roberto Alagna and
Angela Gheorghiu

Publicity and the public tend to follow each other around in circles. At the
centre stands the singer, or 'star' of whatever kind, a more or less willing
prisoner. Alagna and Gheorghiu share their circle, enviably as it might
seem, yet I daresay they sometimes feel like Dante's ill-fated lovers in
theirs, except that the winds which drive our singers forward follow in the
wake of importunate journalists or are generated by the movement of a
million hands applauding.

Of course it is all very necessary and they would miss it if those winds
stopped blowing; but how tired they must get of being the centre of interest
not individually as artists but jointly as a phenomenon.

At the present moment they have been particularly associated in Britain with the re-opening of the Royal Opera House. They gave a special
recital there in the first week, and have now taken part in one of the first
productions of the new regime. They and the house have been kept
prominently in the public eye, at least in as far as anything to do with
opera can make today's news. In both instances it usually seems that the
connection with music is incidental. With the house, the interest has lain
in whether it would open on time, how much money had been wasted, and
how dissatisfied are its clients. With the singers, the questions for the
media are 'Are they still a beautiful couple?', 'Has either of them thrown a
tantrum lately?', and 'Are they reckoned still to be "on form"?'.

That last question might be thought to have something to do with music
after all, but hardly so: it is a kind of barometrical reading as opposed to
experiencing the sun and rain, or an interest in the thermometer amid
indifference to the patient. The music critics themselves, being required to
come up with a story, develop a kind of clinical concern too. Is the
thermometer going up or down? How are they doing, and more particularly
how is *he* doing? And *what* is he doing, silly boy? 'Going to ruin his voice,
if it isn't ruined already.' And so forth. Edith Sitwell remarked about the
Cambridge literary critics that they had the patient air of a dentist probing
a decayed molar. Music critics can be like that too.

But there it is. The circle holds, and all are drawn in. It's the publicity

Roberto Alagna as Rodolfo in *La Bohème*

that has done it: the pair are packaged. That was certainly the feeling at their recital in the newly refurbished Covent Garden. They sang with the orchestra, who as a matter of form played an overture after which the famous couple arrived looking curiously unreal, like celebrities caught in the lights at a prestigious film-premiere. The programme was a mish-mash, the death of Otello followed by the waltz from *Faust* and that kind of thing. At encore-time they dispensed with the austerities of Donizetti and Puccini in favour of something about 'Musica', presumably as better befitting 'The People's Opera House'. They furthered the purposes of publicity by looking in each other's eyes and holding hands. And, with hermetic largesse, they sang.

The very sight of the word 'Otello' on the programme was conducive to critical dentistry. 'Doing quite nicely for the present … just a little loosening down there … and you may have some trouble in the future from this. All right for now.' The love duet, taken slowly, found Alagna singing as though determined to show that he had it in him, prolonging the G flat of his first solo ('immensa') and to that end taking a breath between noun ('l'ira') and adjective. In the process he very slightly sharpened the pitch, reminding us from the start that security of intonation has always been an incidental problem. The voice had certainly filled out since he first sang here. Even so (we reflected), one of the advantages of having a lyric tenor sing Otello's love music is that the quieter, lyrical phrases such as 'E tu m'amavi per le mie sventure' might be quietly sung – but they were not. 'Vieni', yes, that was a genuine *piano*; and 'Venere splende' was held for its full six slow measures. In the Death scene (and what a strange selection for a recital) he sang quite beautifully the tender 'E tu, come sei pallida', but from then onwards held on, as it were, to anything in sight, culminating in the *pianissimo* 'morendo' which was intended to last as long as the breath in his body. It was like a flashback to old times; and similarly at the end of 'E lucevan le stelle', 'tanto' was held for an eternity – as perhaps years ago a folk-hero tenor such as Miguel Fleta might have done to send his fellow countrymen into ecstasies. It doesn't really do in London.

Gheorghiu, in the meantime, sang beautifully as she always does, but with expressive powers limited by the nature of the occasion. Her voice seems hardly to have changed at all in the eight years we have known her. Originally, perhaps, it had a youthful vibrancy that has been smoothed out – indeed, this was given (privately) as the reason why her record company did not rush out waving a contract immediately. She was then the most lovely Micaëla imaginable, a delightful Mimì, and a Nina who won all hearts playing opposite the radiant Chérubin of Susan Graham. Everybody admired her in those days and saw great things ahead. Yet, when they materialised, the beauties of her *Traviata* (1994) and the completeness of her success were still beyond expectation. It is so rare to find a *complete* Violetta (the brilliance as well as the delicacy, the character as well as the voice) that this alone was remarkable; but the real source of joy

240

Angela Gheorghiu

was the voice. Its purity was flawless. She had the kind of translucence that was so exceptional in Mirella Freni, but with a warmer light, a softer, 'rounder' glow. She seems now, on her latest visit, to have lost none of this.

Alagna has been more problematic almost from the start. The story of his discovery by the founder of the Festival at Aix-en-Provence in a Paris pizzeria is more romantic than reassuring, and even the 'breakthrough' success of his Roméo at Covent Garden in 1994 was controversial. My own rather amazed delight in the occasion provoked some thoughtful disagreement from judicious record-collecting listeners who looked out their Fernand Ansseau, Georges Thill and Paul Franz: more style, more feeling, and probably better voices. To me, Alagna's singing of the cavatina 'Ah, lève-toi, soleil' and the suave close-of-scene solo had been the fulfilment of a long-held wish, to find and hear again a tenor who could sing worthily in the best French tradition. Alain Vanzo had been the last, but Alagna seemed to me then good enough to recall what records tell of one of the century's earliest, Edmond Clément (Vol. 2 Ch. 26): he had that slim-lined, clean-cut elegance of tone and a manner to go with it. But then we learned that he was to sing Don Carlos.

This was not as it should be. Don Carlos means Tamagno (first singer in the 1884 revision), Martinelli at the Met, Vickers at Covent Garden. The old, old story, we thought: too much, too soon. Also, despite the opera's French origins, and that being the language of the proposed revival, it suggested a development in the wrong direction, Italian rather than French. In fact, it proved remarkably successful. In the Châtelet opera house Alagna's voice had no lack of volume, measuring up perfectly well to his partners, Mattila, Meier, Hampson and Van Dam. Further reserves of power would no doubt have helped in the great confrontations, but he compensated with intensity for what he lacked in sheer force, and I recall no sense of inadequacy on his part at the time. More disquieting were certain features of his performance in *La Bohème* not long afterwards. Here, as well as some rather blatant solo-acting in an ensemble-opera, he took to opening out those upper-middle notes so as to make a big Italianate sound, and French grace seemed to have been forgotten. And that appeared to establish a pattern: he would push forward in the Italian repertoire ('His plans include *Simon Boccanegra*, *Pagliacci*, *Tosca*, *Il trovatore* and *Luisa Miller*' says the biographical note in the latest Covent Garden programme) at the expense of the more specialised, and more valued, French.

That value has been attested recently by two excellent recordings: *Werther* under Pappano, and *Roméo et Juliette* under Plasson. The Werther is sung with a good clean line and with feeling that does not spill over into self-pity. As Roméo he sings with much, not all, of the grace of 1994, and 'Ange adorable' (a good test-case) is still lightly, finely drawn in the Clément tradition. When heard last in the role at Covent Garden (March 2000) his part in that duet had thickened, and the elegant Edmond no longer came to mind: yet in many ways his singing then had grown richer. This was not so much in tone (which has certainly put on weight) as in maturity. Without coarsening, he had achieved much greater mastery of declamation, and in the inspired exile scene ('Ah, jour de deuil') he rose nobly to the challenge. Gheorghiu was at all times most lovely as Juliette, as indeed she is as Charlotte in the recording of *Werther*. It is sometimes said that their stage-union, following their marriage, is good for neither of them, each being best in what does not necessarily best suit the other. That strikes me as no more than a partial truth, and probably rather mischievous. 'Let me not to the marriage of true voices admit impediments', as Shakespeare might have said, had it scanned.

CHAPTER 49

Renée Fleming

We all write under some immediate stimulus – an encounter, a memory, drink, drug or deadline – and to that extent come high on the list of suspects. Just back from a concert by the world's greatest soprano presently in her prime, even I am suspicious. Was she (is she) as great as all that, and what exactly constitutes this 'greatness' anyway? Plenty of others, many of them sopranos, do a good job, week-in-week-out, contributing to musical life with the steady professionalism we expect of our singers as musicians; and then, every so often, up pops this 'greatness'. And what, after all, is it? So often in my experience, when you try to analyse or abstract it as an element in the whole compound, it emerges as a hairbreadth's distinction of tonal colour or verbal inflection: quantitatively a tiny, luxurious presence in relation to the essentials of performance. And yet this it is that lifts the heart, puts the world to fleeting rights, and sets the pen a-scribbling.

Last evening it was Renée Fleming at the London Barbican. She sang in a memorable programme devoted to the life and work of Emily Dickinson. Ten composers, all American, were represented, and the singer shared the platform with the actress Claire Bloom. This is not a review, but since names are being mentioned I must add those of the pianist, Helen Yorke, the compiler William Luce, and the originator and director Charles Nelson Reilly. Very moving, I found, this concentration of miniatures, set against the lively background of a life that was no life. That, in one sense is by the way. In another, it is highly germane to this manifesto celebrating the power of a singer's art. Many of the songs were new, composed for the occasion; none was really well-known. In these circumstances, a singer's voice becomes identified with the music; and the feelings aroused, by music, the context and the naturally beautiful voice, fuse and enrich one another. Fleming sang with warmth, intelligence, sensitivity – and yet that hardly amounts to 'greatness'. She sang with richness, purity, vibrancy of tone – and that doesn't amount to 'greatness' either. So what does?

The question, I'm afraid, has to stand. But one element noted on this occasion may be suggestive, for as one listened to the voice in these songs, other music, and the emotions associated with it and the singer, seemed to rise in fragments, a kind of spiritual participation or in the biblical phrase 'so great a cloud of witnesses'. Into the voice of Lee Holby's ecstatic 'The Shining Place' or the excited declamation of Robert Beaser's 'I dwell in Possibility' or the cherished pain of Copland's 'Heart, we will forget him' there stole the ghost of Blanche Dubois; behind her, and more dimly, the Marschallin of *Der Rosenkavalier*, Dvořák's Rusalka and Mozart's Countess Almaviva.

Blanche is a rather terrible evocation, yet not entirely inappropriate. This is another example of the way in which a voice becomes attached in memory to the new music in which it is heard. André Previn's *A Streetcar Named Desire* provided Fleming with a great 'creator's role', frightening in its demands upon singer, actress and sheer physical stamina, but proportionately rewarding. Fleming is a lyric soprano, and this role calls for weight. Marvellously, she found it, and appears to have survived. 'The old grim reaper put up his tent on our doorstep': the brass is fierce around this, and the voice has to carry not just vocal but emotional weight, while constantly on call at this point are the chesty low-notes which with her are so temptingly available and embody the will-power of this embattled woman. Those strengthened notes not only came to the aid of Emily Dickinson but also brought the emotional stirrings of *Streetcar* with them. I would not like to say that such a power of association in a voice is the sign of a great singer, but it is certainly a power that many great singers have (think how Claudia Muzio's voice gathered accretions of tragic import so that any one of her arias could seem to be reinforced by all the others).

Come to think of it, Blanche might have been a great part for Muzio had her name been Bianca del Bosco. As it is, Fleming makes it hard to imagine anyone else in the role, and certainly anyone other than an American. Her own national identity contributes to that 'great' which we are still trying to define. She draws upon pop and jazz, an inescapable part of American culture and life, with its liberating ways – its rhythmic frankness and colloquial ease – and with apparent immunity to the coarsening of sensibility which is its reverse side. She began with a jazz trio in college, and sang to the saxophonist Illinois Jacquet who invited her to tour with him. She has the idiom in her bones and blood, where you need them in order to be any good at all in it. A return to jazz is on the cards even now. I (who have it in neither blood nor bone) find it wonderful: she has sometimes sung songs (which I don't even very much like) by Duke Ellington with a fine freedom and a touch of Cleo Laine, and at a recent *Gramophone* Awards ceremony she gave us 'Summertime' combining the gorgeous tone and production of a great opera singer with the improvisatory gift and physical engagement of authentic jazz. The danger of this is that it may infiltrate where it should not. She herself has said that jazz colours her singing of Handel, particularly in the ornamentation of Alcina's arias. Memory recalls nothing obtrusive in the performance heard live in Paris, but the effect is not quite so happy when heard on records. It

244

certainly has no place in nineteenth-century opera, as was clear when ever-so-faintly such inflections became noticeable in a recording with Domingo of the Love duet from *Otello*.

Many excellent American singers elicit in critical commentary the harsh word 'bland' in their dealings with the larger repertory. Fleming's

245

Fleming at the 1999 Gramophone Awards

assimilation of European culture has been almost suspiciously comprehensive and yet the dreaded word seems to pass her by. The 'blandness' in question may refer to tone or timbre as to expression, and it probably arises from American eclecticism, which can pick and choose among the European national schools and often comes up with a mixture from which the idiosyncrasies have been eliminated. Fleming has a timbre of her own, its flavour, as with so many of the most distinctive voices, owing much to the presence of a vibrancy which of itself signposts a singer in the direction opposite to the one marked 'bland'. It is one of the qualities that have made her exceptional among this prolific generation of accomplished Rossini singers. When she appeared, previously unknown to most of us, in *Armida* at Pesaro, the vibrancy registered immediately, not so extreme as the once-common fast vibrato of the Supervia type but as an infusion of this life-giving force, combining with an unusual depth of tone to draw the comment 'A *noble* voice'. She sang with what sounded like total assurance

246

and technical mastery; but then it has been an extraordinary development of our times that so many come onto the Rossini scene and do just that. With Fleming, in this (effectively) debut-opera on stage and on record, there was a certain glamour in the tone, the product of this technical command, vibrancy and depth in combination. In the opera's brilliant finale, made famous by the superb Callas and yet, without a hint of Callas in the singing, Fleming sounded like a queen. There was royalty in the voice and style and yet, in 1993, she had just begun.

At this point the discussion might well be extended to include Schubert, Brahms and Strauss, then on to French opera and song, and beyond into the Russian repertoire with her beloved Rusalka for encore. But another name intervenes, and I wonder whether it is tactless or tasteless to mention it. Not so many years ago another lovely American soprano arose and became Queen, or Crown-Princess at least, and also involved herself in an impressively wide repertoire. It is two or three years now since I have heard her, and almost as long since I have heard *of* her. Apart from gathering that she and Aida did not agree with each other (and she would not have been the first to find that), I know nothing of developments there, but cannot avoid the comparison. Cheryl Studer had a most lovely voice, used it for the most part well, but perhaps stretched herself too far; and there may be a warning there. There is also a contrast, for Studer's voice is not one I can summon readily to mind; a kind of tonal blandness pertains here, and in character, though there was expressiveness, there does not, in recollection, seem to have been a personal warmth. In both respects, Fleming is different.

The scope of her achievements to date is indeed remarkable. Mozart and Strauss she sings within the tradition of which Schwarzkopf is part (Schwarzkopf who was Fleming's teacher for a time and whom she still reveres as a singer supreme in the field). She has triumphed also in Massenet's *Manon* – 'in the great tradition of de los Angeles and Cotrubas' reported Rodney Milnes under the heading 'How to storm the Bastille' (*The Times*, 25 January 1997). Her Rusalka and Desdemona, Eva and Ellen Orford have all won a place in the story. She may even so be her best self in American song and opera, and conceivably around her and her gifted contemporaries there may eventually flourish a real national school of vocal music. Perhaps all of this itself amounts to greatness. One other thing: as was found at the Barbican concert, when she stops singing one still hears her. And that too is a sign.

247

CHAPTER 50

Enrico Caruso

If a doubt about greatness may arise with Renée Fleming in view, how much more insidious and insistent are the whisperings or, worse, the indulgent silences that may now attend the name of Enrico Caruso. He is acknowledged of course: every anthology of voices on records, even if it ignores all the other marvellous singers of his time, has to have its token Caruso. People will say 'I suppose he must have been wonderful really', meaning they can't quite see it. Or 'Of course it's a terrible recording but it gives you an idea', meaning you would hardly play it for pleasure. Others will probe ('But was he really so great? Wasn't it just that in those days ...'). Some will chip away at the edges ('Not much of an actor was he?'). Some will condescend amiably ('Completely natural, instinctive gift', meaning he was a peasant), or informatively ('His singing killed him you know. Oh yes, burst a blood-vessel poor chap'). I remember Compton Mackenzie, with faith, hope and charity in his heart, writing 'every day, somewhere, somebody will hear his voice for the first time and say "This was a singer" ' (*The Gramophone*, July 1924). And I wish I could be sure of such a future, or even such a present.

Possibly it is a necessary first stage in the pursuit of truth to note that Caruso did not always sing well, in the theatre or on records. A Covent Garden programme is sometimes exhibited in which the original owner, of 1907 or thereabouts, has written comments against the names in the cast-list: 'Emmy Destinn v.g; Kirkby Lunn exc; Caruso v.poor.' Compton Mackenzie himself said that most of Caruso's recordings of 'sacred' music would (I think this was the phrase) give a cow a sick headache. Then perhaps it should be acknowledged in all sadness and seriousness that the recordings of his last two years show forms of deterioration, vocal and physical, which in the midst of much that is still magnificent, bode perhaps tragically ill. There was a growing discrepancy between registers: with the existence now of complete editions it is possible to play Caruso's records from the first to the last, a process that uncomfortably exposes the extent to which his high notes came increasingly to be dissociated from the main body of the voice. Then, in some of the very last records, especially the great and inspired 'Rachel, quand du Seigneur' from *La Juive*, the intakes of breath are painful to hear. Modern reproduction has made this so clear

248

Caruso as Canio in *Pagliacci*

that one marvels everybody around him did not hear it and realise that this was a man who had something seriously wrong with his lungs.

No doubt the inexorable demands of truth then lead one to reflect on his lifestyle and character. He was an immensely loved and lovable man: generous, enthusiastic, sincere and affectionate, full of life and unsparing of his own vitality. But the extremity of his emotions made him terribly

249

vulnerable, and the ever-increasing sense of responsibility put lamentable pressure upon him. His incessant smoking (he came to need a cigarette in the wings and might even leave the stage for a quick drag in mid-scene) was entirely relatable to the stress of super-stardom. Coming early in the twentieth century, Caruso's fate was a tragic portent. The new phenomenon of mass-media was largely the cause. Caruso's records sold throughout the world, and in the brilliance of their forward, full-bodied tone, they led people to expect the impossible, most particularly a voice of ear-splitting volume. Caruso knew what was expected of him, and gave prodigiously to meet the expectations. Of humble origins, not a peasant but a townboy, he grew up with a happy disposition and a wondrous gift for the world. He gave it – the gift of song, and also the rich bounty of his generous nature – but became the victim of his own fame. The undermining of his health would nowadays be seen clearly as stress-induced, a large part of it derived from the unprecedented sale of his voice on records. To that extent there is truth in the basically ignorant and superstitious idea that 'his singing killed him'. In more factual terms, he died on 2 August 1921 of emphysema and related causes at the age of 48.

The records are no doubt a priceless inheritance – they are all we have of him as an artist, apart from the hundreds of caricatures he drew with a sure hand, a sharp eye and a love of fun. They have nevertheless been responsible for some harmful notions about singing and even for a mistaken concept of Caruso's greatness. The harm is illustrated by a story told by Herman Klein, who as well as being a music critic and author taught singing. A young man arrived for an audition in such a highly-wrought state that at first he was unable to sing. Then, saying 'I can do it, you know', he summoned every ounce of strength, uttered a few notes fortissimo and collapsed. He had been listening to records. Now, it used to be no very uncommon experience to meet people who had heard Caruso. None of them spoke first or primarily about volume. One whom I met, at, I believe, a party for his seventieth birthday, had tramped some thirty miles in his youth to hear Caruso sing in Liverpool. He decided there and then that this was what he wanted to do in life: to sing like that. And he almost did. For a while Tom Burke enjoyed a career among the great, so that his biography (John Vose, 1982) is called *The Lancashire Caruso*. Because it was the first thing I could think of (and that too is significant), I asked him about his memory of Caruso's voice: 'And was it very powerful?' Well, it *was* powerful, he said, but that clearly was not the point. Essentially it was a matter of quality and style, the natural beauty, the manliness of it. All the contemporary reports of his singing – at least, those that were favourable, and not all were – confirm this. They speak of the sweetness of his tone, the naturalness of his art and its sincerity. These, I would say, are what we are now in a better position to appreciate as the real distinction of his recorded voice. It is powerful, to be sure, but that is not 'it'.

The records are, or can be, such precious possessions that we need to be clear as to what exactly they are. First, they are nothing until played and heard, and what is heard depends on the equipment and the acoustics. Few people now have 78s, so they play on transfers either to long-play or compact disc. This, you may say, is commonplace, true of all records: but with Caruso it matters immensely. His voice ideally suited the early gramophone, which caught in satisfying proportion its qualities of sweetness and power, richness and brilliance. With many systems of modern transfer and reproduction the proportions are altered. In particular, more prominence is given to the higher frequencies, with the result that the brilliance and power have been maximised, the sweetness vying with a harder core of tone to catch the ear, and the richness as it were *narrowed* so as to gain a brighter definition. When the proportions are of this kind, whatever their fidelity to 'the record', they give a false impression of Caruso's voice as we know it to have been through the testimony of people who heard him. Almost any playing of a record by Caruso will give at some point a clear conviction of power and brilliance; the test is whether, in reproduction, it catches the richness and the sweetness. If it does not, it has not 'got' Caruso.

Let's have done now with this clearing of the decks and measuring out of allowances. Our critic's chores are ended; our revels now begin. And with Caruso, what a party! Joining him in duet, trio, quartet, sextet are his esteemed colleagues and our honoured guests. Dame Nellie arrives on the evergreen HMV perpetually single-sided 054129, and how gallantly Caruso softens his notes so that the unearthly beauty of her high C can rise, free, like Ariel, to the elements. His beloved Antonio ('we were like brothers' said Scotti mourning his death) joins for that 'Solenne in quest'ora' where it used to be thought, so baritonal were Caruso's low notes, that they had swapped parts. The mighty Titta Ruffo brings the sweat to his brows for a moment as Otello and Iago exchange vows. Frances Alda and Marcel Journet revive the inspired, dying Saracen in the trio from *I lombardi*, and Alda gives way with only a soupçon of malice as Geraldine Farrar, with the merest glint of a gloat, takes her place for the trio in *Faust*. Then how they pile in for *Rigoletto* and *Lucia* – Sembrich, Tetrazzini, Galli-Curci, De Luca, Amato. And in this party of ours their voices are set free from the constrictions of that little box of a studio out in New Jersey. 'Chi mi frena in tal momento?' asks Edgardo, opening the great sextet from *Lucia di Lammermoor*. 'Niente, nulla, nessuno' we answer. No restraints at this party. *Canta, cantare, sempre cantare.*

When the time comes for a solo, everybody has ideas about what it should be. As at any old-time Italian concert the voices rise, with cries of '*Pagliacci!*', 'Sole mio!', 'Santa Lucia!' But I know what *I* want, and that's what we'll have: 'Guardann' 'a luna'. 'Oi luna lu' sings the incomparable voice, soft and high, in the traditional language of lovelorn Neapolitans. The girl Rusina, apparently, may even now be awake, in which case perhaps the moon would oblige by leading her to him; or she may be asleep

Cartoon from *Punch*, 27 July 1904. Caruso (with moustache and clown's cap for *Pagliacci*) holds a money-bag. On either side of him are Calvé as Carmen and Melba as Mimì. Others include Van Rooy as Sachs, Scotti, Destinn and Mr Punch.

and the moon could help by waking her. But of course she might simply be with somebody else, and if that is so he doesn't wish to know, so the moon can lose itself behind a cloud. Until the last verse Caruso sings quite softly, almost as to himself; then, with broadened tempo and fuller tone he gives to this ordinary, charming song the intensity of his operatic soul, even then leaving reserves which only the passionate bars of its climax will tap. It is a kind of nothing; it is everything. The words, the tune, all utterly commonplace, but all his soul is there, and with it the soul of Italian song; the feeling for when to hold back and when to urge forward, for when to take the world lightly and when to feel its woe.

'As I write this, somewhere, somebody is playing a Caruso record' wrote Compton Mackenzie, and 'every day, somewhere, somebody will hear his voice for the first time and say "This was a singer" '. And so I hope. *In saecula saeculorum.*

Dates, Books and Records

The singers are found here in alphabetical order. After the name (professional name only) their chapter number in this book is given in brackets, and the biographical information which follows is limited mainly to dates, names of teachers, place and role of operatic debut, important first appearances abroad, and world premieres. The list of books and records is selective. Autobiographies are included, though not all will be currently in print. The recordings listed are on compact disc unless otherwise stated, and catalogue numbers have been added where it is thought they may be useful; but of course many are deleted, often with a new reissue on a different number and sometimes another company label. The *Gramophone* Classical catalogue is the best guide to what is available. Of general reference books the most comprehensive is the *New Grove Dictionary of Music and Musicians* (Macmillan 1980) or for opera singers the *New Grove Dictionary of Opera* (1992). Among many other helpful books is the *International Dictionary of Opera* (St. James's Press 1993) which will be found to have interestingly written discursive articles on several of the singers listed here. On the earlier singers and their recordings Michael Scott's *The Record of Singing* (Duckworth, 2 volumes 1977, 1979) can usually be relied on for an informative and stimulating entry, and for the art on records of singers up to 1970 there is *The Grand Tradition* (Duckworth 1974, reprinted as a second edition 1993) by the present writer. Where a number has been dedicated to a particular singer in this series, reference is always given to the *Record Collector*, an invaluable specialist magazine available on subscription and published quarterly. Information from the Editor, 111 Longshots Close, Broomfield, Chelmsford, Essex CM1 5DU, England.

ALAGNA, Roberto (48) French tenor of Sicilian parentage. b. Clichy-sous-Bois 7 June 1963. Spotted by G. Dussurget (founder of Aix Festival) singing in pizzeria. Debut Plymouth (*Traviata* w. Glyndebourne Touring Co.) 1988. La Scala 1990. Cov. Gdn. (*Roméo et Juliette*) 1992. Metropolitan (*L'elisir d'amore*). Paris (*Don Carlos*, Châtelet) 1996. Winner Pavarotti International Competition and Laurence Olivier Award 1995.
Records: complete operas inc. *Don Carlos, Rigoletto, Contes d'Hoff-*

mann, Roméo et Juliette, Werther, La rondine. Solo recitals and good duet recitals w. Gheorghiu.

ALDA, Frances (41) New Zealand soprano. b. Christchurch 31 May 1879; d. Venice 18 Sept. 1952. Studied w. M. Marchesi. Operatic debut Paris (*Manon*, Opéra-Comique) 1904. Brussels 1904-7, Cov. Gdn. 1906, Scala 1908, Metropolitan 1908-29.

Autobiography: *Men, Women and Tenors* (Boston 1937). See also: Simpson and Downes: *Southern Voices* (Auckland 1992); *Record Collector* (vol. 6 no. 10).

Records: Complete 1909-1915 Romophone (further volume planned). Or seek LP collections on Opal and Club 99.

AMATO, Pasquale (21) Italian baritone. b. Naples 21 March 1878; d. Jackson Heights, NY 12 Aug. 1942. Studied Naples Conservatory. Debut Naples (*Traviata*, Teatro Bellini) 1899. Cov. Gdn. 1904. Scala 1907. Metropolitan 1908-21 (inc. Rance in premiere *Fanciulla del West* 1910). Also S. America, Germany, Russia. Last appearance *Tosca* NY Hippodrome 1934.

See: *Record Collector* vol. 21.

Good selections on Nimbus, Pearl and Preiser. Also seek late recordings on Rubini LP.

BARTOLI, Cecilia (47) Italian mezzo-soprano. b. Rome 4 June 1966. Studied Rome Academy and w. parents. Operatic debut Nancy 1986. Pesaro (*Scala di seta* 1988). Scala (*Comte Ory* 1991). Metropolitan (*Così fan tutte* 1996). Also Cov. Gdn, Vienna, Salzburg, Paris. Song recitals in most leading cities.

See: Chernin and Stendhal: *Cecilia Bartoli: The Passion of Song* (NY 1997).

Many recordings inc. *La cenerentola* (Chailly on Decca or 1995 video from Houston). Recitals: Mozart, Rossini, *Arie antiche, Live in Italy.*

BONNEY, Barbara (46) American soprano. b. Montclair, NJ April 1956. Studied at Salzburg. Debut Darmstadt 1979. Cov. Gdn. (Sophie in *Rosenkavalier*) 1984. Scala (*Zauberflöte*) 1985. Metropolitan 1991. Song recitals and other concert work in most leading cities and festivals.

See: J. Allison: *Barbara Bonney* (*Opera* Aug. 1999).

Many recordings inc. *Rosenkavalier* (cond. C. Kleiber), *Nozze di Figaro* (cond. Östman). Recitals inc. *The Best of Barbara Bonney* Teldec 0630-11470-2.

BORI, Lucrezia (2) Spanish soprano. b. Valencia 24 Dec. 1887; d. NY 14 May 1960. Studied in Spain and Milan. Debut Rome (Micaëla in *Carmen*)

1908. Scala (Octavian in *Rosenkavalier*) 1911. Sang Manon Lescaut w. Metropolitan in Paris 1910. Met, NY, 1912-36.

See: *Record Collector* vols. 3, 4, 9, 10, 21, 29; Marion: *Lucrezia Bori* (NY 1962); Rasponi: *The Last Prima Donnas* (1975).

Records: Victor 1914-25 (Romophone 81016-2), 1925-37 (81017-2). Seek LP set *The Adorable Lucrezia Bori* (inc. recordings of farewell perf.). Also 'live' from Met: *Pelléas et Mélisande* and *Peter Ibbetson*.

BOSTRIDGE, Ian (32) English tenor. b. London 25 Dec. 1964. Trained as historian at Oxf. and Camb. before studying singing. Came to notice as winner of Nat. Federation of Music Societies Award 1991 and as recitalist at Wigmore Hall 1993. Official operatic debut Edinburgh (Tamino in *Zauberflöte*) 1994. ENO 1996. Cov. Gdn. 1997. Concert and oratorio work in leading cities Europe and USA.

His book *Witchcraft and its Transformations 1650-1750* is pubd. (Oxford 1997).

Many recordings inc. Schubert: *Schöne Müllerin* (Hyperion Schubert Song ed.) and English song recital (EMI).

BROUWENSTIJN, Gré (6) Dutch soprano. b. Den Helder 26 Aug. 1915; d. Amsterdam 14 Dec. 1999. Studied Amsterdam. Debut (*Zauberflöte*) 1940. Netherlands Opera 1946-71. Cov. Gdn. 1951 (*Aida*). Bayreuth 1954 (*Lohengrin*). Also Vienna, Glyndebourne, San Francisco, Chicago. Roles included Leonore, Sieglinde, Jenufa, Rusalka and large Verdi repertoire.

See: *Opera* July 1959.

Recordings: LP recitals on Philips. Currently on CD: *Meistersinger* (Bayreuth 1956), *Tannhäuser* (Vienna 1963), *Walküre* (Leinsdorf 1961), Verdi's *Requiem* (Solti 1958).

BRUSON, Renato (18) Italian baritone. b. Este 13 Jan. 1936. Studied Padua Conservatory. Debut Spoleto (*Trovatore*) 1961. Successes in Amsterdam and throughout Italy. Metropolitan 1969. Scala 1972. Cov. Gdn. 1976. Also Russia and Far East.

See: Tigano: *Renato Bruson: L'interprete e i personaggi* (Parma 1998).

Records inc. most major Verdi roles for baritone. Also Wigmore Hall recital (Chandos CHAN6551). Seek Donizetti recital on LP (Ars Nova ANC25007).

CABALLÉ, Montserrat (3) Spanish soprano. b. Barcelona 12 April 1933. Studied Barcelona and Milan. Debut Basle (*Bohème*) 1956. NY debut concert perf. *Lucrezia Borgia* 1965. Also Glyndebourne and Metropolitan. Cov. Gdn. 1972. Also throughout Europe and N and S. America. Recitals in most leading cities.

See: Pullen and Taylor: *Caballé: Casta Diva* (London 1994).

Many recordings inc. most of her repertoire in Bellini, Donizetti, Verdi

255

and Puccini. Also (e.g.) *Salome*, Spanish song and zarzuela. Many collections and 'pirate' editions.

CARRERAS, José (19) Spanish tenor. b. Barcelona 5 Dec. 1946. Studied Barcelona. Official debut Barcelona (Flavio in *Norma*) 1971. NY City Centre 1972. Cov. Gdn. and Metropolitan 1974. Scala 1975. Salzburg 1976. Also S. America and Far East. Illness 1987; return to singing July 1988. First 3 Tenors concert 1990.

Autobiog: *Singing from the Soul* 1991 (Sp. original 1989).

Records: well-documented career. Early Verdi (*Giorno di regno, Corsaro, Due Foscari* recommended). Post-1987: *Juive* and *Samson et Dalila*. Many collections.

CARUSO, Enrico (50) Italian tenor. b. Naples 25 Feb. 1873; d. Naples 2 Aug. 1921. Studied Naples. Debut (Teatro Nuovo) 1894 (*L'amico Francesco*). Buenos Aires 1899. Scala 1900. Cov. Gdn. 1902. Metropolitan 1903-20. Premieres inc. *L'arlesiana, Adriana Lecouvreur, Fedora, Fanciulla del West.*

See: E. Caruso Jnr. and Farkas: *My Father and my Family* (Portland, 1991); Scott: *The Great Caruso* (London, 1988); Favia-Artsay: *Caruso on Records* (NY 1965).

Records: best complete ed. Pearl 4 vols., 12 discs. But worth trying others according to taste e.g. EMI for C's first records, selections on Nimbus, or an early LP ed. on Olympus. His records have also been subject to various 'processes', inc. the superimposing of a symph. orch. in the 1930s and a new attempt along these lines by RCA/BMG in their disc *Caruso 2000.*

DELLER, Alfred (31) English countertenor. b. Margate 31 May 1912; d. Bologna 16 July 1979. Chorister Canterbury Cath. and St Paul's. From 1944 prominent as soloist esp in Purcell. Britten wrote Oberon in *MND* for him (1960). Founded Deller Consort 1950.

See: M. Hardwick: *Alfred Deller: A Singularity of Voice* (London 1980).

Records: as soloist, essential HMV 1949-54 (EMI CDH5 65501-2). Also Decca collection (448 247-2DM). Many recitals by Consort on Vanguard and Harmonia Mundi.

DEL MONACO, Mario (17) Italian tenor. b. Florence 27 July 1915; d. Mestre 16 Oct. 1982. Studied Rome and Pesaro. Official debut Milan (Teatro Puccini) 1941 (*M. Butterfly*). Vienna and Cov. Gdn. 1946. Scala 1949. Metropolitan 1950. Also S. America and Russia. Roles inc. Aeneas (*Les Troyens*), Lohengrin and Siegmund (Stuttgart 1966).

Autobiography: *La mia vita e i miei successi* (Milan 1982).

Records: *Otello* 1961 (cond. Karajan), *Forza del destino, Turandot* and many others. Several 'pirate' performances. esp. of *Otello.*

256

FLEMING, Renée (49) American soprano. b. Rochester NY 14 Feb. 1959. Studied in Germany on a Fulbright scholarship. Official debut Salzburg 1986 (Constanze in *Entführung* at Landes-theater). Metropolitan Opera Audition Prize 1988. Met debut Countess in *Nozze di Figaro* 1991. All major opera houses in years following inc. Bayreuth 1996 (*Meistersinger*). Success on records dating from 1993 Rossini's *Armida* at Pesaro. World premieres inc. *Ghosts of Versailles, Dangerous Liaisons* and *Streetcar Named Desire.*

Many records inc. complete *Rusalka* (Dvořák) and *Streetcar.* Exc. solo recitals inc. Schubert songs, Mozart arias and Strauss selections.

FLETA, Miguel (19) Spanish tenor. b. Albalata de Cinquos nr. Huesca 28 Dec. 1898; d. La Coruña 31 May 1938. Studied Barcelona and Madrid. Debut Trieste (*Francesca da Rimini*) 1919. Buenos Aires 1922. Metropolitan 1923. Calaf in world premiere *Turandot* Scala 1926. World tours. After 1928 sang mostly in Spain. Also many concerts and zarzuelas.

See: Valdivielso: *Miguel Fleta: Memoria de una voz* (1986, 1997). *Record Collector* vols. 15, 37, 38.

Records: selections on Preiser and Nimbus.

FRENI, Mirella (24) Italian soprano. b. Modena 27 Feb. 1935. Studied w. Campogalliani, Bologna. Debut Modena 1955 (Micaëla in *Carmen*). Cov. Gdn. and Scala 1962. Metropolitan 1965. Salzburg 1966 (Aida in 1979). Continued singing throughout 1990s.

See: Magiera: *Mirella Freni: Metodo e mito* (1990). Also *Opera* April 1967.

Many recordings inc. *Bohème* and *Butterfly* w. Pavarotti cond. Karajan; also *L'amico Fritz.* Seek early recs. inc. LP recital World Records CM19.

GEDDA, Nicolai (7) Swedish tenor. b. Stockholm 11 July 1925. Studied w. Oehman and later Novikova. Debut Stockholm 1951 (premiere Sutermeister's *Der rote Stiefel*). Scala 1953. Paris 1954. Cov. Gdn. 1955. Metropolitan 1957. Premiere Barber's *Vanessa* 1958. Large rep. songs and oratorio. World tours. Still singing in 1990s.

Autobiography: *Nicolai Gedda: My Life and Art* (Amadeus, 1999).

Over 200 recordings inc. operettas w. Schwarzkopf, *Benvenuto Cellini* (cond. Davis), Salzburg recital 1961. Also seek LP set *The Art of Nicolai Gedda* EMI SLS 5250.

GHEORGHIU, Angela (48) Romanian soprano. b. Adjud, Moldavia 7 Sept. 1965. Studied Bucharest Acad. Won prizes Vienna and Hamburg. Debut Cov. Gdn. 1992 (Zerlina in *Don Giovanni*). Vienna and Metropolitan 1993. Salzburg (*Otello*) 1995. Paris 1998 (*Traviata*). Also concert perfs, many w. her husband R. Alagna.

Recordings inc. the famous Cov. Gdn. *Traviata* of 1994 cond. Solti. Also fine *Rondine* (cond. Pappano) and Verdi recital.

GIGLI, Beniamino (23) Italian tenor. b. Recanati 20 March 1890; d. Rome 30 Nov. 1957. Studied Rome w. Cotogni and Rosati. Won International Competition Parma 1914. Debut Rovigo (*Gioconda*) 1914. Scala 1918. Buenos Aires 1919. Metropolitan 1920. Cov. Gdn. 1930. Retired opera 1953, concerts 1955. Also films.

Autobiog: *Memories* (London 1957). See also *Record Collector* vols. 9, 35.

Complete recordings of operas inc. *Bohème, Butterfly, Tosca*; *Cav. rusticana* cond. Mascagni. Many solos, duets and ensembles. Complete editions Victor (1921-32 3 vols.), HMV (1918-35 2 vols.) on Romophone; songs 1949-55 (4 vols. on Testament).

GOERNE, Matthias (33) German baritone. b. Chemnitz 31 March 1967. Studied w. Beyer, Fischer-Dieskau and Schwarzkopf. Operatic debut Cologne 1992 (title-role in Henze's *Prince of Homburg*). Joined Dresden opera. Salzburg (Papageno in *Zauberflöte*) 1997. *Wozzeck*, Zürich 2000. Important concert career, with successes from 1994 in London and NY.

Records inc. *Winterreise* w. G. Johnson (Hyperion Schubert Song ed.), Eisler *Hollywood Songbook* and Schumann Lieder (Decca).

GRUBEROVA, Edita (25) Slovak soprano. b. Bratislava 23 Dec. 1946. Studied Bratislava, Prague and Vienna. Debut Bratislava (*Barbiere di Siviglia*) 1968. Vienna 1970. Glyndebourne 1974. Metropolitan and Salzburg 1977. Cov. Gdn. 1984.

Recordings from *c.* 1990 on her specially created Nightingale label. Earlier on EMI inc. *Capuleti e i Montecchi, Lucia di Lammermoor* and recitals. Zerbinetta in *Ariadne auf Naxos* on Decca (1979 cond. Solti), also Philips (1988 cond. Masur).

HAMPSON, Thomas (45) American baritone. b. Elkhart Indiana 28 June 1955. Studied Los Angeles and w. Schwarzkopf. Debut Düsseldorf 1981. Many international awards with successes in most leading cities Europe and America, concert and opera. Premieres inc. *Dangerous Liaisons* (San Francisco 1994).

Many recordings in large repertoire e.g. *Don Giovanni* (cond. Harnoncourt), *Barbiere di Siviglia* (cond. Gelmetti), *Don Carlos* (from Châtelet 1996 cond. Pappano), *King Roger, Billy Budd*, Bach cantatas, Schubert (vol. 13 of Hyperion Song ed.), Mahler, American song.

HEMPEL, Frieda (42) German soprano. b. Leipzig 26 June 1885; d. Berlin 7 Oct. 1955. Studied Berlin w. Nicklass-Kempner. Debut Berlin 1905. Cov. Gdn. 1907. Metropolitan 1912. Was the first Marschallin in Berlin and NY. Seems not to have sung Zerbinetta (*Ariadne auf Naxos*) though Strauss reputedly wrote the part for her. Retired opera 1921. Then concert work, inc. Jenny Lind programmes.

Autobiographies: *Mein Leben dem Gesang* (Berlin 1955) and *My Golden Age of Singing* (Amadeus 1998). See also *Record Collector* vol. 10.

Recordings mostly 1906-24. Selections on Nimbus and Pearl.

HEPPNER, Ben (15) Canadian tenor. b. Murrayville B.C. 1956. Studied B.C. School of Music. Won CBC prize 1979 and Birgit Nilsson prize 1988. US debut Carnegie Hall 1988. Stockholm (Lohengrin) then Bolshoi, Moscow 1989. Scala 1990 (*Meistersinger*) also Cov. Gdn., Metropolitan, Vienna. Tokyo 1991. Salzburg 1992.

See: *Opera* Oct. 1995.

Recordings inc. *Fidelio, Lohengrin, Rusalka, Turandot*, Strauss recital.

JANSSEN, Herbert (9) German baritone. b. Cologne 22 Sept. 1892; d. NY 3 June 1965. Studied Berlin. Debut Staatsoper 1922. Cov. Gdn. 1926-39. Bayreuth 1930-37. Metropolitan 1939-52. Also an admired recitalist. Taught NY.

See: *Record Collector* vols. 16, 21.

Records: Wolfram in *Tannhäuser* rec. 1930 Bayreuth. Hugo Wolf Soc. issues. Represented in EMI albums of Schubert Lieder, Schumann and Brahms. Seek 'pirated' perfs. of *Tristan, Götterdämmerung* and *Fliegende Holländer* (Cov. Gdn.).

JURINAC, Sena (5) Croatian soprano. b. Travnik 24 Oct. 1921. Studied w. Kostrencic. Debut Zagreb 1942. Vienna 1944. Cov. Gdn. 1947. Glyndebourne 1948-56. Also Scala, Salzburg, Buenos Aires, San Francisco. Also Lieder recitals.

See: *Opera* 1950 and 1966.

Records: *Don Giovanni* and *Nozze di Figaro* cond. Böhm, *Ariadne auf Naxos* cond. Leinsdorf, *Rosenkavalier* cond. E. Kleiber, also video Salzburg 1960. Good collection EMI CDH7 63199-2.

KIPNIS, Alexander (38) Ukrainian bass. b. Zhitomir 1 Feb. 1891; d. Stanford CT 14 May 1978. Studied Warsaw and Berlin. Debut Hamburg 1915. Berlin 1919. Bayreuth and Cov. Gdn. 1927. Metropolitan 1940. Also Salzburg, Glyndebourne, Chicago. Many song recitals.

See: *Record Collector* vols. 22, 23.

Records: Brahms Lieder and Hugo Wolf Soc. (EMI); 4 vols. song and opera on Preiser. Also good selections Nimbus, Pearl and Sony. Several 'pirated' operas from Met (inc. *Boris Godunov*), Cov. Gdn. and Salzburg.

KOZLOVSKY, Ivan (26) Ukrainian tenor. b. Maryanovka 24 March 1900; d. Moscow 21 Dec. 1993. Studied Kiev w. Lysenko. Debut Poltava

1920 (*Faust*). Bolshoi 1926-57. Many honours in USSR. Wide song rep. and recitals till 1987.

See: *Record Collector* vol. 44.

Records: discography of 279 items, inc. many complete operas. Portrayal of the Idiot in *Boris Godunov* on film; also progs from Russian TV. Single items in collections e.g. Rec. Coll. CDs but no adequate representation yet in Western catalogues.

KRAUS, Alfredo (4) Spanish tenor. b. Las Palmas, Canary Islands 24 Sept. 1927; d. Madrid 10 Sept. 1999. Studied w. M. Llopart. Debut Cairo 1956. Cov. Gdn. 1959. Scala 1960. Metropolitan 1966. Great favourite in Spain and S. America. Continued singing, opera and concerts, till year of death.

See: Vitali: *Alfredo Kraus*, Bologna 1992; also *Opera* 1975.

Many recs. inc. *Werther*, *Contes d'Hoffmann*, *Puritani*, *Lucia di Lammermoor*. Remember early *Così fan tutte* (Böhm) and late concerts e.g. Philips 442 785-2PH (Paris 1994). Also Sp songs and zarzuelas.

KURZ, Selma (12) Austrian soprano. b. Biala, Silesia 15 Oct. 1874; d. Vienna 10 May 1933. Studied Vienna w. Ress and Paris w. Marchesi. Debut Hamburg (*Mignon*) 1895. Vienna 1899. Cov. Gdn. 1909. Also Paris, Monte Carlo, Salzburg. Zerbinetta in premiere of *Ariadne auf Naxos* 1916 version.

See: *Record Collector* vols. 13, 41.

Records: 1902-26. Good selections Preiser and Pearl.

LEHMANN, Lilli (11) German soprano. b. Wirzburg 24 Nov. 1848; d. Berlin 17 May 1929. Studied w. mother, Marie Loewe. Debut Prague 1865. Berlin 1869. Bayreuth (Woodbird and Valkyrie in first *Ring* cycle) 1876. Cov. Gdn. 1884. Metropolitan 1885 (appeared in US premieres of *Tristan*, *Siegfried* and *Götterdämmerung*). Salzburg 1901, also as artistic director. Said to have repertoire of 170 roles. Pupils inc. O. Fremstad and G. Farrar.

Autobiography: *Mein Weg* (Leipzig 1913, trans. *My Way* 1914). Also *Meine Gesangskunst* (Berlin 1902, trans. *How to Sing* 1924). See also *Record Collector* vol. 26.

Records 1905-07. Good selection Pearl GEMM CD 9187. 3-LP album Rococo-Cantilena. Also 78 issues on Historic Masters.

LEHMANN, Lotte (11) German soprano. b. Perleberg 27 Feb. 1888; d. Santa Barbara, Cal. 26 Aug. 1976. Studied Berlin. Debut Hamburg 1910. Vienna 1914-38, inc. premieres *Ariadne auf Naxos* (Composer in 1916 version), *Frau ohne Schatten* (Dyer's wife), *Intermezzo*; also Vienna premiere *Turandot*. Cov. Gdn. 1924-38. Metropolitan 1934-45. Also Salzburg and S. America. Continued in concerts till 1951. Pupils inc. G. Bumbry.

Autobiography: *Anfang und Aufstag* (1937, trans. *Wings of Song* 1938).

Also books on Lieder and singing. See also: A. Jefferson: *Lotte Lehmann* (London 1988); Glass: *Lotte Lehmann: A Life in Opera and Song* (Santa Barbara 1988).

Many recordings well represented on CD. Essential: *Die Walküre* Acts 1 and 2, abridged *Rosenkavalier*. Collections on many labels and some 'pirated' operas from Met.

LEIDER, Frida (13) German soprano. b. Berlin 18 April 1888; d. Berlin 4 June 1975. Studied Berlin. Debut Halle (Venus in *Tannhäuser*) 1915. Berlin and Cov. Gdn. 1924-38. Bayreuth 1928. Metropolitan 1932. Also Scala, Paris, Chicago. Retired 1945 and taught till 1958.

Autobiography: *Das war mein Teil* (Berlin 1959, trans. *Playing My Part*, 1966). See also *Opera* 1988 (D. Shawe-Taylor).

Records: comprehensive selections on Preiser. Polydors 1921-26 Record Collector CD TRC14. Seek *Götterdämerung* Act 2 Cov. Gdn. 1938.

LEWIS, Richard (30) English tenor. b. Manchester 10 May 1914; d. Eastbourne 13 Nov. 1990. Studied w. N. Allin. Debut on tour w. Carl Rosa (*Barbiere di Siviglia*) 1941. Glyndebourne 1947-74. Cov. Gdn. 1947. Premieres of *Troilus and Cressida*, *Midsummer Marriage*, *King Priam*. Also Paris, NY, San Francisco, Boston.

See: *Opera* 1955 and 1991.

Records: *Dream of Gerontius* (cond. Sargent 1954, Barbirolli 1965), *Idomeneo* (cond. Pritchard). Recital Handel and folk songs (Dutton CDCSL 4003).

MARTINELLI, Giovanni (1) Italian tenor. b. Montagnana 22 Oct. 1885; d. NY 2 Feb. 1969. Studied Milan. Debut Milan (*Ernani*, Teatro dal Verme) 1910. Scala (*Fanciulla del West*) and Cov. Gdn. 1912. Metropolitan 1913-46. Premieres inc. *Madame Sans-Gêne*, *Goyescas*, *La campana sommersa*. Also Rome, Buenos Aires, Monte Carlo, Chicago. Reappeared 1967 as Emperor in *Turandot* (Seattle).

See: *Record Collector* vols. 5, 25. *Opera* May 1962 (Shawe-Taylor).

Records: good collection Pearl GEMM CD9184. Complete acoustic recordings 1912-24 Romophone 82012. Also Nimbus. Seek 'pirated' perfs. *Otello*, *Pagliacci*, *Aida* (1937) from Met. Excerpts *Turandot* Cov. Gdn. 1937.

MELCHIOR, Lauritz (14) Danish tenor. b. Copenhagen 20 March 1890; d. Santa Monica, Cal, 19 March 1973. Trained as baritone Copenhagen. Debut (Silvio in *Pagliacci*) 1913. Studied as tenor w. W. Herold. Tenor debut *Tannhäuser* 1918. Later studied w. Beigel and Bahr-Mildenburg. Bayreuth and Cov. Gdn. 1924. Berlin 1925. Metropolitan 1926-50. Also recitals and films. Celebrated 70th birthday singing Act 1 *Walküre*.

See: Emmons: *Tristanissimo* (NY 1990).

Records: near-complete ed. European recordings on Danacord (5 vols.). American recs. RCA/BMG. Complete 'live' recordings from Metropolitan and Cov. Gdn.

MILANOV, Zinka (17) Croatian soprano. b. Zagreb 17 May 1906; d. NY 30 May 1989. Studied Zagreb w. M. Ternina. Debut Zagreb (*Trovatore*) 1927. Metropolitan 1937-66. Also Scala, Cov. Gdn., Buenos Aires.
See: Rasponi: *The Last Prima Donnas* (NY 1982). Also *Opera Quarterly* 1990.
Complete operas on record inc. *Aida* and *Trovatore* (w. Björling) and several, inc. *Gioconda* w. Martinelli, 'pirated' from Met. Also Verdi *Requiem* cond. Toscanini. Collection 1945-59 on RCA GD60074.

MILNES, Sherrill (18) American baritone. b. Hinsdale, Ill. 10 Jan. 1935. Studied w. B. Goldowsky, A. White and R. Ponselle. Debut (Masetto in *Don Giovanni*) on tour w. Boston Opera 1960. Milan (Teatro nuovo) 1964. Metropolitan 1965. Cov. Gdn. 1971. Premiere *Mourning becomes Electra* 1967.
See: *Opera* June 1980.
Many recordings inc. most leading baritone roles in Verdi. Also *Guillaume Tell, Gioconda, Hamlet, Tosca*. Collection Decca 443 929. Seek 2-LP set *The Art of SM* (RCA).

MUZIO, Claudia (20) Italian soprano. b. Pavia 7 Feb. 1889; d. Rome 24 May 1936. Studied Turin and Milan. Debut Arezzo (*Manon Lescaut*) 1911. Scala 1913. Cov. Gdn. 1914. Metropolitan 1916. Chicago 1922. Greatly admired in Buenos Aires throughout career. Premieres: *Tabarro* (NY 1918), Refice's *Cecilia* (Rome 1934).
See: *Record Collector* vols. 17, 30; also Steane: *Voices: Singers and Critics* (London 1992).
Records: early HMVs and Edisons Romophone 81005; complete Columbias Romo 81015. Also good selections EMI and Nimbus.

NASH, Heddle (30) English tenor. b. London 14 June 1894; d. London 14 Aug. 1961. Studied w. M. Brema in London and w. G. Borgatti in Milan. Debut Milan (Teatro Carcano, *Barbiere di Siviglia*) 1924. Cov. Gdn. 1929. Glyndebourne 1934. Much oratorio and concert work.
See: *Record Collector* vol. 41.
Many records well reproduced on Dutton and Pearl. *Dream of Gerontius* (cond. Sargent), *Faust* and *Bohème* Act 4 cond. Beecham, *Così fan tutte* cond. Busch.

NESTERENKO, Yevgeny (36) Russian bass. b. Moscow 8 Jan. 1938. Studied Leningrad. Debut (Gremin in *Eugene Onegin*) 1962. Won Tchaikowsky Prize 1970. Bolshoi 1971. Scala 1973. Vienna 1974. Metropolitan

1975. Cov. Gdn. 1978. Also recitals (inc. Shostakovich premieres). Also *Bluebeard's Castle*, Budapest.

Records: complete *Boris Godunov, A Life for the Tsar, Ruslan and Lyudmila*. Verdi's *Requiem* cond. Muti. Seek Shostakovich *Michelangelo Suite* EMI (Melodiya) SLS5078 and Mussorgsky's *Sunless* cycle ASD3700.

NEZHDANOVA, Antonina (27) Russian soprano. b. nr. Odessa 17 July 1873; d. Moscow 26 May 1950. Studied Moscow. Debut Bolshoi (*A Life for the Tsar*) 1903. Rare appearances abroad (esp. Paris 1913). Retired 1935.

See: A. Polyanovsky: *Antonina Nezhdanova* (Moscow 1970), S. Levik (trans. E. Morgan): *The Levik Memoirs* (Symposium, 1995), *Record Collector* vols. 24, 26.

Records: good collection Nimbus NI7877. Well represented in Pearl *Singers of Imperial Russia* vol. 4.

NORMAN, Jessye (16) American soprano. b. Augusta, Georgia 15 Sept. 1945. Studied Michigan University and Peabody Conservatory, and w. P. Bernac. Debut Berlin (Elisabeth in *Tannhäuser*) 1969. Florence and Scala 1971. Cov. Gdn. 1972. Metropolitan 1983. Also Salzburg, Aix-en-Provence and extensive concert work.

Early recordings inc. *Nozze di Figaro* (cond. Davis), Haydn's *Armida* (cond. Dorati). Wide range of roles inc. Dido (Purcell and Berlioz), Elsa and Kundry, Ariadne and Salome. Fine in Tippett's *Child of our Time* and Schoenberg's *Gurrelieder*. Also solo recitals and many collections.

PLANÇON, Pol (43) French bass. b. Fumay 12 June 1851; d. Paris 11 Aug. 1914. Studied w. Duprez and Sbriglia in Paris. Debut Lyon 1877. Paris 1883. Cov. Gdn. 1891. Metropolitan 1893-1908. Premieres inc. *Ascanio* (Saint-Saëns) and *Much Ado about Nothing* (Stanford).

See: *Record Collector* vol. 8.

Records: complete ed. 1903-08 (2 discs) Romophone 82001. Good selection Pearl GEMM CD9497; also coupled with Emma Eames Nimbus 7860.

PONS, Lily (28) French soprano, b. Draguignan nr Cannes 12 April 1898; d. Dallas 13 Feb. 1976. Studied Paris, later NY w. G. Zenatello. Debut Mulhouse (*Lakmé*) 1928. Metropolitan (*Lucia*) 1931-60. Cov. Gdn. and Paris 1935. Also S. America, world tours (inc. concerts for troops in WW2) and films. Reappeared NY 1972.

See: Drake and Ludecke (ed.): *Lily Pons, A Centennial Portrait* (Amadeus 1999); also *Record Collector* vol. 13.

Records: selections on RCA/BMG and Pearl. 'Pirated' Met perfs. inc. *Fille du Régiment* and *Rigoletto*.

PRICE, Leontyne (16) American soprano. b. Laurel, Miss. 10 Feb. 1927. Studied Ohio and NY. Sang as Bess (USA and European tours) in *Porgy and Bess* 1952. San Francisco (*Carmelites*) 1957. Cov. Gdn. and Vienna 1958. Scala and Salzburg 1960. Metropolitan 1961-85. Premiere: Barber's *Antony and Cleopatra* (opening night new Met) 1966.

Many records inc. major Verdi, and Puccini roles. Also excerpts *Porgy and Bess* and many collections (RCA).

PRICE, Margaret (39) Welsh soprano. b. Blackwood 13 Apr. 1941. Studied London w. C. Kennedy Scott. Debut w. WNO (Cherubino in *Nozze di Figaro*) 1962. Cov. Gdn. 1963. Glyndebourne 1966. San Francisco 1969. Metropolitan 1985. Also Munich, Scala, Paris, Vienna. DBE 1993. Much concert work, also in Far East.

See: A. Blyth: *Margaret Price* (*Opera* 1985).

Records: all principal Mozart operas, *Otello* (cond. Solti), *Tristan und Isolde* (cond. C. Kleiber). Schubert recital vol. 15 Hyperion Complete Song ed. Many collections inc. fine early recs. (Mozart and Liszt) on RCA 09026 61635.

RAMEY, Samuel (44) American bass. b. Colby, Kansas 28 March 1942. Studied Wichita and NY. Debut NY City Opera (Zuniga in *Carmen*) 1973. Glyndebourne 1976. Chicago and Philadelphia 1979. Scala and Vienna 1981. Cov. Gdn. 1982. Metropolitan 1984. Salzburg 1987. Also concert work.

See: *Opera* April 1986.

Many recordings inc. 11 complete Rossini operas. Wide repertoire (Bach, Bartok, Bellini, Bernstein ...). Fine recital on Philips 420 184-2.

SCHOENE, Lotte (28) Austrian soprano. b. Vienna 15 Dec. 1891; d. Paris 23 Dec. 1977. Studied Vienna w. Ress. Debut Volksoper 1922. Berlin 1926-33. Cov. Gdn. 1927. Sang in France (inc. Mélisande) till 1940. Returned after war, retiring 1953.

See: *Record Collector* vol. 20.

Records: exc. selection Preiser 89224 (2 discs). Also Schoene and Tauber in operetta (Nimbus NI78331). Seek 80th birthday album on LP (Rubini).

SCHOLL, Andreas (31) German countertenor. b. Eitville nr. Wiesbaden 1968. Sang as chorister w. Kiedricher Chorbuben. Studied Basle w. R. Jacobs and R. Levitt. Won European awards 1992. *Three Countertenors* disc w. Visse and Bertin 1995. Large Bach repertoire. Operatic debut Glyndebourne (Bertarido in *Rodelinda*) 1998. Recitals throughout Europe, NY, Sydney.

Solo recitals on records: Decca *Heroes* 466 196-2OH, also Harmonia Mundi English lute songs, German solo cantatas, Handel arias, *St Matthew Passion*, *Messiah*, Monteverdi's *Vespers*.

264

SCHREIER, Peter (33) German tenor. b. Meissen 29 July 1935. Chorister w. Dresden Kreuzchor. Studied Leipzig and Dresden. Operatic debut Dresden (*Matrimonio segreto*) 1957. Berlin 1963. Metropolitan, Salzburg and Vienna 1967. Scala and Buenos Aires 1968. Developed opera and concert careers concurrently, later known principally as Lieder singer and conductor.

Autobiography: *Aus meiner Sicht* (Vienna 1983). See also G. Schmiedel: *Peter Schreier* (Leipzig 1976).

Records inc. much Bach and most Mozart operas, also roles in Strauss and Wagner. Vol. 18 of Hyperion Schubert Song ed. Many Lieder recitals. Fine *Winterreise* with Schiff (Decca), also with Richter (Philips).

SCHUMANN, Elisabeth (10) German soprano. b. Merseburg 13 June 1888; d. NY 23 April 1952. Studied Dresden, Berlin, Hamburg. Teachers inc. Marie Dietrich. Debut Hamburg (Shepherd in *Tannhäuser*) 1909. Metropolitan 1914. Vienna 1919-38. Concert tour USA w. Strauss 1921. Cov. Gdn. 1924. Continued song recitals till 1950.

See: Puritz: *Elisabeth Schumann* (London 1993), also *Record Collector* vols. 7, 33, and Schumann's own book *German Song* (London 1948).

Records inc. role of Sophie in *Rosenkavalier*, soprano part in *Mass in B minor*. Good collections of songs and arias on EMI, Pearl, Romophone. Short passages from stage in Koch Schwann *Vienna State Opera* vols. 6, 12.

SEEFRIED, Irmgard (37) Austrian soprano. b. Köngetried, Swabia, 9 Oct. 1919; d. Vienna 24 Nov. 1988. Studied w. father and at Augsburg. Debut (Priestess in *Aida*) Aachen 1940. Vienna State Opera 1943. Salzburg 1946. Cov. Gdn. 1947. Metropolitan 1953. Recitals throughout Europe, USA, Australia. Retired opera 1976.

See: Rasponi: *The Last Prima Donnas* (1982); *Opera* Aug. 1966.

Records: Composer in *Ariadne auf Naxos* (cond. Karajan) (EMI), also on DG cond. Böhm; *Zauberflöte* and *Hänsel und Gretel* (both cond. Karajan). Recitals on Decca, EMI (also duets w. Schwarzkopf), Orfeo, Testament, and exc. 1962 broadcast recital and interview BBCL 4040-2.

SÖDERSTRÖM, Elisabeth (35) Swedish soprano. b. Stockholm 7 May 1927. Trained Stockholm. Debut Drottningholm 1947. Stockholm Opera 1949. Glyndebourne 1957. Metropolitan 1959. Cov. Gdn. 1960. Also Edinburgh, Vienna, Salzburg, Australia. Premieres inc. *Aniara* (Blomdahl), *Aspern Papers* (Argento). Many recitals.

Autobiography: *In My Own Key* (Eng. trans. London 1979); see also *Opera* 1969.

Many records, most important probably *Jenufa* and *The Macropoulos Affair* (cond. Mackerras), *Pelléas et Mélisande* (cond. Boulez), Rachmaninov complete songs w. Ashkenazy (Decca).

SOUZAY, Gérard (8) French baritone. b. Angers 8 Dec. 1918. Studied Paris w. Bernac, Croiza, Vanni-Marcoux. Concert debut 1945, opera 1947. Appeared in opera Salzburg, Aix, (briefly) Glyndebourne, Metropolitan. Recitals worldwide.

Records: recitals, French song and Lieder, on Philips, but better earlier EMI and best earliest Decca. Exc. selection 1947-51 Dutton CDLX 7036.

STEBER, Eleanor (40) American soprano. b. Wheeling, W. Virginia 17 June 1916; d. Langhorne, PA 3 Oct. 1990. Studied w. W. Whitney and P. Althouse. Debut (Senta in *Fliegende Holländer*) Boston 1936. Won Metropolitan Auditions of the Air 1940. Met 1940-63. Also Bayreuth, Vienna, Edinburgh. Concerts inc. E. Europe. Premieres inc. *Vanessa* (1958), *Knoxville* (1948). First US perfs. of *Wozzeck*, *Arabella*, *Owen Wingrave*.

Autobiography: *Eleanor Steber* (NJ 1992).

Records: *Lohengrin* (Bayreuth 1953), *Vanessa*, *Knoxville*, *Les Nuits d'été* (1954). Live recitals and Met performances. Collections inc. RCA/BMG 60521.

STRACCIARI, Riccardo (22) Italian baritone. b. Casalecchio di Reno 26 June 1875; d. Rome 10 Oct. 1955. Studied Bologna. Operatic debut Bologna (*Bohème*) 1898. Scala 1904. Cov. Gdn. 1905. Metropolitan 1906. Also S. America, Chicago, San Francisco, Rome. Retired opera 1944. Pupils include A. Sved, P. Silveri, B. Christoff.

See: *Record Collector* vol. 30.

Records include complete *Barbiere di Siviglia* and *Rigoletto*. Many solos Fonotipia and Columbia. Good selections Nimbus and Pearl.

TEYTE, Maggie (29) English soprano. b. Wolverhampton 17 April 1888; d. London 26 May 1976. Studied London, then Paris w. J. de Reszke. Official debut Monte Carlo 1907. Paris (Opéra-Comique) 1908. Chosen by Debussy to succeed M. Garden as Mélisande. Cov. Gdn. 1910. Chicago 1911. Developed important career in French song. Reappeared NY as Mélisande 1948. Belinda in *Dido and Aeneas* w. Flagstad London 1951. DBE 1958.

Autobiography: *Star on the Door* (London 1959). See: O'Connor: *The Pursuit of Perfection* (London 1979).

Records: EMI CHS5 65198-2 essential collection of French song. Others on Decca and Pearl.

URLUS, Jacques (15) Dutch tenor. b. Hergenrath 9 Jan. 1867; d. Noordwijk 6 June 1953. Studied Amsterdam. Operatic debut Utrecht 1894. Leipzig 1900. Cov. Gdn. 1910. Bayreuth 1911. Metropolitan 1913. Much concert work inc. *St Matthew Passion* and *Das Lied von der Erde*. Continued till late in life (e.g. *Tristan*, Amsterdam 1932).

See: *Record Collector* vols. 26, 27.

Made many records but badly represented on CD. Single items in some collections e.g. Pearl's *Hist. Cov. Gdn.* vol. 3. Seek 78s on Historic Masters and LPs on Rococo and Rubini.

VARADY, Julia (6) Romanian soprano. b. Oradea 1 Sept. 1941. Studied Bucharest. Debut Cluj 1963. Frankfurt 1970. Munich 1972. Also Berlin, Edinburgh, Cov. Gdn., Salzburg, Metropolitan 1978. Premieres inc. Reimann's *Lear* 1978.

Records: much Mozart and Strauss; Spontini's *Olympie*; *Lear* now deleted. Recitals inc. exc. vols. of Verdi. Puccini and Strauss on Orfeo.

VON OTTER, Anne Sophie (34) Swedish mezzo-soprano. b. Stockholm 9 May 1955. Studied Stockholm and w. V. Rozsa in London. Debut Basle (Haydn's *Orlando paladino*) 1983. Cov. Gdn. 1985. Metropolitan, Scala, Salzburg, Paris, Chicago, Tokyo in opera; most major cities in wide range of recital and concert work.

See: *Opera* 1991.

Extensive discography inc. *Nozze di Figaro* (cond. Levine), *Rosenkavalier* (cond. Haitink), *Orphée et Eurydice* (cond. Gardiner). Grieg songs (DG 437 52-2GH), *Lamenti* (DG 457 617-2AH). 1983 recs. re-issued on Proprius PRCD 9008.

WARREN, Leonard (17) American baritone. b. NY 21 April 1911; d. NY 4 March 1960. Studied NY. Won Metropolitan Auditions of the Air 1938. Official debut Met 1939. Buenos Aires 1942. Scala 1953. Tour USSR 1958. Died on stage in *Forza del destino* at Met.

See: Phillips-Matz: *Leonard Warren* (Amadeus 2000).

Records: leading Verdi baritone roles; *Gioconda*; *Tosca*. Good selection Preiser 89145. 'Live' concerts USSR RCA GD 87807.

Cumulative Index of Singers

This index applies to all three volumes in the *Singers of the Century* series. Volume numbers and page references to main entries are given in bold type.

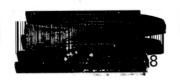

782.0092 STEANE
Steane, J. B.
Singers of the century

WITHDRAWN

APR 0 6 2001	DATE DUE	
JUL 0 6 2002		